Sexual Orientation and Teacher Identity

Sexual Orientation and Teacher Identity

Professionalism and LGBTQ Politics in Teacher Preparation and Practice

Edited by Patrick M. Jenlink

ROWMAN & LITTLEFIELD
Lanham • Boulder • New York • London

Published by Rowman & Littlefield
An imprint of The Rowman & Littlefield Publishing Group, Inc.
4501 Forbes Boulevard, Suite 200, Lanham, Maryland 20706
www.rowman.com

6 Tinworth Street, London SE11 5AL

Copyright © 2020 by Patrick M. Jenlink

All rights reserved. No part of this book may be reproduced in any form or by any electronic or mechanical means, including information storage and retrieval systems, without written permission from the publisher, except by a reviewer who may quote passages in a review.

British Library Cataloguing in Publication Information Available

Library of Congress Control Number: 2019914534

ISBN 978-1-60709-921-5 (cloth)
ISBN 978-1-60709-922-2 (pbk.)
ISBN 978-1-60709-923-9 (electronic)

To all LGBTQ and Straight educators and students committed to
removing hate and violence from our society
and its schools and universities.

Contents

Preface — vii

Acknowledgments — ix

1. Negotiating Identity as LGBTQ Teacher: A Critical Pedagogy of Learning to Teach — 1
   Patrick M. Jenlink

2. Performativity and Disidentification: Subverting Identity Politics through Stereotypical Embrace or Rejection — 11
   Adam J. Greteman and Ira David Socol

3. LGBTQ Teacher Identity: Transgressing the Linear and into the Spherical Identity Model — 33
   Megan S. Kennedy

4. Understanding and Undermining Heteronormativity — 51
   Heather Hickman

5. Shh . . . Out: From Silence to Self — 69
   Janna Jackson

6. Teachers as Sexual Strangers — 87
   Steve Fifield

7. The Personal Is Professional: Understanding Schools as Cultural Institutions through the Identities of Mother/Educator/Lesbian — 103
   Laura A. Bower

8. Dismantling Straight Privilege: Alternate Conceptions of Identity and Education — 117
   Tonette S. Rocco, Hilary Landorf, and Suzanne Gallagher

9 Teaching the Taboo: Including Sexual Orientation in Teacher
   Preparation Courses   133
   Stephanie L. Daza

10 Epilogue: Sexual Orientation, Identity Politics and Teaching:
   LGBTQ Teacher Identities (Re)considered   155
   Patrick M. Jenlink

Editor and Contributors   161

Preface

Over the past twenty years, more local and state American antidiscrimination legislation has been passed that includes sexual orientation and gender identity. Increasingly, antidiscrimination policies in the workplace address the same—some even going so far as to offer domestic partner benefits, even if the state where they are housed may not recognize same-sex partnerships.

However, in spite of changes in legislation and policies that acknowledge the existence of LGBTQ people and allow them to work and live with dignity and security under the law, the fact remains that all too often many heterosexual K–12 teachers and administrators promote homophobia and transphobia in their schools.

In an increasingly diverse society, educators and policy makers face the critically important challenge of fostering educational environments that are inclusive and welcoming to all students and teachers, inclusive of LGBTQ. Today, schools and teachers must consider whether the educational context facilitates learning for all youth, including those who are lesbian, gay, bisexual, transgendered, or queer/questioning (LGBTQ), as well as children who have LGBTQ parents.

In a pluralistic society, administrators must consider whether teachers, aides, or other LGBTQ staff members are hindered in the workplace because of discriminatory policies, practices, or comments. LGBTQ issues in education are relevant from pre-K–12 to higher education, as well as in multiple educational contexts from classrooms and playgrounds to college campuses. Findings from empirically sound research can help us understand LGBTQ topics, specifically as they relate to education, children and youth, schools, and schooling issues.

Problematically, teachers are entering educational settings where difference connotes *not equal*, and discourses of LGBTQ politics, identity, and difference are interwoven with a realization of discrimination and marginalization. Nowhere is this more apparent than when LGBTQ teacher identity and professionalism is framed by misconception, understood not as fact but as perspective. "What is not" defines the boundaries of "what is." The social, historical, political, and cultural contexts in which LGBTQ teachers work and live, and from which LGBTQ teachers derive their identity, play a significant role in shaping the politics, pedagogy, and practice of teacher.

Sexual Orientation and Teacher Identity: Professionalism and LGBTQ Politics in Teacher Preparation and Practice examines the nature of LGBTQ issues and teacher identity as social, cultural, and political constructs. In particular, the contributing authors to this collection present contemporary discourses that will illuminate and critique the practices, structures, and politics in both teacher preparation programs and public school settings that affect LGBTQ teachers and their identity in relation to the struggles teachers as professionals face in obtaining recognition.

Chapter 1 introduces the thesis of sexual orientation and teacher identity. The authors of chapters 2 through 9 focus the reader on critical perspectives and research on LGBTQ issues and teacher identity, drawn from professional contexts in preparation programs and classrooms. Chapter 10 presents an epilogue, focusing on identity politics, and on teaching and (re)considering LGBTQ teacher identity. The authors, again drawing on their personal and professional experiences, give much-needed voice to recognition and the formation of identity from a LGBTQ viewpoint as they relate to teachers, teacher educators, and other cultural workers responsible for shaping professional identities of teachers and for teaching students in schools and classrooms across the nation.

Acknowledgments

The focus on sexual orientation and teacher identity draws into specific relief current cultural, social, and political tensions that exist in our society and its educational system. When I first began to consider this work, I visited with colleagues and former doctoral students who are teachers and administrators in the LGBTQ community. The concerns we discussed, concerns directly related to teacher identity and to the identity of students that enter public school classrooms each day, have been prevalent in society for decades. Our attempt in fostering the chapters presented in this collected work are intended to ensure that the next of generation of LGBTQ teachers entering classrooms are prepared to meet the challenges that society places before them.

Acknowledgement and thanks goes the contributing authors whose insight and experience with sexual orientation and the formation of identities as teachers provide insight and thoughtful considerations for understanding the cultural, social, and political contexts wherein LGBTQ teachers work. The authors bring an understanding to a critically important topic for today's teacher preparation programs: recognizing that one's identity is an invaluable part of the teaching and learning experience.

Acknowledgement is extended to the external reviewers who took time out their busy schedules to review and provide comments and suggestions on the chapters. Acknowledging the value of the chapters and offering constructive feedback was invaluable, as was the affirmation by reviewers for both of the need and importance of a book committed to sexual orientation and the formation of identities as educators.

Likewise, acknowledgement is extended to Tom Koerner and the editorial staff at Rowman and Littlefield Education for their vision in seeing the value of a book on sexual orientation. Likewise, acknowledgement is extended to

Carlie Wall for her work in advancing this work forward in the production process with understanding and caring.

As well, acknowledgment of the production staff at Rowman and Littlefield is in order for their ever-vigilant efforts to move the book through to completion. Working with a quality publisher and the folks that do the work to translate a manuscript into a completed book is a rewarding experience.

Chapter One

Negotiating Identity as LGBTQ Teacher

A Critical Pedagogy of Learning to Teach

Patrick M. Jenlink

At the heart of teaching is a fundamental question of who we are, both as people and as teachers, which revolves uneasily around the notion of a *self*, a coherent, perduring frame of reference that remains constant from one day to the next, over weeks, months, years. For the teacher, such a conception of oneself is challenged by everyday experience, which reveals an undeniable mutability—a structural permeability to change—within one's sense of self. The question of who we are is a question of identity, a question of what it means to be a teacher in the particular social, cultural, historical, and political contexts in which schools are situated.

Nowhere is the challenge of being a teacher in today's schools more difficult than at the intersection of sexual orientation and teacher identity, an intersection that exists in a climate where the two have historically been pitted against each other. LGBTQ[1] individuals entering teaching, as Evans (2002) noted, must negotiate their identity in a heteronormative dominant society. The process of integrating their sexual identities with their roles as teachers are often impelled and impeded by several factors, including community atmosphere, school culture, family status, and a heteronormative view of who should or should not be a teacher.[2]

Alsup (2006) noted that the student entering teacher preparation is faced with negotiating both personal and professional space: "Often this space is in the so-called borderland between identity positions or situated discourses, and is a space of continual becoming rather than an endpoint culminating in a singular identity construction" (2006, pp. 6–7). For the LGBTQ student of teaching, finding a personal and professional identity space is often difficult.

Negotiating identity, either teacher identity or sexual orientation identity, is emotional, in part because of the uncertainty involved (Evans, 2002). That said, teacher educators are confronted with two questions: Do teacher educators and their programs confront issues affecting LGBTQ individuals in society, communities, and schools? If not, why?

STUDENT TEACHERS LEARNING TO TEACH

Learning to teach, for LGBTQ student teachers, is, in part, as it is for their "straight" counterparts, about "negotiating identities, figuring out who one is in the classroom. Some of these negotiations are new: Who am I as I transition from being a student of teachers to a student of teaching to a teacher of students?" (Donahue, 2007, p. 75). Some of these negotiations may be more familiar to LGBTQ student teachers: "How do I define my sexual orientation? To whom and when do I decide to come out? However, even these older negotiations take place in new contexts, school settings where" (p. 75) heteronormativity is the dominant ideology. Both types of negotiations take place simultaneously, with one affecting the other.

Understanding how LGBTQ "pre-service teachers deal with the process of making decisions about coming out in schools amidst the inherent uncertainty of teaching" (Donahue, 2007, p. 76) requires "negotiating the self" in terms of one's sexual orientation and one's identity (Evans, 2002). For new LGBTQ teachers, negotiating the self and simultaneously "learning to teach involves negotiating identity . . . between self in relationship to others and in relationship to historically developed social roles (e.g., teacher, student, heterosexual, homosexual)" (p. 77).

As teacher educators, operating under the precept that we are preparing students to become teachers in classrooms in schools, we must focus on the inherent belief that classrooms are meant to be safe spaces for healthy growth and development by both LGBTQ and straight students alike; we must strive to meet the needs of all students, not just those who fit heterosexual norms. Hill (2006) argues, rightly so, that "this requires us to persistently reflect upon our responsibilities to a culturally diverse student population, including the presence of lesbian, gay, bisexual, and transgender students—their needs must also be met" (p. 153).

As teacher educators, our failure to prepare teachers to enter classrooms and embrace the existence of diverse sexual orientations among our students and "afford them the same rights as others precludes us from creating equitable learning environments that genuinely support student diversity" (Hill, 2006, p. 153). When we as teacher educators are sensitive to the issues surrounding LGBTQ students, we not only advance the formation of identity, we advance the formation of identity is an intersection of sexual orientation and teacher.

TEACHER IDENTITY IN A HETERONORMATIVE SOCIETY

Unfortunately, as DeMitchell, Eckes, and Fossey (2009) note, society's LGBTQ "teachers are often judged by different standards than those that apply to other teachers" (p. 66). Too often, the consistent use of quality teaching practices, the ability to inspire students, and the tenacity to believe in students and to help them achieve more than they thought possible" (p. 66) are overshadowed by heteronormative practices and concerns about the private sexuality of the teacher.

Importantly, "the heteronormative nature of schools and schooling is an impediment for gay teachers as their professional identities can arguably be seen as less authentic than the identities of their heterosexual peers" (Haddad, 2013, p. 29). Schools are often considered microcosms of the greater society they serve, for LGBTQ teachers this is a society fraught with heteronormativity (Haddad, 2013; Mayo, 2008; Warner, 1999). The pervasive effects of heteronormativity are a source of consternation and dissonance for many LGBTQ teachers. The effects of the central position of heteronormativity in institutions like public schooling is significant. As Talburt (2000) noted, research has shown institutional practices both respond to and construct identity.

Increasingly, teachers are entering educational settings where difference "connotes not equal, better/worse, having more/less power over resources, discourses of identity and difference are braided at many points with a discourse of racism, both interpersonal and structural" (Cohen, 1993, p. 293). Teacher identity[3] is often framed by difference, understood not as fact but as perspective. *What is not* defines the boundaries of *what is*. The social, historical, cultural, and political contexts in which teachers work and live, and from which teachers derive their identity, play a significant role in shaping the many different "selves" that are engaged in the social context of a teacher's practice at particular points in space and time.

Point in fact, unequal gender relations and heteronormativity shape the organization of public space, such as schools, in ways that are naturalized to the point of invisibility (Woolley, 2013). Teacher identity is partly shaped by recognition or its absence, often by misrecognition of others (Taylor, 1994). Interwoven with individual identity formation is the development of cultural identity. The system of valuing heterosexuality as the natural and normative sexual orientation in a heteronormative culture devalues all other sexualities of LGBTQ individuals (Page and Peacock, 2013). In this sense, viewing heterosexuality as compulsory and naturally occurring is the result of socialization of individuals, the equivalent of institutionalization into a heteronormative society (Ingraham, 2005).

Recognition as a teacher, the strong and complex identification with one's professional culture and community, is necessary for a positive sense of self and for the making of an involved and active community member.[4] Teachers must learn to examine the consequences that prevailing social practices have jointly had in the creation of their own lives and the lives of their students. The formation of identity process that an individual experiences within social-cultural contexts is replete with multiple encounters that shape identity, one's own and the identity of others. Recognition takes place within a horizon of socially imbued discourses, politically and culturally embedded practices, and normative conditions that work to shape identity circumscribed by those discourses.

CULTIVATING A CRITICAL PEDAGOGY OF IDENTITY

The extent to which teacher educators critically examine and can cultivate in students of teaching a conception of "self" as racially, socially, and culturally constructed texts will, in turn, shape their pedagogies as critical extensions of teacher identity. The intersectionality of sexual orientation and identity as teacher is captured in the questions posed by Asher (2007):

> What do we need to do to enable teachers to identify, engage, and unpack the nuance, context-specific differences at the intersections of race, culture, gender, and sexuality that they encounter on a daily basis? How can we foster critical, self-reflexive ways of teaching that promote equity and democratic ways of being? (p. 66)

Teacher educators "must consider how our approaches to teacher education can explore the struggles and rewards of engaging pre-service teachers as they construct and critique their own cultural self-identities" (Mullen, 1999, p. 151). As well, teacher educators must understand that learning one's identity is intertwined with social agency, and that, as such, agency is "not simply a matter of places, but is more a matter of the spatial relations of places and spaces and the distribution of people within them" (Grossberg, 1996, p. 101).

A critical pedagogy of identity is not about engaging just the positionality of our students of teaching but also about the nature of our own identities as teacher educators as they have and are emerging within and between different social, cultural, political, and spatial discourses and practices. Teacher educators who understand the formation of students' identities are individuals who also understand the formation of their own identities. With respect to developing an identity as LGBTQ and teacher, teacher educators must engage in a critical pedagogy of identity that examines the consequences that dominant discourses and practices, such as those defined by heteronormativity, have had in the creation of their own lives and the lives of their students.

With respect to cultivating a critical pedagogy of identity, it is important to understand, as Spodek (1974) has argued: "All teacher education is a form of ideology. Each program is related to the educational ideology held by a particular teacher educator or teacher education institution, even though the relationship may not be made explicit" (p. 9). As such, spatial discourses and practices shape the identity of both teacher educator and student, often in ways not desired. A critical pedagogy of identity understands that the "embodiment of a teacher identity is an important part of learning to teach" (Alsup, 2006, p. 105). This is equally important for the LBGTQ student of teaching as it is for the teacher educator (LGBTQ or straight).

A critical pedagogy of identity works to mediate the ideological positioning of identity and creates discourses within the preparation program and experiences that address the difficulty of developing a professional identity as teacher (MacIntosh, 2007; Vavrus, 2009). Such a pedagogy understands that "even under the best of circumstances, even though it might be uncomfortable for us and such a discussion might mean revealing some of our own perceived weaknesses," it is a necessary part of rewriting the palimpsest of identity (Alsup, 2006, p. 7).

Teacher educators must necessarily situate LGBTQ and straight students of teaching within spatial discourses as a part of the process of developing a professional identity, drawing on a various discursive genres. As Alsup (2006) argues, situating the student of teaching in spatial discourses concerned with the social, cultural, political, pedagogical, and spatial nature of identity, "and then critically analyzing their relationship to one's developing [a pedagogy of identity], is essential to professional identity formation and the making of a good teacher" (p. 7).

The teacher educator concerned with development of a professional teacher identity in his/her/their students recognizes that creating a critical pedagogy of identity requires also creating "curricular experiences that facilitate complex interpretation . . . [and] creating these 'commonplace locations' for interpretation involves a deliberate process of creating intertextual and interpersonal links among texts, readers, situations, and responses to these" (Sumara, 1998, p. 206).

Such critical pedagogy and curriculum, purposed with developing a professional identity as teacher for LGBTQ and straight students of teaching, is continuously calling into question the location of identity, asking the question: Where is the essence of self located? At the same time, the merging of pedagogy and curriculum as a spatialization of identity recognizes that one's self, one's identity, is somehow circumscribed in one's relation with others within a perceived and contextualized world of significance.

NEGOTIATING IDENTITY AS TEACHER

Importantly, understanding that society at large, and the schools and communities that are microcosms of that society, "prescribes a set model of heteronormative identity development informed by gender socialization. In promoting heteronormativity, all other gender and sexual identities are largely devalued" (Page and Peacock, 2013).[5]

Teacher preparation programs that acknowledge the challenges that LGBTQ individuals face when entering teaching, and the teacher educators within those programs, understand the necessity of providing a space in which one can become the author of one's own interpretations of one's identity as teacher. These interpretations, however, cannot be extricated from one another. The interpretation of the teacher educator and that of the student overlap and intertwine within an ever-evolving and unstable web of contextualized relations. Page and Peacock (2013) explain the complex work of shaping one's identity in an otherwise heteronormative culture:

> Individuals with gender identities and sexual identities that do not conform to the prescribed heterosexual identities must essentially develop their own way, that is, they must privately negotiate their path through identity development and adoption. However, while negotiating their private reality, they must rely on existing concepts of other (i.e., the opposite in a binary system). (p. 651)

Sexual orientation and identities and the identity as teacher are composed of ideas from the larger society about how one should act, think, look, and feel. DeMitchell, Eckes, and Fossey (2009) are instructive on this point when they ask the question, "Who shall teach our children?" (p. 65). Society has long debated this question, perhaps agreeing only on this simple truth: "Who teaches matters" (p. 65). The heteronormative culture the pervades society has, historically,[6] determined the answer to the question, yet the simple truth of "Who teaches matters" is shifting as society realizes that LGBTQ teachers are necessary in today's "age of difference."

CONCLUSIONS

Learning our identity as teacher is often undermined by alterity. As Charles Taylor (1992) reminds us, "alterity reveals the dependence of the self on another at precisely the time when the social guarantee of another is no longer in place" (p. 35). The simultaneous interiorisation of identity (to an interior increasingly other) and the rise of the ideal of social equality means that "[w]hat has come about with the modern age is not the need for recognition but the conditions in which the attempt to be recognized can fail" (Taylor, 1992, p. 35). The work of teacher educators is made even more difficult when we consider that the conditions in schools across society have made it increasingly difficult to become a teacher.

Teacher educators, in preparing teachers, are responsible for defining heteronormativity in relation to what teachers will face in schools and communities. Equally important, teacher educators and students of teaching have an obligation to society to interrupt heteronormativity as an imperative for just and civil society: "the bottom line of teaching is enhancing students' learning and their life chances by challenging the inequities of school and society" (Cochran-Smith, Shakman, Jong, Terrell, Barnatt, and Mcquillan, 2009). Traditional socialization of students of teaching into a profession can no longer just socialize teachers into the metaphorical "mainstream of a profession" because all senses of "normality" with respect to heteronormativity must necessarily be questioned.

The development of a strong sense of identity and agency is more critical now than perhaps ever before. We must understand, as teacher educators, that identity for the LGBTQ and straight individuals is being written each moment of their teaching lives and that their identity is also being written over each moment of their lives, that there are cultural, political, ideological forces at work trying to erase the teacher's identity. Erasure of one's rights is just as much an inscription in the identity of *teacher* as is any "positive" discourse or practice.

NOTES

1. I use *LGBTQ* because this term refers to a range of identities, practices, and representations of individual teachers themselves who self-identify as lesbian, gay, bisexual, transgender, queer, or questioning.

2. Warner coined the term *heteronormativity* in the nineties, explaining that heteronormativity includes those punitive rules—social, familial, and legal—that force members of society to conform to hegemonic, heterosexual standards for identity (Warner, 1993, 1999). Blount (2004) offers an explanation for the heteronormative beliefs found in schools and communities:

> Schools have provided compelling social education for normative sexuality and gender. Schools have defined and regulated gender identities, and school board members and administrators have attempted to hire school workers who model acceptable sexuality and gender norms for their students. (p. 176)

3. The term *identity* refers to how one defines oneself in terms of one's social context and the groups to which one belongs (Beauchamp and Thomas, 2009). I use the word *identity* in the singular here, as a way to talk about how individuals construct who they are in relationship to moments in space, place, and time. *Identity* does not convey a singular and fixed construction; rather, it is nonunitary, evolving within the multiple, shifting contexts in which we live, and is created within and through social and cultural discourse. The intersectionality of sexual orientation and identity is important to consider in the social, historical, and cultural contexts in which we live, and from which we derive our identity. LGBTQ sexual orientation plays a significant role in shaping the many different "selves" that are engaged in the social context of teaching practice at particular point in space and time.

4. Appiah (2005) is instructive in understanding the complexity of forming teacher identity in the diverse and pluralistic society that defines the educational surroundings:

> [T]he social identities that clamor for recognition are extremely multifarious. Some groups have the names of the earlier ethnicities: Italian, Jewish, Polish. Some correspond to the old races (black, Asian, Indian); or to religions (Baptist, Catholic, Jewish, again). Some are basically regional (Southern, Western, Puerto Rican). Yet others are new groups that meld together people of particular geographic origins (Hispanic, Asia American) or are social categories (woman, gay, bisexual, disabled, deaf) that are none of these. (p. 117)

5. The "student of teaching" as I use the designation in this text refers generally to the preservice teacher who is preparing to teach. However, because I believe that teacher educators must also be, as Freire (1998) explained, students of learning to teach, I include the teacher educator as a student of teaching. In this sense, "Whoever teaches learns in the act of teaching, and whoever learns teaches in the act of learning" (Freire, 1998, p. 31). In the context of teacher identity and our role as teacher educator, "The importance of the identity of each one of us as an agent, educator or learner, of the educational practice is clear, as is the importance of our identity as a product of a tension-filled relationship between what we inherit and what we acquire" (Freire, 1998, p. 70).

6. DeMitchell et al. (2009) capture the historical:

> The conduct of American schoolteachers has always been a matter of public concern. While teachers were required to be good employees, they were also required to be good, moral, and upstanding citizens. Thus, the teacher's life was scrutinized inside the classroom as an employee and watched over outside the classroom as a role model for his or her students. (p. 68)

REFERENCES

Alsup, J. (2006). *Teacher identity discourses: Negotiating personal and professional spaces*. Mahwah, NJ: Lawrence Erlbaum Associates.

Appiah, A. K. (2005). *The ethics of identity*. Princeton, NJ: Princeton University Press.

Asher, N. (2007). Made in the (multicultural) U.S.A.: unpacking tensions of race, culture, gender, and sexuality in education. *Educational Researcher, 36*(2), 65–73.

Beauchamp, C., & Thomas, L. (2009). Understanding teacher identity: An overview of issues in the literature and implications for teacher education. *Cambridge Journal of Education, 39*(2) 175–89.

Blount, J. M. (2004). Same-sex desire, gender, and social education in the twentieth century. In C. Woyshner, J. Watras, & M. S. Crocco (Eds.), *Social education in the twentieth century: Curriculum and context for citizenship* (pp. 176–91). New York: Peter Lang.

Cochran-Smith, M., Shakman, K., Jong, C., Terrell, D., Barnatt, J., & Mcquillan, P. (2009). Good and just teaching: The case for social justice in teacher education. American *Journal of Education, 115*(3), 347–77.

Cohen, J. (1993). Constructing race at an urban high school: In their minds, their mouths, their hearts. In L. Weis & M. Fine (Eds.), *Beyond silenced voices: Class, race, and gender in United States schools* (pp. 289–308). Albany, NY: State University of New York Press.

DeMitchell, T. A., Eckes, S., & Fossey, R. (2009). Sexual orientation and the public school teacher. *Public Interest Law Journal, 19*, 65–105.

Donahue, D. M. (2007). Rethinking silence as support: Normalizing lesbian and gay teacher identities through models and conversations in student teaching. *Journal of Gay and Lesbian Issues in Education, 4*(4), 73–95.

Evans, K. (2002). *Negotiating the self: Identity, sexuality, and emotion in learning to teach*. New York: Routledge/Falmer.

Freire, P. (1998). *Pedagogy of freedom: Ethics, democracy, and civic courage.* Lanham, MD: Rowman and Littlefield.

Grossberg, L. (1996). Identity and cultural studies: Is that all there is? In S. Hall and P. du Gay (Eds.), *Questions of cultural identity* (pp. 87–107). Thousand Oaks, CA: Sage.

Haddad, Z. M. (2013). *A multiple case study of gay teacher identity development: Negotiating and enacting identity to interrupt heteronormativity* (Doctoral dissertation, University of Nevada–Las Vegas). Retrieved from https://digitalscholarship.unlv.edu/thesesdissertations/1928

Hill, H. R. (2006). Teach to reach: Addressing lesbian, gay, bisexual, and transgender youth issues in the classroom. *The New Educator, 3,* 149–57.

Holland, D., Lachicotte Jr., W., Skinner, D., & Cain, C. (1998). *Identity and agency in cultural worlds.* Cambridge, MA: Harvard University Press.

Ingraham, C. (2005). Introduction: Thinking straight. In C. Ingraham (Ed.), *Thinking straight: The power, the promise, and the paradox of heterosexuality* (pp. 1–14). New York: Routledge.

MacIntosh, L. (2007). Does anyone have a Band-Aid?: Anti-homophobia discourses and pedagogical impossibilities. *Educational Studies, 41*(1), 33–43.

Mayo, J. B. (2008). Gay teachers' negotiated interactions with their students and (straight) colleagues. *The High School Journal, 92*(1), 1–10.

Mullen, C. A. (1999). Whiteness, cracks, and ink stains: Making cultural identity with Euroamerican pre-service teachers. In C. T. P. Diamond and C. A. Mullen (Eds.), *The postmodern educator: Arts-based inquiries and teacher development* (pp. 147–85). New York: Peter Lang.

Page, A. D., & Peacock, J. R. (2013). Negotiating identities in a heteronormative context. *Journal of Homosexuality, 60*(4), 639–654, DOI: 10.1080/00918369.2012.724632

Spodek, B. (1974). *Teacher education: Of the teacher, by the teacher, for the child.* Washington, D.C.: National Association for the Education of Young Children.

Sumara, D. J. (1998). Fictionalizing acts: Reading and the making of identity. *Theory into Practice, 37*(3), 203–10.

Talburt, S. (2000). Introduction: Some contradictions and possibilities of thinking queer. In S. Talburt & S. Steinberg (Eds.), *Thinking queer: Sexuality, culture, and education* (pp. 3–13). New York, NY: Peter Lang.

Taylor, C. (1992). *Multiculturalism and the politics of recognition.* Princeton, NJ: Princeton University Press.

Taylor, C. (1994). The politics of recognition. In A. Gutmann (Ed.), *Multiculturalism: Examining the politics of recognition* (pp. 25–73). Princeton, NJ: Princeton University Press.

Vavrus, M. (2009). Sexuality, schooling, and teacher identity formation: A critical pedagogy for teacher education. *Teaching and Teacher Education, 25,* 383–90.

Warner, M. (Ed.). (1993). *Fear of a queer planet: Queer politics and social theory.* Minneapolis: University of Minnesota Press.

Warner, M. (1999). *The trouble with normal: Sex, politics, and the ethics of queer life.* Cambridge, UK: Harvard University Press.

Woolley, S. W. (2013). *Identity and difference: Negotiating gender and sexuality in high school contexts* (Doctoral dissertation, University of California–Berkeley). Retrieved from https://escholarship.org/uc/item/2wp2x3q4.

Chapter Two

Performativity and Disidentification

Subverting Identity Politics through Stereotypical Embrace or Rejection

Adam J. Greteman and Ira David Socol

School is a theater with a limited set of roles on the traditional cast list. Like an American play from the early twentieth century, the parts were written for white, middle class, heterosexual, typically abled actors. The ability of others to fill these roles, such as an African American playing King Lear, has usually been defined by their ability to separate who they are in every way from what the audience sees.

Yet within the postmodern condition, the "identity" of teacher has become a struggle as the profession slowly becomes or is argued to need to become less dominated by "white, middle class, heterosexual, typically abled" actors. The traditional theatre of education is in crisis, as it has perhaps always been, as bodies of new teachers struggle to redefine or fit into the traditional cast list.

Three audiences comprise the proscenium of the theater of primary and secondary education. For teachers, the students provide not just an oppositional character on stage but the center of a stunningly critical audience. The students are flanked by the parents—a willing audience, yet one angry about the ticket prices—and the community, a typically silent audience, yet the one most likely to provide a dangerous level of word-of-mouth review. These audiences are each "responsible," in different and complex ways, for how the show goes, what is gained, what is lost, who lives, who laughs, and inevitably what can be "done" in the world.

However, the places of education are not short-term, one-off performances. The roles of educators and students are more involved than roles in long-running stage plays, in the serially conceived film of the 1930s, 1940s, or 1950s, or in weekly television. The performative nature of these ongoing, daily-involved roles create enormous pressures and costs as the performers struggle for identity. In schools, the further a teacher, or a student, stands from the role as written, the greater the potential costs of being unintelligible and not recognized as a subject.

Yet such lack of recognition or intelligibility, although precarious, also provides for critical places for intervention. The costs of these ongoing performances, then, are extremely high, and, in the ongoing roles of teacher in a community, the costs of changing one's performance, of altering the structure of one's identification, might loom as insurmountable.

Disidentification is a basic function of theater, and a basic function of all of the roles in education, but the level of disidentification—and the costs—vary widely. It is a function that is required, is helpful, is destructive, all at the same time. There can be nothing inherently understood as "authentic" in any performance.

The perceived "authenticity," both for the audience and the performer, stems from the construction of the role being played and how that structure meets or challenges the preconception of both parties. Iconic American actors like Jimmy Stewart or Tom Cruise must unify their own understood personas and assumptions with national myths to perform their roles. The roles, although seemingly written for them, require an abandonment of any unique self-concepts, an act of disidentification that may appear cost-free from the audiences' views.

On the other hand, actors such as Judy Garland and Montgomery Clift can be fatally—and somewhat obviously—wounded by the necessary transformation in roles that threaten their own self-images with destruction. However, as theatre has been challenged, so too have the roles and possibilities within theatre, possibilities that allow the audience to see something "new" or for the audience to be surprised, confused, or made anxious by roles no longer filled by the bodies that once dominated the stage.

This requirement that an actor—a teacher—create a consistently understood characterization, often apart from the characterizations they use in other moments of their lives, is a powerful but conflicting task for those on both sides of the proscenium. One might "successfully pass" as straight, or typically abled, or Protestant, or a non–recreational drug user, or as a conservative. In this, actor and audience might be linked in a pact of suspension of disbelief, or it may result in a challenge to expectations ("Why is this person not identifying how we expect them to?").

Or the disidentification might have other intentions. It may take the form of a conversation, through reframing, a conversation designed to gradually reduce tension and anxiety. Or the disidentification might be designed to create gateways of exploration, forcing the audience to doubt their roles by bringing the anxiety to the center of the stage.

For teachers, our interest in this chapter, their identity has been produced in complex and often contradictory ways. Their identity begins away from but related to the role of teacher in a significant way; the steps of (dis)identification with their persona walk a complex line which often borders on "identity treason" (Kannen, 2008).

As with the notion of "race traitors," "straight acting" and "closeted" homosexuals, those who hide "invisible" disabilities, and those with visible disabilities who tend to act as if there is no functional difference, arguably achieve disidentification, contingently, and meet audience expectations (Garvey, 1996). They could be read as reinforcing the perceptions that oppress the "original" identity group, both intrapersonally and within that central student audience. Yet in doing so, they also disrupt or challenge the assumptions of what one's "identity" or "identification" should be.

In moments of (dis)identification, there emerges a paradoxical reinforcing and challenging of identity categories. Teacher identity, within this postmodern play, has become a precarious concept as different critical perspectives have sought to challenge or subvert traditional notions of "identification." As such, preservice teachers and those involved with their initiation into the profession of education, are placed within a space and time where there is a struggle for identity (Britzman, 2003; Segall, 2002).

Preservice teachers ask themselves who they can be, what they can be, and how such decisions will affect their own image and authority as "teacher." Yet, within many teacher education programs, the struggle with identity is rarely engaged with preservice teachers beyond either multicultural courses that focus on student identity or professional development conversations on the role of, for instance, "dress."

For students whose identities are "marginalized" or "controversial," this lack of engagement with their peers and instructors causes further anxiety and fear around entering the classroom space and the complicated process of "becoming" a teacher. For students who may identify as nonheterosexual, nonabled, nonwhite, the process of deciding how to become a teacher and what that becoming means for the various aspects of their lives enters anxious territory. It is in part, then, this anxious territory that this chapter engages to negotiate the politics of identity, their possible subversion, and how such issues relate to or negate various possibilities in education (e.g., recognition, pedagogical, curricular).

One might note here the inherent challenges to identity formation that exist within the act of becoming a teacher for anyone who, even in part, perceives himself or herself as nonheterosexual or nontraditionally abled. The role of teacher, although occasionally linked in "romantic" film to the concept of liberation (see *Dead Poets' Society*), might be more often seen as part of a system of oppression by those who understand their position as that of one on a societal edge (those "lacerated by school," in the nomenclature of Kirsten Olson [2009] or those "on the borderline," in the words of Danish novelist Peter Høeg [1995]).

This is to suggest that the process of becoming a teacher alters the identity conversation long before the teacher enters the classroom. This alteration is, in part, not independent or completely in one's control. Rather, it is a process of becoming that always depends on the discursive possibilities and a becoming that has no end.

Identity is not the enemy, however, and we do not seek to simply throw this critical term aside. For it is identity that, at times, is important for individuals to "put on" as such a "putting on" allows for those individuals to become recognizable within the contexts in which they reside. Although identity has been argued as being essentialist or static, Spivak's (1995) notion of strategic essentialism is inevitably "essential" for us and the political struggles that teachers experience in their contexts.

The different identities that teachers can "put on" are multiple, with each of these identities having its own historical significance and baggage. One can put on the identity of woman or man, black or white, gay or straight, abled or dis-abled; in doing so, one opens oneself up to certain violations and assumptions, but also to possibilities and recognitions.

The notion "putting on" is, of course, more complex then positioned here, as one cannot simply "put on" one's race or gender, class or sexuality. Rather, this putting on, this process of identification, always depends on the context in which one is involved and if one can perhaps pass intelligibly.[1] For the purposes of this chapter, then, we focus on two such identities—"sexuality" and "ability"—to explore the ways in which these identities have been put on in the past and presently, but also how one might not put on such identities or perhaps disidentify with such identities—not to be apolitical or ashamed of what one "is" but to illustrate possibilities in "doing" what one "is" differently—a disruption of the seemingly "natural" identity.

We note from the outset, however, that this engagement is limited, as it will fail to adequately address the relationships sexuality and able-ness have to other identities such as race, class, and gender. For this, we apologize for our inadequacies.[2]

PERFORMATIVITY AND DISIDENTIFICATION

As we begin this exploration, it is important to first clarify some key conceptual terms that will be used throughout our exploration—namely, *performativity* and *disidentification*. Although the theory of performativity, theorized extensively by Judith Butler, has been brought into education contexts,[3] it is still a term that requires explanation and clarification.

Some have read performativity as simply "donning" a costume and being able to simply "be" something different, a seemingly voluntaristic notion. Our use of performativity, however, follows the work of Butler and is one that engages the citational "nature" of the performance. Performativity is not something that can be reduced to *a* "performance" but rather is a repetition of performances.

As Butler (1993) notes:

> [P]erformativity is thus not a singular "act," for it is always a reiteration of a norm or set of norms, and to the extent that it acquires an act-like status in the present, it conceals or dissimulates the conventions of which it is a repetition. (p. 12)

In this, one acts or performs, and such a performance, constrained by certain norms, is repeated and in such repetition becomes seen as "natural" or "normal" or one's "identity." One is compelled to cite such norms "in order to qualify and remain a viable subject" because "subject formation is dependent on the prior operation of legitimating norms" (Butler, p. 232). If a performance does not "line up" with the norms, it is a performance that is often unintelligible and causes violence to be inflicted on the body performing as such to "straighten out" such queerness.

It is these performances, these disruptions to the norms, that in part are of interest to us in this chapter as we argue for or explore the ways in which certain actions—namely the normalized performative of "coming out"—can be challenged to create alternative ways to teach and disrupt the establishment of one's identity as either a "faggot" or a "retard" and inevitably "straight" or "abled."

Important to this exploration also is the concept of *disidentification*. As Munoz (1999) argues, disidentification is, in part, a critical recycling of the term that is "about cultural, material, and psychic survival" as one sets about "managing and negotiating historical trauma and systems of violence" (p. 161).

It is a process that allows for the abject, the outside of "identity," to seek legitimacy—not as a "reverse discourse" but as a way to "rewrite the history of the term, and to force it into a demanding resignification" (Butler, 1993, p. 21). As Munoz (1999) notes, "disidentification is an ambivalent structure of feeling that works to retain the problematic object and tap into the energies that are produced by contradictions and ambivalences" to engage in the practices of freedom and contest the world in which one has been produced in and by (p. 71).

These practices of freedom are not meant to lead to a solidarity between those who identify with the coming out process and those who refute it, but to ask for ways in which such conflicts can be sustained in productive ways as the different groups involved "articulate their goals under the pressure of each other without therefore exactly becoming each other" (Butler, 1998, p. 37). We do not seek to throw away *gay* or *disabled*, but to find ways to resignify them to do something different, to disrupt or challenge the often seen "drive" for such identities to "come out."

PARODY AND PERFORMATIVE AUTHENTICITY

Part of our project is also parodic and ironic. We use these modes of writing and "doing" not to mock the positions we critique but to recognize that the positions we parody are in part necessary for our own work. To disidentify, we need to understand the process of identifying and its political importance.

We, as authors, as teachers, as students, have taken the other position depending on the context and "come out." The intellectual traditions for which "coming out" emerge are a part of our intellectual and personal past. Parody, as Butler (1998) writes, "requires a certain ability to identify, approximate, and draw near; it engages an intimacy with the position it appropriates that trouble the voice . . . such that the audience or the reader does not quite know where it is you stand" (pp. 34–35).

Within the conversation of parody, questions emerge about authenticity and how, through parody, one might be able to do authentic teaching. We might begin with the notion of parodying the concept of "authenticity" and where that parody might lead us. "All representation is misrepresentation," Said (1978) notes, while saying that one possible solution is to retreat to "a make believe world that had no relationship (a) to reality and (b) to the history and actuality of the places we were living in" (p. 272).

Importantly, Said (1978) never sees that kind of retreat, or the other complexities of misrepresentation, as impediment to observation, communication, or the ability to challenge power. As he writes in *Orientalism*, "all cultures impose corrections on raw reality, changing it from free-floating objects to units of knowledge" (p. 67). These units of knowledge, in Said's theory, are worn not as symbols of any actuality, but as costumes designed to either explain as familiar to the audience or to challenge and provoke that audience. Said (2001) himself struggled constantly with the notions of identity, authenticity, and performative narrative, and seemed to conclude that identity was every bit as powerful a concept as it was unreal and dangerous.

Said, Terry Eagleton (2004) wrote, had a "nervousness of orthodoxies" (p. 281), yet he also found identity in the educational audience. Eagleton (2004) cites Said: "I depend very heavily on reactions from my students,"

Said said, noting distinct differences between the types of audiences his work played to, from intellectual representation of the future possibilities of the Islamic world in Europe (ironic in that he was raised a Protestant Christian and principally educated in British-style schools), to "defender of Islam against the evils of the West," in the nations of the Arab world (p. 280, 281).

Can one, in challenging the dominant mode that is imbued with a certain power and authentic recognition, challenge such modes and still be "authentic"? Can one, in working against any expected script or characterization that is accepted as a trope, remain self-aware and comfortable in what feels like "authentic" identity? What "authentic" means, of course, is problematic and contextual but a point that we think important to point out here as the struggle for identity, in part, alludes to becoming one's authentic self.

So, if teachers should "be authentic" with their students, what are possible ways to interpret the concept of authenticity? Is authenticity perhaps an illusion, and a useful illusion to play with as it is the struggle, not the identity, the doing not the being, which the teacher should investigate?

A good teacher is authentic, then, but in such authenticity is able to play with the context of the space and time one is teaching within—an authenticity that is performative or performative authenticity. This performative authenticity in teaching is not about being authentic, but doing authenticity such that "doing" is never about completeness but about impersonating the images of a teacher that may be "productive" or "provocative" in context and getting away with it or being pedagogically useful.

This concept of "doing," however, is not separate from "being," but rather "being" occurs when repetitiously "doing" what is "thought" to be "x" namely "teacher." We each "do" teaching and, in such doing, may "become" a teacher, that is, establish an "identity" that is perhaps part of the problem, as such a "becoming" forecloses other possible ways of engaging and "doing" the world.

The playfulness between "doing" and "being" allows us, as we argue, to not foreclose possibilities that are not yet known, not yet livable or survivable as we can, if brave enough, "do" teaching differently to "be" a different teacher—which is perhaps unrecognizable to some. One might liken this to impersonators who "do" Elvis, but who, in doing repetitiously become a performer of Elvis's persona. This impersonation allows the person doing the impersonation to do the world in a new way, outside of the "normal," and provides space for the viewer to imagine doing something outside the "normal," of new possibilities. None of these impersonations or performances are "universal," but rather are contingent within the context of such performance.[4]

POSSIBILITIES

Judith Butler (2004) writes:

> The thought of a possible life is only an indulgence for those who already know themselves to be possible. For those who are still looking to become possible, possibility is a necessity. (p. 272)

We use this quote to think about ways we may position our students (and ourselves) to do thinking around the impossible not as a task to displace the issues that are present, but to recognize that those issues occlude thinking about the production of such issues. It is our attempt to allow our classrooms to not simply focus on the issues the readings present but think about issues that may be there that are not explicit or visible—issues that may be made visible through our "doings" as teacher as "we" attempt to deconstruct our readings and productions.

Further, it is an attempt to be excessive in thought, to think "big" and go beyond to see what might be there but has been hidden through different discursive moves. To do thinking and teaching in such a way allows for a disruption of the beings (both student and teacher) that are possible to allow for different "doings" that, once accepted and recognizable, become possible. This disruption of the "being" by the "doing" invokes different possibilities in the ever shifting context of the classroom to never simply accept the student body as "natural" and "essential" but as performative, contingent.

Disability studies and queer theory allow us, in this frame, to work the tensions between playing with those already recognizable identities (e.g., gay and lesbian, learning disabled) so that they are livable, but also challenge those identities and how such identities have been discursively constituted to produce other possibilities of seeing such "bodies."

Tom Shakespeare, in the disability studies movement, has worked toward a complex way of doubting those identities—these visions of the bodies and the social structures that offer them as "scripts":

> Being disabled by society is about the twin processes of discrimination and prejudice, which restrict individuals with impairment. This structural analysis is based on the notion of disabled people as an oppressed minority group, and disablement as a collective experience.
> Disability is viewed as a problem located within society—not the individual—and the way to reduce disability is to alter the social and physical environment. (Shakespeare and Watson, 1996, p. 1)

Yet, if this is true, "[o]nce social barriers to the reintegration of people with physical impairments are removed, the disability itself is eliminated" (Finkelstein, 1980, as quoted in Shakespeare and Watson, 1996, p. 3). This notion eliminates any valued notion of human diversity.

When Shakespeare describes "reintroducing difference," he notes that, "[t]hese writers do not see impairment as irrelevant or neutral"—that, as postcolonialists might see it—"the cultural differences forged by history, environment, religion can not be explained away with simple genetics" (Shakespeare and Watson, 1996, p. 4). Those differences, because they alter all parts of the enculturation experience, forge fundamental differences in vision and comprehension.

They become imbedded into both subsequent identity formation and performance. Committed Marxist Terry Eagleton, according to interviewer Laurie Taylor, still saw the Irish Catholicism of his childhood as "a persistent rebuff, a no-go area" (2009, p. 2085), preventing him from embracing what he saw as the extremes of his "leftist" identity.

According to Shakespeare, "We need to focus on disability and impairment; on the external and internal constituents that bring together our experiences. Impairment is about our bodies' ways of working and any implications that holds for our lives. Disability is about the reaction and impact of the outside world on our particular bodies" (Shakespeare and Watson, 1996, p. 6). Such a view of disability allows us to embrace the difference, perhaps to celebrate it, to understand its contributions to that internal sense and the public remaking of self.

Allowing that view of disability creates space for a differing "reading" of any performative character, no matter what role one is about to play or what script one is choosing to work from. "Even the cruelties and stupidities that the Irish Church has perpetrated do not prevent me from recalling how, without it, generations of my own ancestors would have gone unschooled, unnursed, unconsoled and unburied," said Eagleton (Taylor, 2009, p. 2085), despite his years of battling with the church, thus offering a deep acceptance of internal conflict and a willingness to alter his role as the understood needs of both himself and his audiences shift.[5]

This ability to reimagine the beings we are, both experientially and interactively, lead us back to Butler and propels us to ask how we can "do" teaching in a way for new "beings" to become possible, intelligible be that for ourselves as the teacher or for the students sitting in the desks, struggling to survive both "here" in our class and "there" in our future classes.[6] In thinking about these possibilities, we often enter the realm of the fantastical.

In such fantastical space, parody and irony open a safe space for risky thoughts for, as previously noted, these modes require an understanding of that which they parody—the norms and ways the world views or produces "bodies" as intelligible. This fantastical space of doing teaching in this way at times disorients students as they struggle with what to say, while eventually at times engaging conversations that initially were seen as rather humorous or odd questions.

This disorientation in language and understanding can be constructed in this space through challenge and humor and manufactured discomfort.[7] Rejection of "cure" for the "disabled," like rejection of heteronormative standards such as marriage by parts of the gay community, challenge and threaten carefully formed expectations of the role of liberal, progressive societies. Use of terms such as *retard*, *crip*, and *faggot* put the rules of the theater into play as they force reconsideration of the "idea of normality" (Oliver, 1996, p. 6). Discussions of sexuality and disability in ways seen as "inappropriate" for education's stage push students to laugh when "they shouldn't."

The assumption in pushing students in this way is that disorienting students, be it through a question or a reading or our own performances, is educative as it can, if students allow it, challenge them to engage with the topic to become oriented in a different, perhaps slightly altered way, or to reorient themselves to what was familiar.

The question that remains is always whether such disorienting performances are educative.[8] Rather than challenging students to "do" the world differently, do they reinforce why the world is "done" how it is "done"? Is that problematic? Are these, our thoughts on "performative authenticity," really an excuse to maintain the status quo, making the disruptive, the alternative "doings" ridiculous, impractical, excessive, and easily moved past?[9] Is disorientation too disruptive to be "effective" in the time frame of a course?

There is obviously no clear answer to these questions, but there are examples of our own teaching wherein this process of disorientation through performance can be seen and interpreted for the diverse, contradictory results. We move now to present some of these examples to hopefully illuminate the issues introduced previously.

ON COMING OUT

In thinking about the ways that words might wound, Butler (1993) writes,

> Here it is not only a question of how discourse injures bodies, but how certain injuries establish certain bodies at the limits of available ontologies, available schemes of intelligibility. And further, how is it that the abjected come to make their claim through and against the discourses that have sought their repudiation. (p. 223)

We see from Butler's claim that "coming out" is dangerous business. It is a process that, through the injury of forcing an utterance of "I'm gay," or "I'm learning disabled" brings the abject into a space of recognition, but in doing so violates that being. One of the outcomes of "coming out" is a normalization of the subject and a repudiation of the "queerness" of being.

Coming out, as a process or series of utterances, normalizes the possibilities of "being," for instance, gay whereby one can only be recognizably gay through "coming out"—by stating "I'm gay." I become a legitimate subject as I cite the utterance that is "essential" for the healthy, psychologized gay subject. It is the repetition of this "utterance" of the closet, that has since the middle of the twentieth century become a defining aspect of "being" gay and since been taken up in other avenues of "difference" (e.g., coming out as Republican or a chocolate lover).[10]

Yet the power of the utterance is not simply one that normalizes the "gay" subject as it does, in its utterance, disrupt the heteronormative—disrupting the social field that is often viewed as "straight." The dangerous business of coming out is, then, that it is never neutral. It is always rife with problems simultaneously disruptive and normalizing.

Part of our argument is to disrupt the normalizing process of the coming-out utterance for the queer bodies—to illustrate other possibilities of being "gay" or "disabled"—to decipher this utterance and its tie to identity to expose what *can be* rather than what *solely is* in the frame of outness. Foucault (1996) argued in "Friendship as a Way of Life" that "we have to work at becoming homosexuals," illuminating in part that homosexuality is never something completely realized, but something worked toward; it is this process, this "becoming," that disturbs people as it brings about "the formation of new alliances and the tying together of unforeseen lines of force" (pp. 136–138). Using Foucault within our argument, then, individuals who are "queer" in some way have been asked to "out" themselves so as to be intelligible to those around them and, as it is argued, authentic to themselves.

But this outness is not solely a subversive act; rather, it can maintain the status quo whereby one simply "is" what has been possible, rather than becoming something yet realized. One's queerness is stripped away in order to be recognized. Queer bodies, in contemporary twenty-first century discourses, must make such a statement (e.g., I'm gay, I'm learning disabled, I'm crippled) and repeat such a statement so as to be understood, to be properly legible and legitimate.

A subject must "come out" as "x" constantly, and if such a subject does not, one is criticized for not being, say, "out and proud," or of not taking advantage of the resources available. Those who do not "come out" disturb people because such a position challenges what has been "realized," challenging the intelligibility of subjects.

For instance, a "disabled" subject must "come out" to be given proper services that are otherwise denied to subjects that don't or have no "reason" to come out. But this coming out must be a repetition of a certain form of coming out, a certain form of being "disabled." There is violence within this discourse of coming out and being intelligible in doing so.

Outness then is compulsory to become a legitimate, viable subject. Yet such outness for these same subjects is precarious as it asks them to repeat a claim that, while producing them as intelligible, violates in a major way. This compulsory drive depends on the need for assimilation, the need or want to be normal—to maintain the myths already in place about "being" a certain subject. There are legitimate reasons to argue in such a way as such arguments can garner certain rights and protections—the intentions, goals, and success of identity politics.

Yet with such rights and protections, other issues, possibilities, and lives are occluded. As Rich (1980) notes in her exploration of compulsory heterosexuality, women's experience within a heteronormative society limits their ability to explore their bodies and other's bodies outside of the normative, masculine economy of desire. Oliver (1996) watches as the disability movement moves to reject any notion of "cure" or even individual solutions as incompatible with disability pride and identity.

McRuer (2006), taking up this same notion, extends its reach with the concept of compulsory able-bodiedness wherein differently abled bodies are limited in their experiences by the able-bodied norms. And arguably with queer critiques of mainstream gay and lesbian movements, a compulsory homosexuality, or as Duggan (2002) notes, homonormativity, has emerged as LGBTQ politics push for legitimation by arguing to be normal.

Each of these authors' explorations of the compulsory "nature" of norms allow for recognitions of the complexity of identity, the citationality of their performance, and the trouble with normal.[11] The nature of fixed identity, the belief that coming out is mandatory, relies in part on the possibility of normality and its relation to "authenticity." However, as Edward Said (1993) suggests, a belief in "essential and unchanging qualities" is a deliberate decision, made for political and historical reasons (p. 134).

These notions of fixed status among the colonized of any society are constructs that serve political causes (Said, 1978). The fixed "authentic" group identity is critical to theories of power on both sides of any oppressive relationship. In Said's (1993) engagement of Rudyard Kipling's (1901) novel *Kim*, he notes "colonial . . . appropriation requires such assertive inflections" (p. 160), and requires constant affirmation of "the difference between a white man and a non-white" (p 157).

Said goes on to describe Kim's "chameleon" like ability, where Kim is seen as "a great actor passing through many situations" (p. 158). However, Said notes that Kipling constructed this character as an outsider in all situations, "an Irishman in India" (p. 156). Yet this "outsider" status is fixed and genetically constructed in Kipling's world, and in colonizing situations. For the nonheterosexual or non–typically abled pushing against fixed identity notions in the twenty-first century, they may be seen as creating an "inauthentic" identity, with every step taken across the stage creating unresolved conflicts in relation to the past and contingent possibilities in relation to the future.

This question of "authenticity" in the performative raises particular conflicts in the fields of sexuality and ability. "Even though I knew that gender, race, and sexual orientation were unstable designations," Michael Bérubé wrote in the foreword to *Claiming Disability* (Linton, 1998), "I had yet to learn—or to be taught—that disability is the most unstable designation of them all" (p. xi). At the same time, popular international culture has built an apparent, if possibly completely inaccurate, acceptance of sexual instability, an acceptance more easily found via contemporary media technology than through the technologies of the past.

These available instabilities provide a subtext that challenges any sense of certainty, particularly in young teachers at the start of their careers when much of teacher education recommends that they seem certain and sure in front of their audiences. If things seen as "fundamentals" by many in society—sexual preferences, cognitive status, abilities—might shift, is anything solidly grounded? And for teachers, who have often been schooled themselves in "cognitive and emotional dependence" on a school structure and community that seems rigid and unforgiving, this instability, this fear of inauthenticity, removes access to safe harbors of securely perceived identities (Olson, 2009, p. 71).

Coming out, from this frame, then, is precarious. Butler (1997) notes, "But we surely need to take seriously the contention that 'coming out' is intended as a contagious example, that it is supposed to set a precedent and incite a series of similarly structured acts in public discourse" (p. 124).

Although Butler is engaging the role the speech act operates in the heteronormative, paranoid military context, whereby the act of coming out is punished under Don't Ask Don't Tell, it is possible to extend her contention in how it works within the homonormative context, where it is hoped that in "coming out," a contagion is incited whereby the one "coming out" serves as an example for recruits, for (gay) youth. Yet in both of these efforts, one to limit and one to expand the contagion of outness, Butler (1997) exposes the fact that, although "[t]he declaration that is 'coming out' is certainly a kind of act . . . it does not fully constitute the referent to which it refers; indeed *it renders homosexuality discursive, but it does not render discourse referential*" (p. 125).

FAGGOTY ANECDOTAL EVIDENCE

I don't come out in my classroom by making the explicit speech act of "I am gay" or "I am not gay." This puts me at odds with some scholarship in gay and lesbian studies and popular culture that argues for "outing." Some might find such a decision indicative of "internalized homophobia" or not being comfortable in one's own skin. But I "choose" to do this because I want to, in part, put my students in the awkward space of not knowing and explore what it means to need to know the other's sexuality through speech or to position sexuality as an "identity."

In a conversation with one of my classes, this issue came to light as one of my students noted the need for teachers to be "out" because "out" teachers can provide a "role model" for other gay or questioning students, along with students in general. In this, the student made it relatively clear that it is unfortunate for teachers to be closeted because it is, in a sense, a loss for the community.

As the instructor, I felt the gaze of my students as I then noted that such a stance is important and necessary perhaps in showing other possibilities. Others might not "come out" not because of the simple legal realities of potentially losing one's job, depending on the state in which one resides, but to disrupt the necessity of the "speech act," to create a space of questioning and perhaps become comfortable with "not knowing" and moving sexuality away from being an "identity" based solely on "object choice."

I note this stance in part to show that there are alternatives to reinscribing the norms around sexuality and identity, along with exposing a possible stance they, unknowingly, are or were experiencing. Upon putting this stance out there, another student chimed in with the realization that the notion of coming out is not really for the "gay person" but for "us" so we "know" and are not uncomfortable with not knowing.

I found the discussion illuminating as it presented different ways to conceptualize the issue. But as it was being presented I, in a sense, became paranoid as my body was on display and my own performance was being exposed and explored for its pedagogical possibilities. I arguably probably "came out" to them as something by explaining why one might not "come out" as most of them probably assumed my "sexuality" from my performances (e.g., excessive hand gestures, excited speech, stylish dress, cute shoes), my academic scholarship (e.g., queer theory, sexuality, gender), and my personal stories (e.g., Easter at a drag show, experiences in LGBTQ politics).

Was this display, this vulnerability, an aspect of performative authenticity, of being exposed to the pain that students themselves are asked to expose to the teacher? Is this an illustration where my performance as teacher, often not "serious," exposed serious issues that then allowed for the engagement?

Did my students recognize my own vulnerability, opening up my life as I asked them to open their lives to be read as a text (as it always already is) and make a pedagogical point?

Could my students or can students in general "see" this authenticity or this "authentic" doing? Although authenticity seems to at times to rely on the notion of a "true self" that I am being authentic to, would "coming out" make my students see me as more "authentic" than not coming out but engaging the issues "authentically"? Yet my authentic self is perhaps an impersonation of what in a particular moment I think is wanted of me or what I think would be productive to have available to be seen for pedagogical purposes.

After my students discussed this issue about outness, I made the choice to tell a personal story of being at a gay club for Easter and exploring how the scene of the drag show at the club exposed important issues of sexuality, religion, and, because of the space of the story, education.

Did I choose to tell this story, at this moment, to be authentic with them, to give them something that would quench what seemed to be their thirst to "know" if I am "gay" or perhaps to orient them, finally, after a semester of disorientation and querying whether they have a gay teacher who has yet to say he is (or isn't) gay?

RETARDED ANECDOTAL EVIDENCE

I typically tell my students about one of my "disabilities" but not the other. I describe myself as a "dyslexic" early in any course, and I do that for both course content reasons and political ones. There is value to me in "coming out," and so I do. Fully "in character," I express to the future teachers in the room how the ideas of reading and writing that have been taught to them have injured me, and how the technologies I will teach them about have liberated me. I also get the subtle ability to bash "people-first language" and to insist on the notion of "dyslexic" as a societal construct.

I do not like doing this, but I have listened to prior audiences and I know that emotion works when you are making a sales pitch. My one-man show about my K–12 education can leave people crying. Once they are crying, they hear other things I tell them. Once they are crying, I can twist that performance in a way which threatens them: what if my rules applied?

This is difficult stand-up to perform. I personally become uncomfortable when playing a character one step too close to my own self-perception. That proximity threatens my actor's ability to understand and analyze my performance. And yet I find that discomfort fully tolerable in this situation because my goal is to discomfort the audience—and this seems more humane to me if my act of discomforting them discomforts me.

Those issues may not really be the important ones, however, because dyslexia has never been the issue that caused me the most trouble interacting with society. I've always found ways around reading and writing myself. Attention and emotional "differences" that have cost me jobs, ruined personal relationships, left me in economic jeopardy—those matter in my life. And those I present—if I do present them—by not presenting, but by enabling the students themselves to present them as legitimate parts of the course.

There is no explicit statement of disorganization, just an edge to my presentation, a checking of clocks as if anxious for the class period to end, a refusal to lay out any definite agenda for the day, a rather unorthodox set of transitions from one event to another. There is also a random set of "inappropriate behaviors," from unexpected curses to "borderline" comments to strange choices of YouTube video presentations even to the occasional throwing (soft) things.

My performance as an "ADHD" and "emotionally impaired" person in the classroom is a commitment to doubt. I want the students asking, "Is he normal?" "Is he for real?" "Is this what I'll have to deal with?" and I want them constructing performances in response, trying on a series of performances in response to a constantly changing improv environment.

All this, however, is played against a differing backdrop with another audience. Faculty acceptance of disability—especially relating to issues with literacy and attention, twin pillars of the school establishment—is severely limited. If I am in a seminar with the faculty, with an earbud linking my computer and my ear so I can quickly process text with the assistance of text-to-speech software, I am still far more likely to play the insolent, "I'm listening to Eminem's newest," than to appear "retarded."

CONCLUSION

One of our assumptions is that, if language and ideas are dangerous, then putting on or performing the dangerous issues will be the most productive way to engage education, for it is always a performance, a citation of the norms of being.[12] Another assumption is that if all representation is misrepresentation, all identity is disidentification, and all performance is about the struggle to actually perform, then we, as performers on the stage that is "school," have a responsibility to sow doubt in our students at every turn, to make them aware of their performative identities and possibilities.

We could take on the issues of a given course as they are often taken on through a serious reading, a lecture, or a conversation forced into "polite" debate, or we can put them on, performatively playing with serious issues through seriously parodic, ironic, campy readings. We can try to "pass" as something we are engaging our students with to expose the complexity of such issues and "passing"—causing discomfort for them as they can't "pin" us down.

In this, we can use the stage arts of the magician to confound or the simple masks of Greek drama to make the costume obvious while still demanding suspension of disbelief. We can choose the special effects theory of creating Said's "make believe," or we can force the audience in by running through the aisles.

We both recognize that doing teaching this way presents certain dangers to the normal images of "doing" teaching. But we believe that such danger and risk are perhaps the "best" places to evoke reactions and engagement with issues as in such places we can ask that we "try on" these issue to see how it feels, how it works, to be disoriented, to be possible in different ways.

We work, then, as teachers engaging students around diversity, topics they are often "new" to and struggle with, not to tell them the way things are and have to be or to get them to not say certain things, but to recognize the power of words and the possibility of disrupting or undermining such language and in doing such creating, doing a fantastical, fabulous world—not an easy task by any means.

Ira: I try to assault my students on day one. I ask them to read Irish out loud, and to pronounce it correctly. I tell them, bluntly and with a hint of threat, that I can "disable anyone in this room in a heartbeat," that I can make them feel as teachers have made me feel. Then I insist that they fight back, and I encourage them to fight back. I want them to feel the actions of their limbic brains.

Adam: I do not assault my students on day one or at least not purposefully. Rather, I ask them to think with me about the difficult task of education and the trauma that education can inflict on all bodies—differentially—as that will be our task in this particular course. I assume, in part, that all my students have in some context been assaulted by education and as such inform them that the course we are beginning on diversity in education is about engaging such trauma, of being vulnerable enough to recognize the anxious terrain of power and privilege to seek reparation and how such an engagement is important for their "initiation" into education.

However, we assume that our students can handle these approaches. We ask them for feedback and maintain dialogue with them after class sessions via email to potentially provide space and time for them to feel uneasy, to know that it is ok to be uncomfortable, uncertain, or scared because "being" such asks that one "do" something different to "become" something different or do education differently.

But as one looks back on this text and our experiences and thoughts here, one sees that we are rarely concerned with our students learning "something." Rather, we are concerned that they experience something. Perhaps they experience uncertainty or hurt, or laughter or perhaps fleetingly experience a whole gamut of possibilities that their own students might feel, depending on their (the future students) positions and contexts, along with the gamut of possibilities that have been foreclosed for them but also made possible for them.

We want them as students and future teachers to put on, to impersonate doing school, life, in different ways, in different times, in different spaces, to see that it is possible to "do faggots and retards" as teachers, that it is possible to do queer things and in doing such queer things education and the experiences in education are made strange and dangerous.

Adam: Teaching this course, I am challenged to engage my students in the inequalities and injustices that affect the lives of students and teachers in the context of K–12 public education. Yet in doing so, I recognize that my students emerge out of the different educational contexts we "learn" about. As such, they have different experiences and views on education, different "strengths" and "weaknesses" that I must engage as a teacher and use to illustrate how there are different ways to engage the inequalities that are present. I make my decisions about issues (e.g., due dates, writing style) very explicit so they see the pedagogical choices and how such choices produce certain forms of education.

Ira: I insist on making the strategies obvious as the courses progress. "I had a problem and my paper will be late," I'm told. "I don't care if it's late," I say. "Specific time schedules are ableist, aren't they?" And then I add, "Remember this when you are teaching and some kid doesn't have his homework." If we are actors, we are training actors and we have a responsibility to make the performative transparent.

As we conclude, our queerly disabled engagement as teachers through parodying the serious is perhaps indebted to Dewey. We perhaps find ourselves doing the Dewey, concerned with the experience, the "doing" of education where the child and the curriculum playfully play with one another to create educative experiences and possibilities.

Education, for us, is not about being a student who learns information or learns about the other, but rather is about putting on education in perhaps a different way, where students are allowed to do teaching when the teacher is gone without a "real instructor" present, where they are not given answers but asked to struggle, to "do" education, where they see others and are asked to imagine such otherness by doing it, its violence and possibilities, for we are all, at times, the Other and other to our self.[13]

We ask them, often implicitly, to do life, to perform, to impersonate, to experience the disorientation, the risk, the fear of "doing" difference as in such a doing, the "doings" of norms are exposed as not "being" normal but as "doing" the repetitious actions of "x" as "x" has become normalized. Perhaps our doing of "teacher" this way is in part because we are not trained as teachers. As such, we are not concerned about lesson planning, behavioral management, and so on, but rather are concerned with allowing one to do the world in ways, perhaps not yet known, to impersonate someone we admire, we want to "be" and perhaps can become by "doing" them, challenging normative frameworks along the way.

Yet we have no way of knowing how this can be done and we have no idea what it means to "be" a teacher other than our experiences as a student and paying attention to the different pedagogical styles we have encountered and impersonating them at different times to see if such an impersonation comes off as authentic or fake. We imagine that as we teach more, this could change as we repeat our own performances, where our "doings" becomes normal, making us "become" a certain "type" of teacher. Will the reinscriptions of these doings make us become a teacher after doing teaching for a while where our parody becomes "normal" and "safe," and we forget how to "do" and impersonate anything beyond an impersonation of our own self?

When one "becomes" a teacher, then, has one become the epitome of a narcissist as one no longer impersonates the other, but the self as the self knows how to "be" a teacher, a safe teacher, constructed in the images and doings of the self? Is the struggle for an identity as a teacher a struggle that cannot be solved or overcome? Rather, must it be deciphered, deconstructed and constantly struggled with in order to never be comfortable, to always be, in part, disoriented, queer at times? In such a "state of becoming," are we allowed to recognize the production of identity and its power to do violence but also to provoke possibilities?

NOTES

1. For different engagements with the notion of passing, see Judith Butler (1993); Howard Griffin (1977); Sirk (1959).

2. For collections of work that engage these intersections see McCarthy, Crichlow, Dimitriadis, and Dolby (2005); Johnson and Henderson (2004); Rodriquez and Pinar (2007).

3. See for example Alexander, Anderson, and Gallegos (2004); Giroux (1997); Marshall (1999); Sedgwick (2003).

4. In using the notion of *impersonator*, we do not want to imply that one can simply take on and off different ways of "being." One may try different "doings" that disrupt one's "being" but such "doings" are, we believe, anxiety ridden and complex and do not automatically construct a "being."

5. For an example of Terry Eagleton's ongoing battle with the Catholic Church, see Eagleton, T. (2005, April 4) The Pope has blood on his hands. *The Guardian*, p. 1. Retrieved from http://www.guardian.co.uk/world/2005/apr/04/catholicism.religion14.

6. For instance, I make lesson outlines on a yellow legal pad that is thrown out at the end of the semester. I do this so as not to archive my practices beyond my memory, forcing me to do teaching differently, although similarly, each semester.

7. This disorientation may be likened to the concept of "cognitive dissonance" from a cognitive psychology frame. We do not use this phrase in part because it focuses on the "mind" and neglects the body's implication in being disoriented or in experiencing "dissonance."

8. Such a question begs to engage the work of Dewey and his thoughts on experience in education. We will engage this, albeit briefly, in the conclusion of this chapter.

9. The risks appear to go in two directions, as established in postcolonial theory (see Ignatiev [1995], Kiberd [1996], Willinsky [1998]). One can separate oneself so far from the audience that empathy is lost (the terrorist bombing might work to attract attention but not when children are targeted), or the performance can be so accessible as to become parody in and of itself, what the Quebeçois call *Cajunification*, in which French culture becomes simply a tourist attraction.

10. For an extended engagement with the notion of the "closet," see Eve Sedgwick (1990). *Epistemology of the closet*. Berkeley: University of California.

11. The phrase "the trouble with normal" is, in part, an ode to Michael Warner's *The Trouble with Normal: Sex, Politics, and the Ethics of Queer Life* (1999), which provides a critique of mainstream gay politics.

12. We take this insight from readings of Foucault, Derrida, and Said.

13. We draw this from readings of Lacan and Zizek's engagement of Lacanian psychoanalysis.

REFERENCES

Alexander, B. K., Anderson, G. L., & Gallegos, B. (2004). *Performance theories in education*. Mahwah, NJ: Lawrence Erlbaum.

Britzman, D. (2003). *Practice makes practice: A critical study of learning to teach*. New York: State University of New York Press.

Butler, J. (1990). *Gender trouble: Feminism and the subversion of identity*. New York: Routledge.

Butler, J. (1993). *Bodies that matter: On the discursive limits of sex*. New York: Routledge.

Butler, J. (1997). *Excitable speech: A politics of the performative*. New York: Routledge.

Butler, J. (1998). Merely cultural. *New Left Review, 227*, 33–44.

Butler, J. (2004). *Undoing gender*. New york: Routledge.

Duggan, L. (2002). The new homonormativity: The sexual politics of neoliberalism. In R. Castronovo, D. D. Nelson, J. Dayan, and R. R. Flores (Eds.). *Materializing democracy: Toward a revitalized cultural politics* (pp. 175–94). Durham, NC: Duke University Press.

Eagleton, T. (2004, March 28). The last Jewish intellectual. *Lenin's Tomb* [Blog]. Retrieved from http://leninology.blogspot.com/2004/03/terry-eagleton-on-edward-said.html.

Foucault, M. (1996). Friendship as a way of life. In S. Lotringer (Ed.), *Foucault live: Interviews 1961–1984* (pp. 308–12). New York: Semiotext(e).

Ignatiev, N., & Garvey, J. (1996). Race traitor. New York, NY: Routledge.

Giroux, H. (1997). *Education and cultural studies: Toward a performative practice*. New York: Routledge.

Griffin, J. H. (1977). *Black like me*. New York: Houghton Mifflin.

Høeg, P. (1995). *Borderliners* (B. Haveland, Trans.). New York: Farrar Strauss and Giroux.

Johnson, E. P., & Henderson, M. G. (2004). *Black queer studies*. Durham, NC: Duke University Press.

Ignatiev, N. (1995). *How the Irish became white*. New York: Routledge, 1995.

Kannen, V. (2008). Identity treason: Race, disability, queerness, and the ethics of (post)identity practices. *Culture, Theory and Critique, 49*(2), 149–63.

Kiberd, D. (1996). *Inventing Ireland: The literature of a modern nation*. New York: Vintage.

Linton, S. (1998) *Claiming disability: Knowledge and identity*. New York: New York University Press.

Marshall, J. (1999). Performativity: Lyotard and Foucault through Searle and Austin. *Studies in Philosophy and Education, 18*, 309–17.

McCarthy, C., Crichlow, W., Dimitriadis, D., & Dolby, N. (2005). *Race, identity, and representation in education*. New York: Routledge.

McRuer, R. (2006). *Crip theory: Cultural signs of queerness and disability*. New York: New York University Press.

Munoz, J. E. (1999). *Disidentifications: Queers of color and the performance of politics*. Minneapolis: University of Minnesota Press.

Oliver, M. (1996). Defining impairment and disability: Issues at Stake. In C. Barnes and G. Mercer (Eds.), *Exploring the divide* (pp. 29–54). London: The Disability Press.

Olson, K. (2009). *Wounded by school: Recapturing the joy in learning and standing up to old school culture*. New York: Teachers College Press.

Rich, A. (1980). Compulsory heterosexuality and lesbian experience. *Signs, 5*(4). 631–60.

Rodriquez, N., and Pinar, W. (2007). *Queering straight teachers: Discourse and identity in education*. New York: Peter Lang.

Said, E. (1978). *Orientalism*. New York: Vintage.

Said, E. (1993). *Culture and imperialism*. New York: Vintage.

Said, E. (2001). *Power, politics, and culture: Interviews with Edward Said* (G. Viswanathan, Editor). New York: Vintage.

Sedgwick, E. K. (2003). *Touching feeling: Affect, pedagogy, performativity*. Durham, NC: Duke University Press.

Shakespeare, T., & Watson, N. (1996) "The body line controversy": A new direction for disability studies? Conference paper Hull Disability Studies Seminar. Hull, United Kingdom. Retrieved from http://www.leeds.ac.uk/disability-studies/archiveuk/Shakespeare/The%20body%20line%20controversy.pdf.

Segall, A. (2002). *Disturbing practice: Reading teacher education as text*. New York: Peter Lang.

Sirk, D. (Director). (1959). *Imitation of life* [Motion picture]. United States: Universal International.

Spivak, G. (1995). Can the subaltern speak? In B. Ashcroft, G. Griffiths, and H. Tiffin (Eds.), *The Postcolonial Reader* (pp. 24–28). New York: Routledge.

Taylor, L. (2009). Tragic hero: Laurie Taylor interviews Terry Eagleton, *The New Humanist, 124*, 4. Retrieved from http://newhumanist.org.uk/2085.

Warner, M. (1999). *The trouble with normal: Sex, politics, and the ethics of queer life*. New York: Free Press.

Weir, P. (Producer). (1989). *Dead Poets Society* [Motion picture]. United States: Touchstone Pictures.

Willinsky, J. (1998). *Learning to divide the world: Education at empire's end*. Minneapolis: University of Minnesota Press.

Chapter Three

LGBTQ Teacher Identity

*Transgressing the Linear and into
the Spherical Identity Model*

Megan S. Kennedy

We are often afraid to discuss our identities within classroom settings, but it is these very identities that influence what we teach and how we teach it. For many educators with marginalized identities, whether it is sexual orientation, race, class, or another, the opportunities to have those identities affirmed in the classroom and school setting are few and far between. This chapter is an opportunity to listen to these marginalized voices, the voices of lesbian, gay, and bisexual educators in a conservative state in the western United States.

To set the context for the chapter and the eventual implications for schooling at any level, one must first have an overview of the theoretical framework of queer theory as well as the pertinent literature on identity-development models. A brief discussion of the methodology and the participants leads into an examination of these teachers' stories from the six different themes that emerged throughout the research. The six themes discussed are experience with discrimination, personality, philosophy, isolation versus support, nonnegotiables, and sense of self. The chapter concludes with implications these six themes have on the current identity-development models and possible areas to explore in a new inclusive identity-development model.

THEORETICAL FRAMEWORK

Queer theory's origins are rooted in a social reform movement. The theory has been developed in a variety of ways. Some authors understand it as a method (Britzman, 1995; de Lauretis, 1991; Foucault, 1990; Fuss, 1991;

Zuckerman, 2001) and some as content (Katz, 1990, 1997; Rubin, 1984), whereas others see the theory as performance (Butler, 1991). No matter which of these three contexts it is understood in, queer theorists have used the theory to depart from identity politics (Butler, 1991; Foucault, 1990; Fuss, 1991; Seidman, 1995) and as a way to both disrupt the normal and normalize the identity (Anzaldua, 1998; Butler, 1991; de Lauretis, 1991; Kumanshiro, 2001; Seidman, 1995).

Teirney and Dilley (1998) argue, "Queer activism seeks to break down traditional ideas of normal and deviant, by showing the queer in what is thought of as normal, and the normal in the queer" (p. 60). Queer theory looks to use the tools of activism and to "[question] what (and why) we know and do not know about things both normal and queer" (p. 62).

Through queer theory, the binary of sexual orientation (heterosexual–gay) and gender (man–woman) are challenged, identities are decentered, and power is being embodied discursively and through the politics of provocation. Queer theory recognizes that versions of lesbian, gay, or bisexual subject positions are inscribed everywhere and that the deviance paradigm is abandoned to give way to transgression (Plummer, 2005). Morris (2000) argues, "Queer theory attempts to disconnect sex and gender by suggesting that the two are not necessarily related" (Morris, 2000, p. 22).

This separation also makes queer theory applicable and relevant to the field of education. The complexities of identities are evident in the students being educated in PK–12 classrooms, as well as the teachers leading this educational endeavor. As Davis and Sumara (2000) posit:

> Co-opting the term "drag"—which, for the most part, has been used in reference to men dressing as women—we came to understand that each of us continued to perform "teacher drag" in our classrooms, schools and universities. Teacher drag had become for us a signifier for robing and disrobing we felt must take place in order to re-complexify our teaching identities—that is, to acknowledge and announce our complexities in schooling practices we considered oppressive, particularly for those who identity as "other." (p. 106)

Beyond identities,

> queer theory is not simply about the studying of people whose sex lives are not heterosexual, or even the positionalities of those people; at its core, it is about questioning the presumptions, values, and viewpoints from those positions (marginal and central), especially those that normally go unquestioned. (Dilley, 1999, p. 462)

Queer theory is complex and, by the very nature of its assumptions, fluid. It challenges the researcher to recognize multiple perspectives and to ensure that voices are not lost by remaining fixed on one particular position. If the researcher does not remain cognizant of the fluidity required by a queer framework, the researcher could unintentionally exclude or silence other aspects of identity.

For example, queer theory can help a lesbian or gay researcher center the often overlooked concerns of race, ethnicity, and class (Beasley, 2005). Queer theorists recognize that intersectionalities of identity inform and offer insight into the other. The researcher worked to acknowledge these intersections through the interview questions and data analysis.

IDENTITY DEVELOPMENT MODELS

An area of literature that was significant in grappling with the research design, data, and eventual conclusions was identity development. The most prominent identity development models contain a final stage addressing identity integration (Cass, 1979; Coleman, 1982; McCarn and Fassinger, 1996; Minton and McDonald, 1984; Troiden, 1988). Identity integration can be understood as the recognition of one's sexuality as part of the whole person, and is also defined by the understanding that sexual orientation is only one facet of a person's identity. Eli Coleman (1982) created a five-stage development model in which the final stage is a level of integration. This is marked by a person's ability to be "fully functioning" within society. Vivian Cass (1979) developed a theory of lesbian and gay identity development, which terminates in *identity synthesis*. A person who reaches this point will likely have found a way to mediate a lesbian or gay identity within a heteronormative world. There is less division of self, as the lesbian or gay identity becomes just one factor of an identity and not one's only lens through which a person negotiates the world.

Trioden's (1988) identity development model is divided into four stages. The final stage is *commitment*, which is highlighted by a significant same-sex relationship. During this stage, individuals create new stigma-management strategies such as "blending, covering, and conversion" (p. 112). Lesbian, gay, and bisexual individuals are now able to fully integrate their once-dissonant images and identities.

Minton and McDonald (1984) created a nonlinear model in which growth is based on the interaction between societal values, beliefs, and the individual. The end goal of this model is to achieve *identity synthesis*, which requires the integration of all aspects of one's personal identity. Once one has fully integrated the lesbian, gay, or bisexual identity into other aspects of identity such as race, religion, and class, one has reached the *universalistic* stage.

McCarn and Fassinger (1996) developed a model of sexual identity development that separates the developmental tasks into two types of categories: individual sexual identity development and group membership identity development. These categories are independent of one another and can evolve at different paces. The final phase is *internalization/synthesis*, during which the individual integrates both the personal identity and the group identity into the whole.

The qualitative study[1] that serves as the basis for this chapter was not about setting the notion of being "out" as better, but rather about helping teachers consider wholeness and synthesis within their identities. Defining what constitutes a good teacher means looking beyond the teaching methodologies employed and the curricular theory enacted. It requires looking at the person who is in the classroom.[2] Teachers, teacher educators, and administrators need to understand the varied intersections of identity and integrity when seeking to support teachers, who in turn support students.

The study investigated one specific aspect of identity, sexual orientation, but the ideas of wholeness, identity, and integrity have implications for all teachers. From personal reflections, the times when my students did not get a whole and present teacher were when I felt out of integrity or in conflict with my personal identities. Palmer (1998) notes that "a good teacher must stand where personal and public meet, dealing with the thundering flow of traffic at an intersection where 'weaving a web of connectedness' feels more like crossing a freeway on foot" (p. 17).

The research methodology considered congruence with the selected theoretical framework of queer theory. Nelson (1999) articulates potential ways that queer theory might inform an inquiry approach to research, such as a qualitative method that acknowledges that the domain of sexual identity may be important to a range of people for a variety of reasons; examines both subordinate and dominant sexual identities; looks at divergent ways of producing and reading sexual identities across cultural contexts and discourses; identifies prevailing competing and changing cultural norms pertaining to sexual identities; explores problematic and positive aspects of this identity domain; and, lastly, considers sexual identity in relation to other acts of identity and vice versa.

Queer theory provides a flexible and open-ended framework for approaching this research project. As Nelson (1999) notes, "Furthermore, a queer approach recognizes that sexual identities are not universal but are done in different ways in different cultural contexts, and it calls for a close look at how identities are produced through day-to-day interactions" (p. 378). This focus is in close alignment with the research questions.

SIX THEMES

Understanding the experiences of lesbian, gay, and bisexual educators as they manage their sexual orientations within a teaching role requires extensive representation from a diverse community. This study is a step toward that end as each narrative further adds to the depth of knowledge. Using the six themes as a guide, the reader can begin to appreciate the complexities and nuances of how one manages sexual orientation in a teaching role. All six themes are needed to help illuminate the larger context of the experiences, both personally and professionally, and should not be separate from one another, but rather seen as pieces of a puzzle.

Theme One: Experience with Discrimination

Experience captures the specific events, moments, and periods that collectively shaped the personal and professional life of each participant. For some individuals, this was their first "coming out" experience or achievement of tenure in the public school system. The *experience* theme was explicit first at a microscopic level and acknowledges the importance of looking at the "who" behind the story.

Carissa's story is a prominent example of the *experience* theme. Her experience of getting fired for being perceived as a lesbian shaped and defined her. It influenced her choice of career and guided her down a different path from one that she described as "a calling." In her words:

> But I did apply to a few schools. . . . I showed the department chair my resume and she said, "I am exhausted reading this resume," because of all the stuff I had done. She called me back and said, "Well, I talked to the principal and he said he made a phone call to your school and said that we will not be hiring you." I was just like, "What am I going to do?" . . . [W]hen I went a couple of places and had that same experience I was just like, "What is going on?" I didn't know what the hell to do. I don't know what a person does in a situation like that.

Carissa looked at herself differently because of these experiences and this moment stood out among all the other experiences she shared around her "coming out" process and her upbringing. Her narrative resonated with others regarding how they regrouped from what others described as their worst nightmare. Her narrative enriches the understanding of what it means to be both a teacher and lesbian, gay, or bisexual.

Religion was also a relevant *experience* that was coded for ten of the fourteen participants. For Carissa, Rachel, and Andi, religion was a place of hate. Carissa explains,

> I had to figure out how to not send myself to hell. . . . [I]t was huge and especially growing up in evangelical Christianity. I mean it was like what am I gonna do with everything I've been believing for the last fifteen years. How am I going to not send myself to hell? And so I had to totally reconfigure my whole belief system, because of this, you know.

Rachel discussed coming from a fundamentalist Christian home where she and her siblings were isolated from much of mainstream culture. She attended Christian private schools, which made their views on homosexuality very clear to students.

> We were taught to hate, basically. We were taught that homosexual people were horrible, horrible people. . . . I'll always remember hearing the story about the boy that they hung upside down on a bar and they like pinched his testicles and did crazy shit to him—these homosexual people.

In contrast to Carissa and Rachel's experiences, Andi articulated his fear of hatred from his religious peers, not toward himself.

> [C]hurches are big in Texas, literally and figuratively speaking. . . . I had a lot of Christian buddies who . . . every now and then would bring up gay subjects like, if I knew a gay was here I'd beat them up or kill them or etc. Just their whole homophobic fear mentality would come out especially in conversations, which I would try to change the subject or avoid.

Other individuals talked about religion as a source of conflict and something that was important to resolve. Andi's statement, "[w]hy would I want to be a part of something that hates me and something I can't really control, at least willingly?" was repeated by many participants. The religious aspect of the *experience* theme was about understanding some of the complexities of decision-making processes as well as subjects' personal motivators.

The theme of *experience* illustrates how the whole of a person's experience as a lesbian, gay, or bisexual educator can be shaped by exclusion and hate. These experiences serve as narratives that continue to inform their teaching identities.

Theme Two: Personality

Personality, the second theme, is the elusive but defining aspect of personality that supported navigations for each participant personally and professionally. Participants self-identified as introverted or extroverted in interviews or described themselves using such words as "goofy" or "genuine." As a theme, *personality* was evident in the ways in which participants shared stories and as they discussed their classroom practices.

Personality was one method used by some participants to navigate their lesbian, gay, and bisexual identities in the classroom and in their personal lives. Sean's identity as an activist is connected to his view of himself as extroverted. He draws on these extroverted tendencies when he has difficult conversations or is a media representative.

> So I am very extroverted, very up and out. . . . I think that helps with being an activist, is being an extrovert. But I also do think people like Gandhi who were not extroverts, can still be an activist, it's just in a different way. . . . I do a lot more for societal reasons in the future than I do for me, myself. I am a masochist in some ways, unfortunately. That's sad but it happens. I think you have to have great pain to be a great activist. Because if you don't have the pain, the difficult conversations don't occur.

This point in Sean's narrative was important on a myriad of levels. First, Sean's approach is threatening for many individuals. Later in his interview, he mentioned a lesbian teacher who left his school out of the fear of being associated with him. Second, he wanted introverts to know that, although approaches and styles may vary, they can still address the larger concern of discrimination. Finally, Sean invited others to embrace their own personality to inspire change at school and district levels.

In the interview context, Andi's introverted nature was readily apparent. In discussing how personality helped him navigate the classroom, he said:

> [I] feel a little bit awkward sometimes in social situations, I'm not quite misanthropic but I'm close. I've thought a lot about that, why do I act that way sometimes because I can be really serious sometimes and reverting back to my military discipline and then sometimes I have this whole theatrical side to me where I just want to like act crazy.

This offers a counternarrative to Sean's extroverted nature. I feel it is important to acknowledge both aspects, and at the same time recognize how people move, especially introverts, and struggle to move fluidly between the two circles of personal and professional lives.

The title of Rachel's narrative, "Oh yeah, still crazy people," is the epitome of the *personality* theme. Rachel moves through the classroom and her personal life with flair that is indicative of her vibrant personality. She described how her students responded to her transition from a lesbian to a more feminine, straight-identified woman.

> So, all throughout the year, it was kind of like, "What's going on? What are you doing? Why are you wearing those shoes? Why are you wearing that shirt?" So, kind of all throughout the year this evolution and then it's really funny because I left last summer. . . . I was still wearing my basketball shorts and my tee-shirts to now skirts and tighter fitting shirts and longer hair and sometimes heels. And, they're like, "What are you doing?" So, it's been confusing for everyone involved . . . that's some of the things that the kids would say is they'd be like, "Well, as long as you're still crazy." Oh, yeah, still crazy, people. Let's get that one straight.

The importance of personality for Rachel and others is that she maximized a personal strength to help her in the classroom. Even as she has experienced extensive personal changes, her *personality* component has remained a constant. Rachel remained true to herself and her personality as she navigated a potentially stressful journey.

Theme Three: Philosophy

The theme of *philosophy* emerged as a point of intersection of the personal and professional for many participants, where one was often used to help define the other. *Philosophy* developed as a theme in through the analyzed interview sections focused on two interview questions: What, if any, steps have you taken toward being out or open in your personal life or school life? What have been the motivating factors and effects of each of these steps?

Many participants wove in educational philosophical stances as part of their answer. It became clear that they felt that this is the point at which the personal and philosophical intersected. Each participant's educational philosophy appears to be an evolving set of standards, which guides their instruction and decision-making process that molds how they present themselves in the classroom as a lesbian, gay, or bisexual educator.

Brian's educational philosophy is grounded in the high value he places on positive relationships with students. He expresses concern that being more "out" with the students could result in discomfort. This discomfort is in direct contradiction to the core of his educational philosophy of relationship building. Therefore, he has carefully considered changing his current situation to be more "out" in the classroom, which could potentially cause students discomfort.

> I'm not comfortable with telling kids because they're going to react differently, and I think, part of it is my ultimate job is to teach them. Some kids are going to be fine with that and some of kids may have a real problem with that and that affects my purpose for being with them in the first place if that's going to make them uncomfortable.

Additionally, Brian's contradiction is evident as he talks about lying to the students even when he recognizes how important trust and openness can be in relationship building.

> [Y]ou can't teach unless you build relationships with the kids. And you build relationships with the kids by talking about yourself, and asking about them.... And so, that's frustrating because I have to pretend that this part in my life doesn't exist, and if kids ask me about it, I just kind of ignore it, or something. I don't say, you know, "My personal life is none of your business."

Brian's depiction of *philosophy* highlights the struggle many lesbian, gay, and bisexual educators experience when their personal philosophy and professional philosophy meet at points of incongruence.

Karly's remarks about philosophy provide an interesting comparison to Brian's. She also believes in strong relationships with students, and her educational philosophy was actually part of her decision-making process to be "out" in the classroom. She did not want to deceive the students and impede her ability to build relationships. Her goal in teaching is to create better conditions for future lesbian, gay, and bisexual teachers, and she defines herself as a "pioneer."

> And I still sometimes visualize myself as a pioneer. I think it's really important for me to be as open as I possibly can so for people behind me it won't be as bad. I encourage people to ask questions and I offer them sometimes probably more information than they want to know. But I think they need to know it.

Thus she is willing to be "a first" and present herself openly as a lesbian educator, in the hope that this "outness" and openness builds authentic relationships with colleagues and students. Her personal and professional lives reached a point of intersection and choice. In her decision-making process it is clear that Karly used her personal philosophy to guide her educational philosophy.

Theme Four: Isolation versus Support

The fourth theme, *isolation versus support*, is best visualized as a continuum. On one end is *isolation*, which is often reflected in words like *shame* or *fear*, progressing to the opposite end, *support*, which depicts the highest level of support offered by colleagues, families, friends, communities, and districts. The role and the importance of the ally were often denoted in this theme.

A theme may not be traditionally constructed as a continuum, but in data analysis it was impossible to separate these two ideas into individual themes. There was such situational movement back and forth between the two identifiers, depending on the period being discussed or the individual or group involved. This movement required that both ideas be connected and interpreted together.

Alec's story is a pertinent example of the theme of *isolation versus support*. He discusses the movement from a conservative school where he was in the closet to a more liberal environment where he was not the only "out" teacher.

> When I went to interview . . . it seemed like a more welcoming place. And I was very frustrated not being out [at my current school]. . . . I quickly discovered that there were a number of out gay teachers. At least out in the faculty.

> Some out to everybody . . . and the other gay teachers on the faculty, they were sort of this little club . . . that turned out, to be almost, I would say almost a lifesaver.

Woven in his story are examples of how individuals in his personal and professional life helped and offered strong *support*; he discussed his family and sister, the social network of teachers at school, as well as a significant personal relationship. However, while sharing these points, he also discussed *isolation* and being "in the closet" at his church.

> And so the only place that I was still closeted was the church. I even got the paying jobs through music at my very little parish. So I could be out to the other musicians and the pastor didn't care. And nobody else knew because I wasn't from their neighborhood and so I was still Catholic, but still semi-closeted there.

His story illustrates how many gay, lesbian, and bisexual teachers feel strong moments of *support* at the same time as they feel *isolation*.

Carissa's narrative is also worth revisiting under the theme of *isolation versus support*. Her story is an example of how an individual can change over time, and her narrative depicts moments of *isolation* and how they can eventually be transformed into *support*. In her case, Carissa needed to find support in herself to accept her own story to balance her experiences of *isolation* and *support*.

> I couldn't answer that question for a long time. Why aren't you teaching anymore? . . . I probably could now. I could do anything I want right now. But it really wasn't until I believed my story that I realized that look, this did happen. And there's not another explanation, really. But now things are coming around where I've learned from a lot of experiences. . . . I don't feel the shame so I don't feel like I'm defending myself anymore. I'm not a victim anymore. This thing just happened. That's why it ends up being a really great thing that happened because now I've got so much fun ahead of me, that kind of stuff, that I would never have been able to experience. It was the shame that kept me in that for so long. . . . But now I've gotten the closure. But no, I've never been ashamed ever, ever of being a lesbian ever.

The final point to note under *isolation versus support* is the role lesbian, gay, and bisexual educators play for each other. Participants discussed the pressure applied by others in the community to "come out" or be more visible. This pressure was expressed as negative and pushed participants closer to *isolation* as they felt alone in the process and unsupported by their own communities.

Other participants spoke about their need to be more explicit in their support for other lesbian, gay, or bisexual colleagues, who were in different points of "coming out." Additionally, participants often spoke of a previous lesbian, gay, or bisexual teacher or mentor who supported them either in word or in presence. This substory of how lesbian, gay, and bisexual educators foster *isolation versus support* for each other is an area that needs further examination.

Theme Five: Nonnegotiables

The theme labeled *nonnegotiables* represented the point of least flexibility for participants. This theme was often identified by the tone or strength in which the participants conveyed their thinking about the written and unwritten rules that they closely followed. For example, participants precisely described rules of not lying when directly asked if they are gay or that matters *must* be handled if they include any aspect of discrimination, as defined by law.

Sean's *nonnegotiable* centered on the characteristic of discrimination. Whenever a situation is presented to him that has this characteristic, he is motivated to act. He never dismissed a student, school, or district seeking his expertise. Neither would he ignore a situation that was rooted in discrimination.

> In one situation, I had a parent who didn't want [his child] being taught by a gay teacher. I had to deal with that, saying, "No, you can't do that. What if a white supremacist didn't want their children being taught by an African-American? We wouldn't change it." I'm not sure it's a choice in the fact [to raise or confront issues] I won't allow them to be discriminatory. And I think I choose that route because I know in the long run, it would actually help the student who was actually removed . . . that's more of what I do; I make sure the policies are enforced and applied equitably.

Often Sean gains little from these situations, but they are impossible for him to ignore; they are his *nonnegotiable.*

The "unspoken" is how Alec described his *nonnegotiable.* Alec's work on a local magazine sparked his understanding of lesbian, gay, and bisexual youth, which in turn opened his eyes to his own school environment for these youths. Alec's nonnegotiable is not allowing people to be silenced. As a teacher he consistently tries to give voice to the silent. One example of how he gave such voice is the case of a popular, closeted former student. Alec believed this student's story would be an eye opener to the faculty peers who are blind to the realities facing lesbian, gay, and bisexual youth:

> I would really like to be able to say, Do you remember this kid, do you remember? Yeah, he was on the committee to hire our new principals, you remember and you had no idea he was gay. And he went through, at the time he was just really heavy, and when he started coming out he started losing

weight, and he is really looking good now. And you had no idea how internalizing all of this . . . you saw a good, good kid. But you just had no idea how difficult it was for him, and we just have to make things different for these kinds of kids.

Other participants have a "no-lying rule," which means that when asked directly by colleagues they will answer honestly. Evan stated,

I never got to a place where I felt like I was lying really with anyone in my building because whenever I was asked I was always honest. I have a feeling that they might know, but I really don't honestly care.

These nonnegotiables shaped teacher identity behaviors inside and outside the classroom. These nonnegotiables also shaped their lesbian, gay, and bisexual identities.

Theme Six: Sense of Self

The theme *sense of self* captures the presence of wholeness and the inner dialogues used by participants as they make decisions on personal and professional levels. This theme offered the most fluidity and flexibility through a person's life, but progressively showed strength as the narrative worked its way to the present day. Examples of this theme included discussions of internalized homophobia and how that has changed over time. *Sense of self* also explains how allies explored their sexual orientations as part of their progression through ally development.

It is said that wisdom comes with age and this was evident in this study. Participants were able to articulate a greater level of confidence and self-acceptance as the number of years that they have been "out" increased. In the classroom, this often was manifested as a willingness to be more visible or outspoken. It also resulted in a greater intolerance for being "in the closet" or the ability to more easily dismiss the oppressive practices from others and not seeing these as personal. The *sense of self* was evident in either the participants' direct phrases or through a holistic analysis of their narratives.

Sense of self was also coded in individual transcriptions when participants explained their classrooms and how they viewed themselves as educators. For some participants who had been in the classroom fewer than three years, the struggles of the classroom often superseded struggles around being a lesbian, gay, or bisexual educator. They were often described as separate entities, because participants had not had the space to examine how they connected. They were still coming to know the "self" as teacher.

Andi is about to enter the classroom and is forthright in his *sense of self* explorations. He is exploring threads of this theme, how one understands the self or individual who teaches, and how this understanding is influenced by personal and professional forces. Andi is at the very beginning of a journey that other participants took more than fifteen years before him. His codes of *sense of self* look very different than those of the veteran teachers.

He was coded at points in his narrative where he discussed the questions he is seeking clarity on, as he explores what it means to be a gay educator. Because he lacks teaching experience, he is currently exploring different mediums, like videos, to help him work through some of these questions.

> I think it would just have to depend on the situation and being a new teacher, I'd be very concerned with keeping a new job and maintaining good relations or whatever. But after watching that *It's Elementary* video, which was real eye opening, it actually gave me a little more confidence that there are people that are stepping out of their comfort zone whether they're straight or gay. I thought it was cool that there were some straight people teaching that.

Both allies went through moments of personal exploration and questioned their identities as heterosexual women. Jill grappled with identifying strongly with lesbian, gay, and bisexual individuals to the point of questioning her own conservative, religious upbringing.

> But I've never come out myself and I'm not gay. Although, when I started identifying so strongly with all of these people that . . . I mean, I have a lot of gay friends. And I certainly did go through that process myself thinking have I just repressed this? I mean, what's really the . . . 'cause I would feel fine about being gay. I'm like and I kind of laugh at it now because I would take myself through a process of things. I just never got attracted to women. And I would think am I repressing 'cause you know the way you were raised? And I would imagine being with a woman and think, yeah, no.

Ava, on the other hand, asked herself the question, but quickly connected it to larger issues in society instead of her own experiences.

> I was always so interested in being an ally and at many times questions like "Am I really gay? Why is this important to me? What is so . . . why is this so important to me?" And I think it's just a basic human rights thing. It's like the reason like sexual abuse is super important to me and victim recovery because it's just the basic human right to be treated well.

Thus, in different ways, both sought clarity regarding the question of why they are passionate advocates for lesbian, gay, and bisexual individuals. Their *sense of self* was deepened after their personal exploration. Their sense of self made them active allies and more effective teachers.

One of Molly's dominant traits is her ability to metacognate around her own sexuality and how sexuality is perceived in the world. It is this trait that resulted in many examples of *sense of self* in her interview transcriptions.

One of the best examples is her response to the question, "What does it mean to be a bisexual educator?"

> What does it mean to be a bisexual educator? Well it means that sexuality is probably a little bit more on the forefront of my brain than it is someone who is just falling into the mainstream. Because it's just something that I've thought more about. And so I am more cognizant of sexual matters when it comes to social constructions of sexuality within the classroom, specifically within texts that I am teaching. Social constructions in general is something that I'm always trying to bring to my students' attention whether it be it the freshman or the adult students I have now.

Other participants were coded as they described the answers they found to similar reflective questions they posed in the early days of their classroom experiences.

THEME IMPLICATIONS

The primary research question of the experiences of lesbian, gay, and bisexual PK–12 educators was explored and understood through the themes of the data as well as voices of these marginalized individuals. To begin to consider the subquestion of this study on the applicability of the current identity development models for lesbian, gay, and bisexual educators, the different model stages were compared with the original data and the seven themes. Through this analysis, a clear disconnect emerged.

Traditional identity development models equate wholeness with identity synthesis (being "out" is better) (Cass, 1979; Coleman, 1982; McCarn and Fassinger, 1996; Minton and McDonald, 1984; Troiden, 1998). If this is true, many of the participants in this study failed to reach this arbitrary state of wholeness. Part of this failure, however, is not on the part of the participants; rather, it is due to the nature of the school community, school rules, and state and federal laws that set up many teachers for failure and underestimate the power of school environments. The participants all spoke about teaching as a passion or as a "calling"; many described how teaching is a core identifier for them.

With that said, to reach definitional identity synthesis, both identities— that of an educator and a lesbian, gay, or bisexual individual—would need to be merged. Part of that merger, as outlined by the theories, includes not hiding one identity, possessing the ability to be an outspoken advocate for the identity, having strong social networks connected with the identity, and reaching a point where all identities are in harmony.

Many participants have contemplated these merger points in their personal lives, but the identity of lesbian, gay, or bisexual is still not in harmony with their identity as an educator in the school context. As demonstrated by the participants, teachers still conceal their sexual orientations, they question to varying extents the support they have around them, and they are overshadowed by a society that still supports discrimination legally and as a culture. This does not make them "lesser" or any less self-aware.

These individuals grapple with identity on a daily basis when they confront students' and colleagues' questions; when they select literature and stories for their classrooms; in determining the manner in which they frame questions; how they defuse hate language in the hallways or on the playing field; and in their performance of lesbian, gay, bisexual, or ally teacher. It is part of how they make decisions, balance safety and risk, and define who they are to themselves and to others.

Traditional research and models have created a two-dimensional version of identity (e.g., gay and male) that place individuals in specific identity boxes. However, individuals are not two dimensional; they are in reality multidimensional (e.g., lesbian, female, educator), and possess identities that have not been expressed in the traditional models. Identity research cannot be conducted in a sterile environment; it removes the complexity of reality and therefore creates an unreal version of the individual.

CONCLUSION

This research has exposed multiple factors of identity that could not be developed in the traditional models because of their "flatness" or either–or mentality: identity synthesis as zenith or "closeted." The themes explored in this research create a whole person taking into account the individual; the context of the experience as a lesbian, gay, or bisexual individual; and the role as educator.

The use of queer theory in future research on identity can create a whole or spherical view of the individual, rather than the flat continuum perspective offered by the previous models. This spherical perspective of individuals' identity is fluid, ever changing, and takes into account the contextual experience. This view does not place individuals in the either–or box as "out" or "closeted," and therefore creates an affirming space for individuals to develop and find wholeness in their own sphere.

The development of new, more spherical models can create this affirming space in the theoretical sense, but multiple individuals must create this space in the practical space. Teachers, administrators, and policy makers' actions foster environments of inclusivity or exclusivity in the school environment. For lesbian, gay, or bisexual educators to find wholeness in the classroom, researchers and practitioners alike need to revision identity development with a queer theory lens, as this research has done.

Additionally, all educators must begin to address issues of teacher identity exploration, the binaries that currently exist within the school culture, the environment of PK–12 schools, and the teacher education programs that foster teacher identity development, while also creating affirming environments for all teachers to explore their marginalized identities.

NOTES

1. The research study used a qualitative methodology of heuristics. The study included a three-series interview protocol, transcript reviews, and participant follow ups for accuracy. Each interview was coded individually and then comparisons were made across the participants offering a rich cross-analysis and deeper understanding of the theme implications. Heuristics was best suited for this research study, primarily for its ability to capture marginalized voices and teacher experiences in a politically conservative state.

Heuristics is a "process of internal searching through which one discovers the nature and meaning of experience and develops methods and procedures for further investigation and analysis" (Moustakas, 1990, p. 9). The researcher is present throughout the process, and the research questions and ensuing methodology are structured around an "internal search to discover, with an encompassing puzzlement, a passionate desire to know, a devotion and commitment to pursue a question that is strongly connected to one's own identity and selfhood" (Moustakas, 1990, p. 40). There were two research questions for this project:

First: What are the experiences of lesbian, gay, and bisexual PK–12 educators in a conservative state in the United States?

Second: How do the lesbian and gay identity development theories match the experience of lesbian, gay, and bisexual PK–12 educators?

2. Participants in the study included fourteen lesbian-, gay-, bisexual-, and ally-identified teachers. The participants possessed more than 116 years of teaching experience; one individual has more than thirty years of teaching and another is just entering his first year. The participants included eight females and six males. Of these, four identified as lesbians, six as gay, one as bisexual, one as "straight but open," and two as allies. Allies were included in the call for participants so that referrals of potential participants did not "out" people. However, even though participation was not anticipated, two allies expressed interest in participating in the research, and the decision was made to complete the interviews. Additionally, the participants varied in their level of "outness" to colleagues, parents, and students.

REFERENCES

Anzaldua, G. (1998). To(o) queer the writer: Loca, escritora y chicana. In C. Trujillo (Ed.), *Living Chicana Theory*. Berkeley, CA: Third Woman Press.
Beasley, C. (2005). *Gender and sexuality: Critical theories, critical thinkers*. Thousand Oaks, CA: Sage.
Britzman, D. P. (1995). Is there a queer pedagogy? Or stop reading straight. *Educational Theory, 45*(2), 229–38.
Butler, J. (1991). Imitation and gender insubordination. In D. Fuss (Ed.), *Inside/out: Lesbian theories, gay theories*. New York: Routledge.
Cass, V. C. (1979). Lesbian, gay, or bisexual identity formation: A theoretical model. *Journal of Lesbian, Gay, or Bisexuality, 4*, 214–35.
Coleman, E. (1982). Developmental stages of the coming-out process. *American Behavioral Scientist, 25*, 469–82.
Davis, B., & Sumara, D. J. (2000). Another queer theory: Reading complexity theory as a moral and ethical imperative. In S. Taulburt and S. R. Steinberg (Eds.), *Thinking queer: Sexuality, culture and education* (pp. 105–27). New York: Peter Lang.

de Lauretis, T. (1991). Queer theory: Lesbian and gay sexualities: An introduction. *Differences: A Journal of Feminist Cultural Studies, 3*(2), iii–xviii.

Dilley, P. (1999). Queer theory: Under construction. *International Journal of Qualitative Studies in Education, 12*(5), 457–72.

Douglass, B. G., & Moustakas, C. (1985). Heuristic inquiry: The internal search to know. *Journal of Humanistic Psychology, 25,* 39–55.

Foucault, M. (1990). *The history of sexuality volume 1: An introduction* (R. Hurley, Trans.) New York: Vintage Books.

Fuss, D. (1991). Introduction: Inside/out. In D. Fuss (Ed.), *Inside/out: Lesbian theories, gay theories* (pp. 1–10). New York: Routledge.

Katz, J. N. (1990). The invention of heterosexuality. *Socialist Review,* January/March, 7–33.

Katz, J. N. (1997). Homosexual and heterosexual: Questioning the terms. In M. Duberman (Ed.), *A queer world: the centre for lesbian and gay studies reader* (pp. 177–80). New York: New York University Press.

Kumanshiro, K. K. (2001). Queer students of colour and antiracist, antiheterosexist education: Paradoxes of identity and activism. In K. Kumanshiro (Ed.), *Troubling intersections of race and sexuality: Queer students of colour and anti-oppressive education* (pp. 1–26). Lanham, MD: Rowman and Littlefield.

McCarn, S. R., & Fassinger, R. E. (1996). Revisioning sexual minority identity formation: A new model of lesbian identity and its implications for counseling and research. *The Counseling Psychologist, 24*(3), 508–34.

Minton, H. L., & McDonald, G. J. (1984). Lesbian, gay, or bisexual identity formation as a developmental process. *Journal of Lesbian, Gay, or Bisexuality, 9,* 91–104.

Moustakas, C. (1990). *Heuristic research: Design, methodology, and application.* Newbury Park, CA: Sage.

Morris, M. (2000). Dante's left foot kicks queer theory into gear. In S. Taulburt and S. R. Steinberg (Eds.), *Thinking queer: Sexuality, culture and education* (pp. 15–28). New York: Peter Lang.

Nelson, C. (1999). Sexual identities in ESL: Queer theory and classroom inquire. *TESOL Quarterly, 33*(3), 371–91.

O'Driscoll, S. (1996). Outlaw readings: Beyond lueer theory. *Signs: Journal of Women in Culture and Society, 22,* 30–51.

Palmer, P. J. (1998). *The courage to teach: Exploring the inner landscape of a teacher's life.* San Francisco: Jossey-Bass.

Plummer, K. (2005). Critical humanism and queer theory. In N. K. Denzin and Y. S. Lincoln (Eds.), *The Sage handbook of qualitative research* (third edition) (pp. 357–72). Thousand Oaks, CA: Sage.

Rubin, G. (1984). Thinking sex: Notes for a radical theory of the politics of sexuality. In C. S. Vance (Ed.), *Pleasure and danger: Exploring female sexuality* (pp. 267–93). Boston: Routledge.

Ruffolo, D. V. (2006) Queer(ing) scholarly research: Decentering fixed subjects for implicated subjectivities, *Higher Education Perspectives, 2*(2), 1–22.

Seidman, S. (1995). Deconstructing queer theory or the under-theorization of the social and the ethical. In L. Nicholson and S. Seidman (Eds.), *Social postmodernism: Beyond identity politics* (pp. 116–41). Cambridge, MA: Cambridge University Press.

Sumara, D., & Davis, B. (1999). Interrupting heteronormativity: Toward a queer curriculum theory. *Curriculum Inquiry, 29,* 191–208.

Tierney, W. G., & Dilley, P. (1998). Constructing knowledge: Educational research and gay and lesbian studies. In W. E. Pinar (Ed.), *Queer theory in education* (pp. 49–71). Mahwah, NJ: Laurence Erlbaum Associates.

Troiden, R. R. (1988). Homosexual identity development. *Journal of Adolescent Health Care: Official Publication of the Society for Adolescent Medicine, 9*(2), 105–13.

Zuckerman, J. B. (2001). *Queering the life of a progressive, urban, elementary school: Genealogical ghost stories.* New York: Teacher's College.

Chapter Four

Understanding and Undermining Heteronormativity

Heather Hickman

The confluence of knowledge, power, and heteronormativity produces one body of struggles that teachers and students who are lesbian, gay, bisexual, transgender, transsexual, and queer/questioning (LGBTQ) face in schools. A review of literature in these areas shows that textbooks, which teachers and students encounter regularly, represent knowledge in many schools. Because such books are developed through intricate power structures, the result is often heteronormative. Scholarship on heteronormativity already reveals a plethora of struggles faced by teachers, administrators, and students in schools. When combined with the knowledge and power of textbooks, the marginalization is exacerbated.

This chapter explores the literature as well as the data from a deep investigation of one high school literature textbook over time.[1] It details how the books harm the teachers and students exposed to them by silencing authors, gendering nongendered speakers, and ignoring critical questioning, among other things, to perpetuate heteronormative stereotypes.

Building on work from Kincheloe (2008), Duncan-Andrade and Morrell (2008), and others, this chapter looks at how critical pedagogues, queer theorists, and classroom teachers can disrupt that marginalization and move beyond it through critical questioning and activism. Classroom examples are used to demonstrate how teachers can disrupt the heteronormative status quo and create space for students to accept their own identities and learn about those of others.

CONFLUENCE OF KNOWLEDGE, POWER, AND HETERONORMATIVITY

The literature on LGBTQ issues demonstrates that "learning to transgress the heteronormative order is at best a process that occurs by fits and starts" (Koschoreck, 2003, p. 46). Of specific concern with these fits and starts is the problem of heteronormativity in public schools. Unlike other issues that have brought reform for social justice and equity, conversation about sexuality is still shunned by many educators (Tooms, 2007). The literature shows how "heteronormativity permeates all social institutions (family, religion, work, leisure, law, education)" (Filax, 2006, p. 140).

Despite efforts to the contrary, "students, teachers, and administrators in the public schools continue to experience intolerable levels of discrimination and harassment as a result of their actual or perceived sexual differences" (Koschoreck, 2003, p. 28). This finding from Koschoreck is particularly striking because, as he says, one need only be perceived as LGBTQ for harassment to occur. Once a perception exists, LGBTQ students and faculty experience regular marginalization. For example, students considered "powerless, weak, and unmanly" are frequently referred to as "fag" in schools (Pascoe, 2007, p. 157).

This experience along with others causes students who are LGBTQ to miss class because they feel unsafe, which results in "having lower GPAs than students who were less often harassed" (Kosciw, Diaz, and Greytak, 2008, p. 168). Students who are marginalized because of heteronormativity are also at risk for "depression, alcohol and drug abuse . . . risky sexual behaviors, and elevated levels of suicide attempts" (Koschoreck, 2003, p. 28).

In addition to the marginalization faced by students, faculty members who have "desired others of the same sex or wished to transgress traditional gender bounds" are forced to try to "fool" their colleagues or remain quiet about their lives in order for their colleagues to "tacitly agree to leave them alone" (Blount, 2005, p. 1). Those who are clear about their identity "risk ostracism, parental outrage, punishment, and even dismissal" (Blount, 2005, p. 1). This explicit marginalization is evidence of heteronormativity.

Meyer, who considers bullying and harassment from a feminist frame, reinforces what the previously cited scholars suggest. As a public high school teacher, Meyer recalls the destruction of one student by her peers. She says,

> During my first year of teaching, I observed a very bright and athletic student—a leader in the school—dissolve into depression, drug use, and absenteeism as a result of how her friends were treating her. She had fallen in love with a young woman she had met that summer, and her classmates made sure she felt their disapproval. (Meyer, 2008, p. 35)

This tragic example is one, the literature suggests, that occurs quite frequently (Kosciw, Diaz, and Greytak, 2008). Unfortunately, school faculty is often complicit in the harassment for a variety of reasons.

School teachers and administrators in particular face many challenges in dealing with the harassment that students face as well as that which they and their colleagues may face. For example, Tooms (2007) talks about a concept called *fit*, which she describes as "a game of being specific to the politics and relationships between school administrators and the community that they serve" (p. 606). This game is played by administrators not only so that they will keep their job, but also so that they can effect change. However, working to fit may mean that the administrator "inadvertently or purposefully perpetuate[s] community norms" (Tooms, 2007, p. 606), often heteronormative norms.

This can be seen as administrators in Tooms's (2007) study note that they keep their "personal lives away from their work lives" (p. 619). Despite this assertion, however, each allowed their personal lives to influence their work lives when they avoided "queer advocacy within their districts" for fear "it would draw attention to their own stigmatized status and this would compromise their fit" (p. 619). This situation highlights the difficulty in advancing social or curricular issues supportive of students and faculty who are LGBTQ.

The problems faced by LGBTQ students, faculty, and administrators that are created by non-LGBTQ students, faculty, and administrators are exacerbated by other areas of public schools. Implicit and explicit curriculum represented through textbooks is another such area of public schooling that perpetuates the problem of heteronormativity.

In a 2003 article, Lugg calls to address the marginalization that results from heteronormative curricula. She "promote[s] a queer-infused curriculum as an expanded understanding of multicultural education across the K–12 spectrum of offerings" (p. 120). She further calls to reform curricula so "public students learn that there are multiple ways to be, including various ways to be queer and non-queer" (p. 120). Authors, selections, questions, projects, and other aspects of textbooks have the potential to address Lugg's call to action or to reproduce heteronormativity and continue to marginalize LGBTQ students and faculty. Current literature (Meyer, 2008) suggests they are doing the latter.

Textbooks as a form of curriculum are physical embodiments of the knowledge students are expected to learn. That knowledge is, of course, not arbitrary. Instead, "curricular materials project images of society, as well as of other aspects of culture such as what constitutes good literature, legitimate political activity, and so forth" (Sleeter and Grant, 1991, p. 79). Mandated knowledge development, projected through curricular materials, is regulated by the federal government, state governments, local school boards, and individual teachers, as well as by textbook companies.

Although the federal government delegates education to the states, federal legislation can and does shape what knowledge is transmitted by public schools. Likewise, state legislatures can mandate public school educators to cover a variety of topics. In some districts, scripted curricula are an attempt to ensure conformity to local, state, and federal mandates (Apple, 2006). In others, individual teachers are responsible for using the materials of the school to develop the students' knowledge.

Most often, the materials used in schools to facilitate scripted curricula are textbooks and workbooks produced by commercial textbook companies (Apple, 2006; Schubert, 1986; Sleeter and Grant, 1991). In short, "in the absence of an overt national curriculum, the commercially produced textbook . . . remains the dominant definition of the curriculum in the United States" (Apple, 2006, p. 46).

As Apple (1993, 2006) discusses, the widespread use of textbooks has myriad implications. Not only do they dominate classroom time, they also influence student learning. Apple (1993) cites Down as saying,

> Textbooks, for better or worse, dominate what students learn. They set the curriculum, and often the facts learned, in most subjects. . . . The public regards textbooks as authoritative, accurate, and necessary. And teachers rely on them to organize lessons and structure subject matter. But the current system of textbook adoption has filled our schools with Trojan horses—glossily covered blocks of paper whose words emerge to deaden the minds of our nation's youth, and make them enemies of learning. (p. 50)

The system Down refers to is that of mass statewide adoptions, which cause textbook companies to produce books that "confuse, mislead, and profoundly bore students" because their content is watered down while "making all of the adults involved in the process look good" (Tyson-Bernstein cited in Apple, 1993, p. 50). In short, "the texts made available to the entire nation, and the knowledge considered legitimate in them, are determined by what will sell in Texas, California, Florida" and other southern states (Apple, 1993, p. 51). This is important because Texas, for example, "mandates texts that stress patriotism, obedience to authority, and the discouragement of deviance" (Apple, 2006, p. 46).

The view that textbook content is in many ways controlled by a few states who adopt texts statewide is reinforced by Apple and Christian-Smith (1991), who say that texts:

> are at once the results of political, economic, and cultural activities, battles, and compromises. They are conceived, designed, and authored by real people with real interests. They are published within the political and economic con-

straints of markets, resources, and power. And what texts mean and how they are used are fought over by communities with distinctly different commitments and by teachers and students as well. (pp. 1–2)

Because textbooks are "a form of cultural politics," they represent a window into the culture that produced them (Apple, 1993, p. 51). Unfortunately, this window often exposes a culture that perpetuates rather than eschews marginalization.

Textbooks are a key place to analyze what kind of knowledge about LGBTQ issues, if any, is produced in public schools or how they instead perpetuate heteronormativity. Because they "symbolize the capitalistic system in action" (Schubert, 1986, pp. 326–327), they signify social and cultural values. As noted previously, they "give us 'official' knowledge, arrived at by a complex interaction of economic, cultural, and political factors. They are what Voltaire said history was: the propaganda of the victorious" (Fishwick, 1992, p. 168).

Exposing knowledge that is victorious in the textbook propaganda race also exposes what has been ignored, which is often referred to as the *null curriculum*, "the curriculum not taught" (Schubert, 1986, p. 107). Textbooks are part of the null curriculum because many things are left out, and their exclusion produces knowledge.

Schubert (1986) says, "We need to realize that students in our schools continuously meet curricula that provide an absence that converts them in many ways" (p. 107). The power of the null curriculum drove activists in the 1960s and 1970s to lobby for the inclusion of African-American perspectives and women's perspectives among others, because the exclusion of those views conveyed a message that there was nothing important contributed from these groups.

Although there have been "literally thousands of studies of textbooks over the years . . . most of those remained unconcerned with the politics of culture" (Apple and Christian-Smith, 1991, p. 1), which highlights the need for such studies. Those that have considered the politics of culture are limited and demonstrate that, although modest changes have been made in the inclusion of African-American and women's perspectives, other areas of difference continue to be excluded (Sleeter and Grant cited in Apple and Christian-Smith, 1991).

Marginalization and heteronormativity found in the overt and null curriculum of textbooks are perpetuated because of power. Kincheloe (2008) suggests that "the power of knowledge (episto-power) plays its role in reinforcing . . . forms of power by placing the various peoples . . . into hierarchical categories" (p. 3). This hierarchical placement is often done via discursive power. Discursive power is a specific consideration in the literature on power as it refers to access and control over often "complex communicative events" (Van Dijk, 2001, p. 356).

Textbooks are connected to this form of power because, as noted earlier, textbooks produce knowledge through content that was agreed upon in part by political factors, which are inherently tied to power. According to Foucault (1973), "behind all knowledge, behind all attainment of knowledge . . . is a struggle for power" (p. 32). Because knowledge is produced through power relations, including knowledge presented in textbooks, any study of textbook knowledge must also include a study of power. For Foucault, the type of power that creates knowledge is not repressive power, or that which comes from the top down, but rather discursive power, which often emanates from the bottom up (1976, p. 98).

In *Discipline and Punish* (1977a), Foucault argues that institutions, like schools, use discourse to reproduce that which is considered reality. Kincheloe would call this discursive power "episto-rays" or knowledge weapons (2008, p. 4). He says, "indeed, the episto-rays [knowledge weapons] move us to support—under the flag of high standards—schools that obscure more than enlighten" (Kincheloe, 2008, p. 4). Because textbooks include some forms of knowledge and exclude others, they are using knowledge as a weapon to reproduce a specific reality.

To understand discursive power, it is important to understand how it is created. Van Dijk (2001) suggests that several factors come together to form discursive power. These include understanding who controls content, context, and topics experienced by individuals. These factors can be explored in media discourse and political discourse but also in curricular discourse. In the case of textbooks, for example, an understanding of who influenced the content, who structured the context, and who arranged the topics can illuminate the ideology behind the text. Although students may never consider such things, those factors influence the textbooks, which influence the production of knowledge in the students themselves.

The discursive power at the heart of access to and control over context and topic, as well as at the core of mind control, which is another area of discursive power that van Dijk (2001) considers, can be particularly insidious because the structures created have lasting implications. The results of discursive power can occur in explicit ways, but it can also occur in more implicit ways, which can have a longer, lasting effect.

Foucault's work gives foundation to van Dijk's argument. His work suggests that discursive power makes it explicit that knowledge produced by textbooks does not "only mean the juxtaposition, coexistence, or interaction of heterogeneous elements . . . but also the relation that is established between them" (Foucault, 1972, p. 72). Therefore, as van Dijk (2001) suggests and as noted previously, power fills discourse as a result of the relationships among structures of content, context, and topic, among others. For this reason, discursive power is indicative of specific types of knowledge production.

HETERONORMATIVITY IN ONE HIGH SCHOOL LITERATURE TEXTBOOK

To demonstrate the point at which knowledge (conceived as textbook curricula), power, and heteronormativity meet, four consecutive editions of one high school literature textbook were analyzed to see how each perpetuated heteronormativity. The research was grounded in queer theory (Plummer, 2008; Wilchins, 2004) and carried out using the understandings of critical discourse analysis (van Dijk, 1989, 1993, 2001) and several axioms developed by Sedgwick (1985, 1990) in her work challenging the dominant heterosexual narrative.

Several aspects of the textbooks were considered for their perpetuation of heteronormativity. The first aspect examined was the authors; second, the biographies provided in the textbooks about those authors; third, the stories and their content; and fourth, the questions provided for student consideration.

A total of 135 authors were represented in the textbooks and of those, fourteen can be identified through biographical information as being LGBTQ or writing with dominant LGBTQ themes. These authors include W. H. Auden, Truman Capote, Constantine P. Cavafy, Emily Dickinson, Audre Lorde, Amy Lowell, Mary Oliver, Edna St. Vincent Millay, Langston Hughes, Claude McKay, Saki, Stephen Sondheim, Alice Walker, and Walt Whitman. Over time, six of these authors were eliminated from later editions of the textbook, with the most recent edition having only eight LGBTQ authors represented.

As noted earlier, queer scholars and research on students exposed to a curriculum reflective of LGBTQ issues demonstrate that heteronormativity can be challenged through positive discussion of sexuality in school. The presence of any authors in the textbooks offers an opportunity for such discussion to begin. However, the research shows that despite the representation of LGBTQ authors, there is no mention of sexuality in the textbooks.

A review of the author biographies provided by the textbook reveals that none of the authors who are LGBTQ or who write with dominant LGBTQ themes are so identified by the textbook biographies. Instead, the biographies, although irregular in content, expose things such as the authors' upbringing, their education and honors, their military experience, ideology, the marginalization they experienced, the causes for which they are active, their marital status, and any disabilities they faced.

Although some of these categories provide opportunity for the textbooks to reveal the sexuality of the authors, the struggles they faced as a result of sexuality, or the work they do to expose inequity based on sexuality, none of this is included. Instead, issues such as financial ruin, alcoholism, and divorce are covered. In revealing these aspects of authors, but not sexuality, the textbook's hidden curriculum conveys a message that sexuality is worse than financial ruin, alcoholism, and divorce. It is not hard to imagine what messages such silences send to students and teachers who are struggling with their own sexuality and identity in schools.

More than the consideration of author biographies in the textbooks, the stories themselves reveal other silences that further marginalize students and faculty who encounter the textbooks. Although the fourteen LGBTQ authors included among the textbooks represent about 10 percent of all the authors included, their work represents 11 percent of all the stories, play and novel excerpts, poems, and other works included in the textbook anthologies. Although the textbooks place each work into a themed unit, my analysis revealed themes in the literature that are markedly different than the themes used by the textbooks to categorize the stories.

These included stories focusing on heterosexuality; gender concerns; racial and cultural concerns; physical, mental, and emotional struggles; and consequences for nonconformity. Although some of these themes do reflect a beginning critical stance, there is a notable absence of a consideration of sexuality. Moreover, just as the sexuality of authors is silenced in the biographies in the textbooks, ambiguous sexuality and unstated gender are masked in poetry.

The gendering of nongendered speakers in poems is one of the more startling findings in the research. Although this finding alone is interesting, more interesting is that, of the eleven poems for which a gender is assumed for the speaker, seven are from LGBTQ authors. With more than forty poems represented among the textbooks, it is noteworthy that 63 percent of those that have the gender of the speaker assumed come from LGBT authors.

In all but two cases, the assumed speaker takes on the gender of the author. The two poems that do not merely assume a speaker whose gender matches that of the poem's author are by LGBTQ authors. The poems are "A Narrow Fellow in the Grass" by Emily Dickinson and "Oh, What Is That Sound" by W. H. Auden. In "A Narrow Fellow in the Grass," the speaker reflects on the illusiveness of snakes and portrays fear on the part of the speaker. Despite the fear, however, the speaker mentions "stopping to secure it" (Dickinson cited in Applebee et al., 2006, p. 554).

This act could be what prompted the textbook publishers to refer to the speaker as a male, whereas in every other poem where an assumption is made the assumption is that of the gender of the author. The other poem that does not merely assume the speaker as the gender of the author is Auden's "O

What Is That Sound." In this poem, there appear to be two speakers commenting on approaching sounds, which are apparently caused by nearing soldiers. Toward the end of the poem, there is an exchange between the speakers:

> O where are you going? Stay with me here!
> Were the vows you swore deceiving, deceiving?
> No, I promised to love you, dear,
> But I must be leaving. (Auden cited in Applebee, et al., 2006, p. 143)

I believe that it is this passage that prompted the reference to the speakers as "husband and wife or a pair of lovers" (Applebee et al., 2006, p. 714). Although a "pair of lovers" does not necessarily imply heterosexual lovers, by prefacing it with "husband and wife," the text sets the reader up to imagine a man and a woman. The authors of each of these pieces is LGBTQ; it appears the textbook is sidestepping any attempt to have that information brought into the discussion of the poetry.

In addition to the silencing of authors and the gendering of nongendered speakers in poetry, among other things, the textbooks also ignore opportunities for critical questioning. Generally, the latest edition of this textbook (2008) has questions that reflect careful attention to technical and literary analysis, plot recall, literal interpretation, and patriarchy.

This focus has caused the elimination of critical questions from earlier editions of the textbook. For example, five questions related to five different stories in the earlier editions of the textbook challenge structures of power. One asks students to consider the line between "hunters and huntees" (Connell in Applebee et al., 2006, p. 58), and another asks students about the necessity of chasing wealth and status. These questions and others like them are important because they push students toward an analysis that challenges the status quo.

Although no questions from either edition ask students to consider or challenge heteronormativity, there are questions that ask students to consider other forms of marginalization. One such question asks students to outright articulate a definition of *justice*. Such a question has the potential to open discussion as students pose various perspectives. Because this question is tied to an excerpt from Mandela's speech to reunify South Africa, it clearly alludes to questions of racism in relation to justice.

Other questions provide similar opportunities. One asks about the role of censorship, which could lead to conversations about challenged books, many of which have LGBTQ characters or situations. Others ask about whether or not there is evil in people or if there are benefits in revenge. These questions can illicit responses from students that reflect their own experiences, many of which could be the result of their own marginalized status.

One of the most frequently occurring themes in the questions is that of race and culture. Unlike the other themes mentioned, nearly half of these questions are found in the 2008 text whereas the others are in the 2006 text. These questions deal specifically with issues related to racial and cultural differences. For example, a question following an excerpt from King's "I Have a Dream" speech asks whether the dream has come true.

Similarly, a question at the end of an excerpt from *Black Boy* (Wright) asks whether the aspirations of African Americans are limited by society today as they were in the story. In addition to these questions about race, "The Future in My Arms" (Danticat) and "A Voice" (Mora) ask about issues of culture. A question following "The Future in My Arms" asks students to compare social views on child rearing and responsibility in their experience to those in the story. One question after "A Voice" asks explicitly about the necessity to preserve culture.

These questions others like them, which I categorized as reflective of race and culture, provide students an opportunity to explore tough issues, but they can also be steps toward other understandings. For example, "The Tropics of New York" (McKay) is a poem in which the speaker considers the fruit he has in his New York window in contrast to what the fruit would be like if he encountered it in the tropics.

Despite the text's assumption that the poet is the speaker, it does ask an interesting question about how the author experiences his race given the content of the poem. What is missed, however, because the book ignores sexuality, is how the poem reflects the author's experience with sexuality. Again, the text does not address this, but the question about race leads a reader to ask questions about a variety of experiences.

A last category of questions deals with issues of gender. These questions can be found in both the 2006 and the 2008 editions in nearly equal numbers. These questions vary from asking students to consider what expectations we have of women and men, respectively (what roles each should take on), to asking for consideration of specific character traits such as intuition and expressiveness. One of the most interesting questions relates to Auden's poem "O What Is That Sound," which was discussed earlier in this chapter because the 2008 text suggests that the speakers are "husband and wife or a pair of lovers."

Despite its assumption in an introduction to the poem, the 2008 text also includes a question about who the two speakers are, which leaves their genders open to interpretation. This question provides an opportunity for discussion about why students make the decisions about the speakers' genders that they do.

In addition to the obvious opportunity to discuss LGBTQ issues in "O What Is That Sound," several of the other questions from stories listed under the theme of gender provide similar openings for discussion. The story

"Brothers Are the Same" (Markham) deals with boys completing rites of passage.

A question following the story asks about rites of passage in a general way. This would allow students to consider on their own whether LGBTQ students experience different rites of passage than non-LGBTQ students. Questions for other pieces that direct students to consider what expectations we have of women and men can also provide students an opportunity to consider where the line between women and men becomes blurred, which allows them to challenge typical gender stereotypes.

Many of the questions that fall into the themes outlined here provide opportunity for students to have further discussion about challenging topics. Unfortunately, not all stories included such questions. Instead, through omission, the questions following some stories silence conversations that could challenge gender norms, explore LGBTQ speakers in poems, or expose the conformity society expects from individuals.

Specifically, a question about the speaker in "A Narrow Fellow in the Grass" (Dickinson) would allow students to explore both the speaker's fear of the snake and the speaker's desire to pick up the snake and how these elements shape assumptions of gender. A similar question about "The Raven" (Poe) would expose flaws in assumptions that the speaker is male. These omissions are reflective of the ways in which these textbooks use discursive power to perpetuate heteronormativity.

Although there is more to the research in this study, these key points demonstrate how the confluence of knowledge and power as represented by textbooks meet with heteronormativity to create a curricular product that stifles strong identity development and expression in students and teachers who encounter them. Given this knowledge, it is critical to explore what can be done to undermine the inherent marginalization.

QUEER THEORISTS, CRITICAL PEDAGOGUES, AND CLASSROOM TEACHERS

Queer theory is the starting point for both understanding and undermining heteronormativity. Queer theory is a paradigm that draws from "feminism and the postmodern sensibility" (Denzin and Lincoln, 2008, p. 33). It also traces its roots to the civil rights movement (Wilchins, 2004). Denzin and Lincoln (2008) note, "It uses methods strategically . . . for understanding and for producing resistances to local structures and domination" (p. 33). Such domination creates binaries, one side that is deemed good and one side marginalized as the other.

Although often not explicit in discourse such as textbook content, othering "tends strongly to be done in the name of politics," a politics of heteronormativity (Filax, 2006, p. 21). In these ways, queer theory also has much in common with critical theory, which calls for understanding "diverse forms of oppression including class, race, gender, sexual, cultural, religious, colonial, and ability-related concerns" (Kincheloe and McLaren, 2008, p. 407).

However, queer theory, unlike critical theory, relies on the postmodern tradition and focuses on the "endemic crisis of homo/heterosexual definition" and "deconstructing the sex/gender divide" (Plummer, 2008, p. 488). By deconstructing these binaries and recognizing both explicit and implicit othering in discourse, queer theory responds to what it sees as more limited frames in feminism and gay and lesbian studies.

More specifically, queer theory works at "exposing the deep injustice of both homophobia and heterosexism" and understanding how "gender, sex, desire, and sexuality organise all human behaviour" (Filax, 2006, p. 139). Such work is intent on causing social change, which is not a goal of all theories or classroom practices. To arrive at such change, queer theorists both in the research field and in the classroom must "show that there is no fixed, unified, biological, essential, or pre-discursive self" (Filax, 2006, p. 141). Instead, it must show, through discourse analysis, that individuals are created through discourse.

Sedgwick (cited in Barber and Clark, 2002) notes that "saying something can be doing something" (p. 9). It is through discourse that meaning and identities are created. For example, "in order for heterosexuality to function as the normal, natural, and given, it must have its abnormal, unnatural, absent other: the homosexual" (Filax, 2006, p. 143).

Whether that other is actually part of the explicit discourse or not, discourse analysis can demonstrate that the explicit mention of heterosexuality implicitly maligns the homosexual position—saying something does something, just as Sedgwick suggests. Queer research reveals the commonness of such discursive othering, and it can and should be carried out in the classroom through such projects as the textbook analysis described here.

Following a queer theoretical perspective, it is through a critical pedagogy that classroom teachers can begin to challenge the marginalization of heteronormativity as well as other forms of marginalization. Aronowitz and Giroux suggest that the challenge "is to combine the intellectual work of cultural reclamation with the work of pedagogy. This would entail a deliberate effort to avoid the tendency toward exclusivity on the part of intellectuals" (Aronowitz and Giroux, 1991, pp. 221–22).

One form of pedagogy moving away from exclusivity and toward cultural reclamation is critical pedagogy. Kincheloe (2008) says, "[I]t is the charge of critical pedagogy to throw a monkey wrench into a system of knowledge—an episteme that Foucault labeled his regime of truth—that perpetuates such [marginalizing] perspectives and the human suffering that accompanies them" (p. 3). Going back to Aronowitz and Giroux, however, the fear of dealing with this politically charged topic must first be overcome by academics before the system of knowledge can be not only challenged but also changed.

Koschoreck challenges the episto-power that Kincheloe refers to and eschews the fear of this topic; he discusses his own classroom experiences in his article on transgressing heteronormativity. He says, "the individuals in my examples, then, might very consciously be persons of color, elderly individuals, women, gay men, lesbians, or persons of differing abilities" (Koschoreck, 2003, p. 37). This allows him to not only address heteronormativity but also demonstrate overall inclusiveness.

A reconceptualization of high school curricula found in textbooks can make similarly deliberate decisions about the examples of authors, texts, questions, and images included for study. If this is done, we can meet the challenge of critical pedagogy and, as Kincheloe says, embrace the notion that "elementary and secondary schools as well as colleges and universities must become 'trading zones' of intercultural exchange and global meeting places" (2008, p. 7).

Critical pedagogy in the language arts does not suggest omitting all material traditional to a neoconservative canon. Rather, it suggests using that canon along with additional material to understand and challenge the regimes of power. Duncan-Andrade and Morrell (2008) say that critical pedagogy in literature starts with the hegemonic texts that perpetuate marginalization because "these are the very texts that need to be critiqued, contextualized, and ultimately re-written by critically empowered and critically literate citizens" (p. 53). From this study, additional texts (visual, audio, print, etc.) are brought in to link the traditional with elements of students' own culture.

Like Koschoreck's work, this allows critical pedagogues to be inclusive of LGBTQ literary examples but also of other marginalized groups. This is vital because, as Apple (2006) notes, one reason the conservative right has so much influence is because the progressive liberal agenda is fractured.

To become trading zones of intercultural exchange that Kincheloe, Koschoreck, Duncan-Andrade, Morrell, and others recommend, the textbooks used as curriculum must be reconceptualized. An ideal textbook would do a variety of things. First, it would encourage students to explore the information that they are presented and judge whether it is factual or opinion. This work forces students to evaluate what they are presented and why they view things in the way that they do. Textbooks should also include autobiographical information from the authors where possible in lieu of the textbook-created biographies.

Although these autobiographies would be cut by textbook editors, using authors' own words would eliminate some of the masking in which existing biographical accounts engage. Further, such excerpts would force students to look at the editing choices of the editors, noting where words, phrases, and sentences are omitted and where words are added. Considering such editing will further develop students' ability to be critical of what they are presented.

As this review of queer theory and critical pedagogy demonstrates, there is need for both theory and practice. Although critical pedagogy is often criticized for being too theoretical, I have shown through the work of Koschoreck and others that it can truly be applied in the classroom. I have also seen such theories work first hand in the classroom.

As a secondary literature teacher, I encounter texts like the one described in the analysis here. From my own queer theoretical lens I employ critical pedagogy in asking students to challenge dominant discourses. For example, in a unit titled "Injustice," students begin by brainstorming forms of injustice. Students readily identify racism and sexism. When pushed, they will identify classism. It takes much questioning for them to acknowledge marginalization based on religion, culture, and ability, and even more for students to consider marginalization based on gender and sexuality.

Yet, when the list goes up, students lose their surprise and few challenge that there is discrimination based on these and other categories. Students are not even confounded by the differences between sex and gender; they immediately relay stories of gender discrimination that they've experienced or witnessed. This demonstrates the mere need for a forum to discuss such elements of our society that our students experience daily. As Duncan-Andrade and Morrell (2008) suggest, this does not take away from the standard curriculum, which allows students to operate in the dominant society.

Rather it adds a new dimension to it. Students use such a list to consider the treatment of characters in classic texts such as *Oedipus the King* and *The Inferno*. Such a critical pedagogy acknowledges the dominance and gives students the tools to play in the field of dominance while simultaneously challenging them to confront and undermine the dominance.

Students can also be taught to challenge dominance in much more subtle ways. When confronted with poetry, such as that found in the previously discussed data, in which the speaker's sex or gender is not identified, students can be pushed to think outside of their dominant frame. Take, for example, the poem by Aleksandr Solzhenitsyn, "Freedom to Breathe." In this poem the speaker's gender is not explicit. Students and textbooks often assume the speaker is male because the poet is male and because the speaker says, "not even a woman's kiss is sweeter to me than this air" (Solzhenitsyn, n.d.).

However, when pushed, students can acknowledge a variety of assumptions that they've made about the poem that suggest their dominant thinking. When considering the possibility that the speaker is a woman they point out how in the beginning of the poem the speaker is especially in tune with nature, which the students associate with women.

> I stand under an apple tree in blossom and I breathe. Not only the apple tree but the grass round it glistens with moisture; words cannot describe the sweet fragrance that pervades the air. I inhale as deeply as I can, and the aroma invades my whole being; I breathe with my eyes open, I breathe with my eyes closed—I cannot say which gives me the greater pleasure. (Solzhenitsyn, n.d.)

They also note that a man is more likely to be in prison and notice the noises noticed by the speaker at the end of the poem.

> This, I believe, is the single most precious freedom that prison takes away from us. . . . No matter that this is only a tiny garden, hemmed in by five-story houses like cages in a zoo. I cease to hear the motorcycles backfiring, radios whining, the burble of loudspeakers. (Solzhenitsyn, n.d.)

Such a conversation is missed without critical pedagogy emanating from a queer theory. With this conversation, students never challenge their own dominant thinking, and therefore never challenge dominance in other areas of their lives.

Although I recognize that these are small examples and I, too, have far to go in infusing my courses with a critical pedagogy, I am taking the initial steps that all educators can take to undermine stereotypical identities and challenge students to consider how and why such identities exist. To take it a step further, I must continue to challenge both myself and my students to take the knowledge of domination and use it to undermine heteronormativity and also other forms of marginalization.

CONCLUSION

This chapter considers how knowledge in the classroom can be conceived as that which comes from textbooks. It also explored how power shapes those textbooks in the form of our dominant heteronormative culture. The literature shows clearly how such curricula harm the teachers and students exposed to them. Through a study of one high school literature textbook over time, it is evident that authors are silenced, students are expected to accept the gendering of nongendered speakers, and both teachers and students are to ignore critical questions that could challenge dominance.

Together, queer theory and critical pedagogy offer a frame from which educators can begin to develop a critical dialogue in their classrooms and offer students an opportunity to affirm their identity, whether it is LGBTQ or not. Examples from both the literature and my personal experience demonstrate how the theories come to life in the classroom. Although minimal, these demonstrations show that it is not difficult for educators, regardless of their own gendered and sexual identity, to be critical in the classroom, and to therefore produce students who can be critical of dominance and have the language to challenge marginalization of all forms.

NOTES

1. Research is from the unpublished dissertation of the author:
Hickman, H. (2009). *Knowledge, Power, and Heteronormativity: A Deep Investigation of One Text and Its Evolution Over Time*. (Doctoral dissertation, Lewis University, Romeoville, IL).

REFERENCES

Apple, M. W. (1993). *Official knowledge: Democratic education in a conservative age*. New York: Routledge.

Apple, M. W. (2006). *Educating the "right" way: Markets, standards, God, and inequality* (second edition). New York: Routledge.

Apple, M. W., & Christian-Smith, L. K. (1991). The politics of the textbook. In M. W. Apple and L. K. Christian-Smith (Eds.), *The politics of the textbook* (pp. 1–21). New York: Routledge.

Applebee, A. N., Bermudez, A. B., Blau, S., Caplan, R., Elbow, P., Hynds, S., et al. (Eds.). (2006). *The language of literature*. Evanston, IL: McDougal Littell.

Applebee, A. N., Bermudez, A. B., Blau, S., Caplan, R., Elbow, P., Hynds, S., et al. (Eds.). (2002). *The language of literature*. Evanston, IL: McDougal Littell.

Applebee, A. N., Bermudez, A. B., Blau, S., Caplan, R., Elbow, P., Hynds, S., et al. (Eds.). (2000). *The language of literature*. Evanston, IL: McDougal Littell.

Applebee, A. N., Center on English Learning and Achievement. (1991). *A study of high school literature anthologies*. University at Albany Center on English Learning and Achievement. Retrieved April 2, 2008, from http://cela.albany.edu/reports/applebee/ applebeestudy/index.html.

Aronowitz, S., & Giroux, H. A. (1991). Textual authority, culture, and the politics of literacy. In M. W. Apple and L. K. Christian-Smith (Eds.), *The politics of the textbook* (pp. 213–41). New York: Routledge.

Barber, S. M., & Clark, D. L. (Eds.). (2002). *Regarding Sedgwick: Essays on queer culture and critical theory*. New York: Routledge.

Blount, J. M. (2005). *Fit to teach: Same sex desire, gender, and school work in the twentieth century*. Albany, NY: State University of New York Press.

Denzin, N. K., & Lincoln, Y. S. (2008). Preface and introduction: The discipline and practice of qualitative research. In N. K. Denzin and Y. S. Lincoln (Eds.), *The landscape of qualitative research* (pp. vii–43). Los Angeles: Sage.

Duncan-Andrade, J. M. R., & Morrell, E. (2008). *The art of critical pedagogy: Possibilities for moving from theory to practice in urban schools*. New York: Peter Lang.

Filax, G. (2006). Politicising action research through queer theory. *Educational Action Research, 14*(1), 139–45.

Fishwick, M. W. (1992). The politics of the textbook. [Review of the book *The politics of the textbook*]. *Journal of Popular Culture, 26*(2), 168.

Foucault, M. (1972). *The archaeology of knowledge and the discourse on language* (A. M. Sheridan-Smith, Trans.). New York: Pantheon Books.

Foucault, M. (1973/2000). Truth and juridical forms (R. Hurley, Trans.). In J. D. Faubion (Ed.), *Essential works of Foucault 1954–1984: Vol. 3. Power* (pp. 1–89). P. Rabinow (Vol. Ed.). New York: The New Press.

Foucault, M. (1976). Two lectures (C. Gordon, L. Marshall, J. Mepham, and K. Soper, Trans.). In C. Gordon (Ed.), *Power/Knowledge: Selected interviews and other writings 1972–1977* (pp. 55–62). New York: Pantheon Books.

Foucault, M. (1977/1995). *Discipline and punish: The birth of the prison* (A. Sheridan, Trans.). New York: Vintage Books.
Kincheloe, J. L. (2008). Critical pedagogy and the knowledge wars of the twenty-first century. *International Journal of Critical Pedagogy*, *1*(1), 1–22. Retrieved March 3, 2009, from http://freire.mcgill.ca/ojs/index.php/home/article/view/48/16.
Kincheloe, J. L., & McLaren, P. (2008). Rethinking critical theory and qualitative research. In N. K. Denzin and Y. S. Lincoln (Eds.), *The landscape of qualitative research* (pp. 403–55). Los Angeles: Sage.
Koschoreck, J. W. (2003). Easing the violence: Transgressing heteronormativity in educational administration. *Journal of School Leadership 13*(1), pp. 27–50.
Kosciw, J. G., Diaz, E. M., & Greytak, E. A. (2008). *The 2008 national school climate survey: The experiences of lesbian, gay, bisexual, and transgender youth in our nation's schools*. New York: Gay, Lesbian, and Straight Education Network.
Lugg, C. A. (2003). Sissies, faggots, lezzies, and dykes: Gender, sexual orientation, and a new politics of education? *Education Administration Quarterly*, *39*(1), 67–93.
Meyer, E. J. (2008). A feminist reframing of bullying and harassment: Transforming schools through critical pedagogy. *McGill Journal of Education*, *1*(1), 33–48. Retrieved March 3, 2009, from http://mje.mcgill.ca/article/view/1077/2086.
Pascoe, C. J. (2007). *Dude, you're a fag*. Berkeley: University of California Press.
Plummer, K. (2008). Critical humanism and queer theory. In N. K. Denzin and Y. S. Lincoln (Eds.), *The landscape of qualitative research* (pp. 477–99). Los Angeles: Sage.
Schubert, W. H. (1986). *Curriculum: Perspective, paradigm, and possibility*. Upper Saddle River, NJ: Prentice Hall.
Sedgwick, E. K. (1985). *Between men: English literature and male homosocial desire*. New York: Columbia University Press.
Sedgwick, E. K. (1990). *Epistemology of the closet*. Berkeley: University of California Press.
Sleeter, C. E., & Grant, C. A. (1991). Race, class, gender, and disability in current textbooks. In M. W. Apple and L. K. Christian-Smith (Eds.), *The politics of the textbook* (pp. 78–110). New York: Routledge.
Solzhenitsyn, Aleksandr (n.d.). *The global classroom: Linking the world, one classroom at a time*. Retrieved March 15, 2009, from http://www.sad34.net/~globalclassroom/Library/Russiathreeprosepoems.
Tooms, A. (2007). The right kind of queer: Fit and the politics of school leadership. *Journal of School Leadership, 17*(1), 601–30.
Van Dijk, T. A. (1989). Structures of discourse and structures of power. In J. A. Anderson (Ed.), *Communication yearbook*: *Vol. 12* (pp. 18–59). Newbury Park, CA: Sage.
Van Dijk, T. A. (1993). Principles of critical discourse analysis. *Discourse and Society, 4*(2), 249–83.
Van Dijk, T. A. (2001). Critical discourse analysis. In D. Tannen, D. Schiffrin, and H. Hamilton (Eds.), *Handbook of discourse analysis* (pp. 352–71). Oxford: Blackwell.
Wilchins, R. (2004). *Queer theory, gender theory*. Los Angeles: Alyson Books.

Chapter Five

Shh ... Out

From Silence to Self

Janna Jackson

In an interview-based qualitative study of nine self-identified gay and lesbian teachers designed to find answers to the question "How do K–12 gay and lesbian teachers see their experiences as gays and lesbians as informing their teaching?" data analysis showed that answers were neither uniform nor universal. Instead, exploring how participants viewed the process, conditions, and consequences of merging gayness and teaching revealed that internal and external factors impinged on processes of developing gay and teacher identities in complicated ways, which, in turn, shaped classroom practice. In this chapter, I focus on how participants developed their identities as gay teachers.

All participants constructed their personal and professional histories as intricately intertwined and marked by distinct stages: *preteaching*, *closeted teaching*, and *post–coming out*. The *preteaching* stage included participants' experiences before becoming teachers. Once they became teachers, all participants entered the *closeted teaching* stage, or teaching without disclosing their gayness. For openly gay participants, coming out to students created a shift in thinking and teaching, providing a catalyst for the *post–coming out* stage. Although individual experiences of participants were unique, their overall processes were remarkably similar.

Even though all these stages occurred in a linear progression for these nine participants, the stages varied in intensity and duration across participants, with some overlap between stages. For example, one participant was closeted during his student teaching but came out almost immediately upon becoming a teacher, whereas others spent years in the closet. Within these stages, participants experienced phases, areas of development more fluid and flexible than movement between stages. In other words, participants sometimes displayed aspects of both phases at the same time, sometimes moved linearly from one phase to the next, or sometimes moved back and forth between phases.

The first *preteaching* stage contained the *coming into gayness* and *coming into teaching* phases, experiences that laid the groundwork for their gay and teacher identities. The *closeted teaching* stage involved the *super-teacher* phase during which participants tried to become perfect teachers and the *on the verge* phase where participants contemplated coming out to students. The *post–coming out* stage included the *gay poster child* phase, during which participants were acutely aware of their new status as an openly gay teacher, and the *authentic teacher* phase, during which participants integrated their gay and teacher identities. In this chapter, I explore the nuances of these stages and phases in order.

SETTING THE STAGE: THE PRETEACHING STAGE

Whether or not to become teachers and whether or not to accept their gayness were two decisions all participants confronted. Examining participants' accounts revealed that these two decisions were easier for some than others, occurred at varying ages, and occurred at different times in relation to each other.

Individual participant accounts uncover how participants came to these two decisions about gayness and teaching and how their accompanying experiences resonated throughout the rest of their personal and professional lives. The *coming into gayness* phase explores participants' acceptance of their sexual orientation, a step necessitated by "compulsory heterosexuality" (Rich, 1993) and the *coming into teaching* phase explores participants' journeys to becoming teachers.

Comparing *coming into gayness* and *coming into teaching* illustrates that these two phases often resembled each other, even though they occurred at different times and at different rates for each participant and across participants. Some participants portrayed gayness as a preexisting condition: "I look back and go, 'Well, I was a lesbian all my life'" (Summer[1]). Several participants described teaching in a similar fashion: "I always thought that I was naturally born to be a teacher and knew that that was going to happen. So I don't say that as a career statement like, 'I have a job as a teacher.' I think of it more as an identity, as a part of my being is to be a teacher" (Duncan).

Just as participants described coming out to themselves as discovering who they were meant to be, Carolyn described teaching as "what I was meant to do," Duncan described becoming a teacher as coming into his "natural self," and Tony used the term *calling*. Even participants who initially pursued other careers described coming into teaching as a discovery, just as some participants described realizing they are gay as a discovery. When reflecting back on their lives, several participants expressed that a desire to teach was always there, but for some it took a certain self-acceptance, just as with gayness.

Glen, Carolyn, and Patrick initially avoided teaching because they saw it as lacking respect, but eventually they took pride in teaching, just as they moved from shame to pride with their gay identities. Glen describes this transition:

> I felt it was not that impressive a job, that people would see me as not achieving my potential professionally. So I really resisted it. I went from, *shame* is not the word, thinking it would be embarrassing, that people [would] look down on me. Now it's a huge badge of honor. It's something I'm really proud of.

For these participants, self-acceptance as gay and as teachers moved from shame to pride.

Another parallel between the *coming into gayness* and the *coming into teaching* phases involved an "identity lag," a term Ponse (1978) uses to describe the period between recognizing same-sex desires and identifying as gay and experienced by some participants:

> By the time I was in fourth grade, I knew that I was gay. Probably seventh grade was when I could look in the mirror and say it out loud. Ninth grade is probably when I stopped crying myself to sleep every night, praying to God . . . that I'd wake up and be changed. But I didn't really come out to people until college. (Glen)

Just as coming out to oneself did not necessarily coincide with identifying with the gay community, for some participants becoming a teacher did not coincide with identifying as a teacher. For example, Patrick did not identify as a teacher until two years into his teaching career: "I taught at public school and that was the beginning of my career, my identifying as a teacher. Up until then I had been teaching but I didn't consider myself a teacher," which led to him spending "an entire summer looking for a job and myself at the same time."

Despite this, Patrick claimed, "I've identified with [being a teacher] since I was in college, even before I started college." He explained this discrepancy between identifying with teaching earlier than his self-acceptance as a teacher as being tied to his shame about teaching. Becoming a teacher and identifying as a teacher, like becoming gay and identifying as gay, did not occur simultaneously for all participants as experience as self-acceptance played a role.

Not only did I, as the researcher, see connections between identifying as gay and identifying as a teacher through data analysis, participants saw these connections as well. Because coming into gayness and coming into teaching coincided for Patrick, discovering both involved the same questioning process: "I started thinking about what makes me happy and one of the things I realized was teaching does make me happy. So it was more than identity as far as sexual orientation is concerned. It was, 'Who am I? What am I meant to do?'" For Lauren, these two processes also meant finding answers to longstanding questions:

> It's like I'm unaware that's something there. No, that's not right. I know that something's there, like, with being gay. I knew something was wrong. I knew something was just not fitting. It was really getting to me by college. It was like, "What the hell is with this world? I don't think it's all me." And then when that guy I was with said, "Have you thought you might be a lesbian?" I realized and it was like, "Ok. Cool." I have the word. I have a gay–straight framework because I've been looking. It fit. The same is with the classroom teaching. It was like, "Cool, I like this." So it was that the cognitive dissonance was there and when the explanation showed up that fit what I was having problems with.

Lauren and Patrick came into teaching and gayness by answering the same questions about what gave their lives meaning. The *coming into gayness* and *coming into teaching* phases paralleled each other and laid foundations for participants' lives as gay teachers. After deciding to become teachers, all participants left the *preteaching* stage and entered the *closeted teaching* stage, a stage during which they bifurcated their personal and professional identities.

BEHIND THE SCENES: THE CLOSETED TEACHING STAGE

No matter if journeys to teaching were smooth or rocky, entering teaching was problematic for many participants because they saw teaching and gayness as mutually exclusive: "You can't have a gay teacher. I thought that was one of the rules." For Lauren, going into teaching meant going back into the closet: "I didn't feel like I had a choice." For Patrick, returning to the classroom meant returning to an environment associated with teasing and bullying, a concern expressed by participants in other studies (Jennings, 1994; Woog, 1995).

For some participants, the boundaries of the school closet extended beyond school walls. For example, Lauren avoided Pride, an annual celebration of gay culture, during her closeted years. For some, closets not only expanded beyond school, but also extended into the future:

> I want to get married and have kids. I think about what are the parents gonna do? What's the administration gonna do? Where's my backing going to come? What's gonna happen when Ms. Flowers who isn't married gets pregnant? I think about that a lot. Sometimes I think about actually leaving teaching to pursue that since I don't want to have to deal with all the shame that goes along with it. (Stephanie)

Actively avoiding disclosure pervaded every aspect of participants' lives, a phenomenon reported in other studies (Epstein and Johnson, 1994; Woods and Harbeck, 1992).

Participants gave many reasons for entering the closet. Some participants felt the need to please others, as Patrick explained: "It was so important to me to get their acceptance, which was detrimental to me at the beginning because I was not willing in any way to show who I was because I was terrified of that rejection."

While in the closet, Carolyn thought if people labeled her as *gay*, they would read her only as gay, inhibiting them from seeing her as she really is: "I want people to know me for me first and not have to sift through and see me through this veil of, 'Ohhh. She's gay.'" Carolyn hypothesized what parents might think: "Well, is she gonna molest the [students]? Are they gonna be safe with her? Is she gonna say inappropriate things? Or expose them to things we don't think are age appropriate?" Patrick expressed similar fears: "I'd never want parents to wonder if I'm looking at their kids weird" but also worried about the reaction of his students:

> When I first started teaching I was terrified by the stereotypical football offensive lineman who might be sitting in my classroom who I would assume that if he knew I was the gay teacher he would immediately shut me off and want nothing to do with my classroom.

Current events fomented these fears, as Carolyn pointed out: "You read in the newspaper and you hear over time . . . about people losing their jobs." This fear added stress to teaching, an already stressful profession, as Duncan described:

> There was always that undercurrent of fear, the notion that I could be exposed at any moment. I never knew when the accusation was going to come. So I was always walking this really fine line between exposure and concealment and it just put me on edge all the time. I would be hot with tension.

The closet defined participants' professional and personal lives.

Upon entering the classroom, most participants felt the need to enact their image of the ideal teacher. This desire for perfection, common for beginning teachers but exacerbated by the closet, constituted the *super-teacher* phase of the *closeted teaching* stage. As participants tried to establish themselves as teachers in their classrooms and schools, they took on a teacher persona by personifying what they thought a teacher should look like. Carolyn attested to this pressure to be flawless: "As a younger teacher you want to be able to be that great perfect teacher for everyone." "Maintaining an image," Patrick's words, led to high stress as participants tried to conform to an unattainable ideal.

Being the perfect teacher meant having no flaws, as Duncan explained: "I used to have to be the expert on everything in class. I hated to be wrong. I had to know everything." Having no flaws for Duncan meant not asking for help: "I hadn't been able to allow other people to tell me what I'm doing wrong or I was afraid to ask or I built up a nice wall that I wouldn't let them in close enough to let me know." For Patrick, it also meant establishing authority over the classroom: "My first year teaching . . . I wanted constant control." This constant control for Duncan entailed "yes or no at my command. It meant don't contradict me." In the *super-teacher* phase, these beginning teachers put up a façade of being infallible.

Ironically, participants directly linked teacher and gay identity development in the *super-teacher* phase because it involved separating them. This was because being infallible meant not being gay, at least at school: "There were two selves." For participants, being gay reinforced and accentuated the need to be a super-teacher, and being a super-teacher reinforced and accentuated the need not to be gay. In this phase, they viewed perfection as protection, as Duncan explained:

> All those good things I did would make me beyond reproach and certainly not gay. People who are beyond reproach in education can't be homosexual. That was crazy but it kept me busy and it kept me straight, kept me closeted for a long time. . . . The more respectable and presentable and beyond reproach I became, the deeper the closet I was creating. That made coming out even more difficult because I had to reverse the entire process.

Duncan explained how being the perfect teacher "was about creating excellence that couldn't be confused with the evil of homosexuality." In the *super-teacher* phase, participants thought being the perfect teacher placed a teacher beyond reproach, as Glen described:

> You don't want any part of you to be questioned. If you do things that lead kids to asking some questions, then perhaps they might ask others. So I definitely think there's that connection between being a super-teacher and being closeted because there's no room for questions.

Duncan also saw "a direct link actually. Yeah, absolutely because I was so busy being respected and so busy being impeccable in my character that, again, you'd never accuse me of that thing. 'He's too good a teacher. He's too perfect.'" Other studies about gay teachers note this connection between perfection and denying gayness (Grayson, 1987; Jennings, 1994; Lipkin, 1999; Woog, 1995). Participants in this study and others exercised similar strategies of working hard to work against being gay.

Another aspect of being perfect meant doing everything, such as leading extracurriculars as Patrick did: "I tackled everything that I could. . . . Yeah, I mean I just, if I listed all the things that I did in my first two years of teaching, I just can't believe it." For Duncan, this resulted in leaving teaching for a while: "I guess I burned out. I was like Mr. Teacher. I was doing every club, doing all these things. Mr. Pep Rally. And I thought, 'Wow. I can't do this.'" For these participants, the perfect teacher image included getting involved in school activities.

Similar to connections made between perfection and protection, participants also made connections between over-commitment and protection. Just as being the perfect teacher in the classroom lessened the chances of someone asking questions, so did keeping busy:

> The busier I was, the more active I was, the less opportunity people had to slow me down to get into me. So, part of that hyper-busyness, hyper-teaching, and hyperactivity was to avoid slow motion where someone could grab me and stop me and ask me a question. (Duncan)

Duncan's "always moving theory" for Patrick operated to such an extreme that he was too busy to question himself: "There was really no time for thought or anything to deal with [being gay]." For Patrick, "always moving" also had the added advantage of being an excuse for not dating women. Keeping busy kept others', and their own, questioning minds at bay.

Because participants perceived being gay as a flaw in a teacher while in the *super-teacher* phase, they excluded any part of themselves that exuded gayness, as Carolyn described:

> Worrying about the unknown plus you're in a new job and you don't know the principal that well. . . . You're trying to impress your department chair. You want to get tenure. You haven't even proven yourself yet. You don't . . . want to throw in that other piece that could potentially be used against you.

Preventing gayness from seeping into teaching meant a constant vigilance about monitoring appearance: "Starting teaching, I started to change the way that I dressed . . . because I didn't want people to think that I was gay"; physical contact: "It was an appropriate moment to hug and I kind of was doing a handshake kind of thing"; and speech: "When I have to guard my speech, then I can't be relaxed really about anything because you never know when something's gonna slip." Participants in other studies also described guarding their actions, monitoring their appearance, and censoring their speech (Evans, 1999; Sears, 1993; Woods and Harbeck, 1992). Being on guard built walls, making closeted participants "impenetrable in many ways" (Duncan).

This self-editing applied to curricular content as well. Carolyn deliberately made sure people did not suspect anything: "Before I came out, I worr[ied] about if I tried to push for more, talk about gay and lesbian stuff in the curriculum, then maybe people might think I was gay." Just as fears of discovery prompted curricular censorship, fears of having an agenda prompted ensuring parents did not think "that I'm trying to get across some kind of political message. Not necessarily recruit, but have my own sort of agenda. Maybe not recruiting kids to be gay, but recruiting kids to think that gay is cool" (Caroyln). When closeted, participants purged their teaching of anything remotely gay.

If gayness did come up in school, closeted participants would avoid it, which Glen described as "blocking, parrying, deflecting it." This habit caused Summer inadvertently to make a faux pas: "One girl one time asked how lesbians made love. And I said, 'That's something you should ask your mother.' I just called her mother a lesbian." She can laugh about it now, but at the time, she would "shy away from things. Anything even indirect I would bounce it off or go someplace else. The word would make me shiver if somebody said something about lesbian." Tony explained that "the most dangerous time is when you're closeted and kids ask that stuff."

Deflection also involved allowing students to make the heterosexual assumption instead of correcting it. For example, Carolyn did not correct students when they said, "Ms. Walls has a boyfriend." By becoming experts at manipulating conversations, closeted participants managed to conceal their gay identities at school.

Despite all the effort spent removing gayness from the classroom, it largely informed participants' actions and speech while in the school closet, as Patrick described:

> It infiltrated every single part of my life for a while. . . . I used to go to school and put on the show. . . . Coming back into the high school classroom, I immediately felt the need to be a jock. I felt the need to guard what I say. . . . That's what I mean about trauma. It was such a huge part of my job, although ironically I did everything I could to keep it out of my job. Any part of my personality that would suggest that I was gay I would completely remove from my classroom. That's why it was such a huge thing. Everything I said, the way that I walked down the hallway, I guarded everything. It really made my job stressful.

Some participants, like Duncan, not only eliminated "gay" attributes, but also went to extra efforts to appear heterosexual:

> Growing up with the apprehension, always being prepared for the slap, always being prepared for the punch in the gut, metaphorically, puts you on guard. I'[d] do things to avoid detection. You know, playing the straight game is certainly a result of my experiences of being gay, watching people who are gay being harassed, hearing peers and students demeaning gay people.

Passing meant acting in gender-typical ways, including pretending to be straight.

Being a super-teacher created a lot of stress for participants and was "exhausting," in Duncan's words. Trying to "disguise the fact that you're gay ... has some pretty negative effects" according to Carolyn. One of these effects was having a double-life like Duncan led when in the closet:

> You are pretending. You're playing a game. You create a wall. There were two selves. There were double lives. . . . There was certainly a façade, a very well-structured façade, that was my teacher life. . . . It wasn't connected to the piece behind it.

Patrick explained how it "affected every single daily interaction because that's all I thought about was what I need to do here, what do I need to say, how I need to act, how I need to walk, how I need to talk. And it was my greatest insecurity by far." Stephanie put this more succinctly: "Teacher by day. Lesbian by night."

As participants became more comfortable with teaching and with themselves, they shared more of themselves with their students. This made it more and more obvious that they were hiding a vital piece of themselves, as Duncan stated: "It was easy to be closeted when I was not fully myself anyway. As I was becoming more myself with the kids, that other missing piece became far more visible to me." These feelings of lying and hypocrisy prompted some participants to move from the *super-teacher* phase to the *on the verge* phase while in the *closeted teaching* stage.

As tensions of teaching from the closet increased, participants weighed either leaving teaching or coming out to their students. The stress and the exhaustion of monitoring every move constantly pushed several out of the closet, like Carolyn: "The more closeted I was, the more self-conscious I was of how are people perceiving me, doing that sort of double thing, like, 'Ok, this is what I'm doing but how are they perceiving what I'm doing.' . . . And it's like too much effort." For Lauren, stifling the freedom she felt when she finally realized she was a lesbian was too much: "I just couldn't stand being closeted. I just couldn't stand it. You know I'd been so happy when I figured it out and I was just out all the time and who cares."

Others also described feeling like a fraud, which stemmed from many disconnects. Some participants, like Carolyn, felt their outside persona did not match their inner selves: "Dissonance between who I was on the inside and who I was being on the outside and I didn't like [this] distance between who I am and what I'm saying." Duncan described a piece of himself as missing from the classroom:

> That piece of me, that bit of foundation, you need a foundation to teach from solidly, my foundation wasn't complete because it was a lie. There was a piece, a chunk that wasn't added to that. So it was always on the brink of teetering. So it was the last, the last piece . . . was just the point that it was balanced on. It was the fulcrum. And so when I added that piece, my foundation was officially firm and so whatever I said was from an honest place.

As participants brought more of themselves into their teaching, what they were leaving out became more and more obvious.

As their efforts to deliberately eliminate gayness from their teaching became more apparent, some realized that lying by omission sent harmful messages to students. For Summer, conveying this message of shame contradicted other messages of integrity: "I was trying to teach them to feel good about themselves and then I'm not telling them who I am . . . [so] it's difficult for me to try to make them comfortable with themselves if I couldn't be comfortable with who I was."

For Duncan, that glaring contradiction prompted him to come out in an unpremeditated manner when he was telling his students, "If you show pride in who you are, no matter what that is, then people tend not to attack people who are sure of themselves." Participants used similar language to describe the urge to purge themselves of the closet. Many termed incongruences as "lying." Remedying this meant teaching in an "honest" manner and teaching with "integrity."

As these reasons compounded, participants became more likely to come out. Participants in other studies cited similar reasons for coming out (Jennings, 1994; Rensenbrink, 1996; Woog, 1995). For example, a teacher justified coming out by saying, "I will be damned if I will remain closeted and help teach another generation of young gay and lesbian people to hate themselves" (Jennings, 1994, p. 27). The guilt of being in collusion with the prejudice that damages gay students' self-esteems prompted participants in this study and in others to come out at school.

Unlike Duncan, who came out without forethought, all other openly gay participants took more deliberate measures to prepare themselves and others for the moment. This involved what Glen called "testing the waters," or bringing up gay subjects to see how others would react. Stephanie pursued more subtle means of doing this: "But I was like, 'I heard on the radio that Ricky Martin's gay' because I wanted to put it out there and see what the kids would say." Others brought it up more directly, feeling responsible to let administrators and others know their coming out plans, as Glen explained: "No administrator ever likes to be surprised."

When Carolyn followed this advice, she was greeted with a positive reaction from her union representative ("you are saving lives"), but a negative one from her principal ("Why are you doing this?"). To avoid this, Glen made the focus the students when he approached his administrators: "When you talk about your need to come out because otherwise you're sending these really horrific messages to young people, it's difficult for them to argue against that." "Finding allies" among peers for support acted as a buffer to negative reactions for Carolyn and Glen. Gauging people's reactions to gay topics, finding supportive peers, and talking to administrators were some of the steps participants took to prepare to exit the *on the verge* phase and, by doing so, the *closeted teaching* stage.

The culmination of the *on the verge* phase was coming out to students, the most significant marker in this theory of gay teacher identity development, as it meant a huge transition in thinking and teaching for the openly gay participants in this study. Carolyn described consciously shifting her thinking:

> A lot of times people are conditioned to think, "How is the straight student going to react?" but you also have to think, "How is the kid who's in your class who's gay or might be gay or questioning reacting to this?" And I started thinking more about them. I always thought about things from more of a fear perspective or a negative perspective like, "What are the bad things that could happen?" And then I started thinking about, "What are the good things that could happen?" And I realized that I had come to a point in my career and my life that I was willing to accept whatever bad things that might happen.

"Getting over wanting everyone to like you," as Carolyn put it, freed participants up to like themselves. This decision marked the most significant transition point in the gay teacher identity development process as participants discussed how coming out at school radically altered their personal and professional lives.

FIFTEEN MINUTES OF FAME: POST–COMING OUT STAGE

Entering the last stage of the gay teacher identity development process required coming out at school. For many, this involved several steps—coming out to family, to parents, to fellow teachers, and to administrators. But participants clearly viewed disclosing their gayness to students as the real mark of coming out at school, as Duncan stated: "I couldn't be even outer if there is such a phrase. So that's been since I came out to the kids, I told them . . . 'This is my last closet. You are my last closet. The door is open. Done.'"

Coming out to students took different forms for each openly gay participant, but all came out in the context of their curriculum. For example, Carolyn, during a health lesson on homosexuality, asked her students to raise their hands if they knew anyone gay and then told her students, "All of your hands should be up because I'm gay." For participants who have been out for many years, their gayness became a given, as Summer described herself as being "about as out as you can get." For Carolyn, who came out recently, having colleagues and students talk openly about her partner was "another layer of coming out."

Coming out marked a huge transition in all out participants' careers. Glen stated how coming out makes gay teachers' career paths different from nongay teachers:

> A lot of people think about their first year of teaching and then their next couple of years and then their veteran years. And I, it's funny, because I combine that first year and a half as my pre-coming out . . . [which] seems a whole different part of my teaching career.

For Carolyn, it "was a pretty big step" because "you let it out, you can't ever bring it back in." Similar to a leap of faith, she said "you kind of just go off the cliff and you can't go back." Openly gay participants distinguished between teaching pre– and post–coming out, explaining that coming out opened up their teaching.

Coming out served to bring two major aspects of participants' identities together, aspects they previously viewed as irreconcilable. Like other participants, merging these two identities signified a shift in thinking about Duncan's own gayness and teaching: "It was always, 'I am good but I am gay.' They were two separate worlds. But then I realized 'gay' and 'good' could be the same thing. And so, as it happened personally, it happened professionally." The results of this merger for out participants were largely positive.

The fears of backlash expressed in the *closeted teaching* stage, for the most part, were not realized in the *post–coming out* stage. Reflecting back on closeted years, participants described these fears as stemming from their own minds. Carolyn realized "a lot of the discomfort around being out was my own fear of what might happen." Similarly, Duncan attributed his fear to internal machinations: "I would invent fear. I would invent a negative expectation." Duncan explained, however, that he did not fantasize these fears. They were based in reality: "I created fears based on things I knew to be true. They just weren't true for me."

As the basis of these fears, participants cited current and past events, such as the heterosexual teacher fired for teaching an E. M. Forster book about a gay man. Most participants' fears did not come true: "Nothing happened. Nothing negative," "There's been absolutely nothing negative that's come up," and "Nobody has yet said anything to me because I'm lesbian." Ironically, some of these participants who reported a lack of backlash actually did recount individual negative incidents.

For example, both Duncan and Summer had parents pull students from their classes. Summer had a student who made a death threat and her car window was smashed. Instead of allowing these incidents to scare them back into the closet or out of teaching, these participants downplayed the seriousness of the backlash. For example, Duncan verbally dismissed his principal's negative reaction: "My principal telling me that coming out to my students was inappropriate. It wasn't professional. I wasn't teaching when I did that. And so those were blips to me. And now they're not even blips. They're little rocks or something."

Participants may have reported a lack of backlash yet described negative incidents because participants viewed these incidents as isolated, and therefore not as collective backlash. Perhaps the benefits of being out far outweighed individual negative reactions. Perhaps they were "willing to accept whatever bad things might happen," as Carolyn stated. Whatever the reason, it is clear that none of these openly gay participants regretted their decisions to come out at school.

In addition to a lack of negative repercussions, or a lack of significance attached to them, participants who came out related positive outcomes, as Carolyn did:

> [Coming out] helped me to feel a lot more comfortable as a teacher. I didn't feel like there was something I was hiding and therefore, if the students found out, then it would be like, "They know. What does that mean and what's gonna happen?" It's just already out there.

Metaphorically, Duncan described this as "when I came out, something else emerged. . . . Something inflated. Something got bigger. The fog lifted somewhere in there." Freeing themselves from the tensions of being in the closet allowed openly gay participants to concentrate their energies and focus on teaching, a process Carolyn described: "You can just sort of let go of all that emotional energy that it takes to kind of think and worry about that stuff and just direct that toward something else more productive." This implies that the closet can siphon off stamina necessary for teaching.

Outside the classroom, openly gay participants like Carolyn no longer feared personal conversations: "You don't have to cringe in terror when someone says, 'What did you do this weekend?'" Duncan created an ally out of a homophobe:

> [My colleague] said, "I need to tell you that you've changed me. You've totally changed the way that I look at being gay." He was very serious and very sad. "I was one of the ones who would have called you faggot. I was one

of the ones who would have beat you up with a bat. That would have been me. I was full of that. . . . I was up until I met you and until I realized, because you're a wonderful teacher, the kids respect you so much, that you were gay." Then he started crying. He gave me this huge hug and I was high. I just welled up.

In the *post–coming out* stage of gay teacher identity development, new doors were opened for relationships with colleagues instead of closing them as participants feared.

After coming out, many participants initially felt like gay ambassadors, resources to all about everything gay, in other words, like a *gay poster child*. For example, a student checked in with Glen to make sure she did "the right thing" when responding to homophobia. Similarly, a heterosexual student came to Lauren after her same-sex friend expressed a romantic interest in her, to ask if she handled it correctly.

Administrators also viewed out teachers, such as Summer, as resources: "If anything comes through on gay and lesbian issues, [administrators] funnel it right to me: 'Oh, look, we have one in this school.'" After coming out, Glen's department chair saw him as a "[an]other voice [to bring to] the curriculum." For many participants, coming out, in Glen's words, "changed the culture of . . . my school" as they served as resources and as catalysts for change.

Out participants recognized the power they had as representatives of the gay community, as Carolyn stated: "I think [being out] is a lot more meaningful and powerful a message than any lecture or lesson about homophobia or homosexuality could be." Realizing, as Glen did, that for some students they may be their first openly gay person ("At this point I am what they know of gay men. It's like me and Jack McFarland on *Will and Grace*"), participants were mindful of how they came across to students. Feeling like lone representatives of the gay community, they felt pressure to represent gayness by being gay, but not too gay, in this *gay poster child* phase.

To counter negative stereotypes about gay people, Lauren "care[d] that people see a self-confident lesbian leading her life as she sees fit." Out participants were careful not to appear as though gay rights was their only focus, as Glen stated: "It was really important for me to get up and do something that's not LGBTQ specific so people don't see that as my sole focus in the classroom." They also intentionally tried to convey the message that gay people are not the only ones concerned about these issues: "If there are LGBTQ issues that need to be addressed, I'm not the one who does it . . . because people need to recognize that issues that affect lesbian, gay, bisexual, and transgendered people should be cared about by all of us."

According to out participants, the important message to get across is that LGBTQ issues are "one piece of the larger umbrella under which all of these issues fall" (Glen). Openly gay participants educated others about gay and lesbian issues although they carefully manipulated who voiced those messages.

Ironically, in the *gay poster child* phase, participants still monitored their image and their actions, as they did in the closeted stage, as they became hyperaware of being known as "the gay teacher": "At first when I came out I was really careful about not touching a kid on the shoulder, not slapping him on the back, not doing any of that kind of stuff." Some participants also emphasized aspects of themselves that conformed to gender norms, as Glen described:

> When I first came out it was so important that I be the poster child and not the stereotypical poster child. And so it was so important that when there was a faculty softball game, that I was good. It was so important that I won the faculty free throw competition [because] I was gay. That it was really important to me still to not perpetuate the stereotypes.

Although coming out freed them from many of the constraints of the closet, openly gay participants in the *gay poster child* phase still felt the need to present a certain face. As participants merged their gay and teacher identities, however, they dismantled this façade.

Coming out at school was a vital step toward feeling like an authentic teacher. This involved bringing together two aspects of identity that were previously seen as mutually exclusive and was pivotal to self-actualization, as Glen articulated:

> I very much believe that when you can integrate all parts of your identity is when you're truly happy. I mean that is if you're living as a son but not as openly gay together, you're never gonna be whole and complete until you can be the openly gay son. And the same way in the classroom.

Duncan also portrayed coming out at school as a completion of identity:

> I was relieved actually because I'm the fullest because every piece of me is defined. I'm a whole teacher. I'm a whole person in the teaching job. Where I was, I wasn't quite a cipher, but definitely a fraction of who I was. An important piece was missing or was misinterpreted or mistaken. People thought one thing when I'm really another and so I am now an accurate person. I am now accurate. I'm authentic.

Being an authentic teacher was not the teleological end of the gay teacher identity process; instead, some participants described themselves as constantly evolving.

When transitioning from the *gay poster child* phase, participants recognized that, as gay representatives, presenting themselves as one-dimensional was a disservice, as Glen explained:

> I came to realize that I can be the [gay teacher] who likes Broadway show tunes and has dinner parties. I'm still, though, very much aware of being a role model. I still do take that seriously and I do think it's important for me to balance that because for some people I am the only real live openly gay person so from me, they are really making great generalizations. I am realizing that what I need to do is present the widest possible portrait of what that [looks like]. So I don't try to play this butch persona in the classroom. I very much demonstrate my full range of humanity. Some of those things I'm sure fit neatly into a box that might be in their heads and others are simply expanding the size of that box.

Duncan saw this human side as essential to being a successful teacher:

> Because good teaching, effective teaching, comes from the teacher's self.... Many people could stand up there with a book and the material, give it out, and maybe even teach and the kids can learn. But I think good teaching is having a full passion for the material, put yourself into what it is you're teaching. It's about embodying information and you need to fulfill the information with your own self, otherwise you could do it from the book. It's like running on all your spark plugs. I had eight spark plugs in me, eight plugs in me but only seven were firing because the gay one was shut down, then, you know, you were not getting my full power.... It's definitely with Mr. Kemper you're getting everything because I'm not holding back the piece of me which might lead to the conclusion that I'm gay for fear of that accusation. So I can make a gay joke in my classroom ... but before I'd never. My humor has been totally opened up because I can use myself as a piece of humor and that defines me. I'm giving to them a definition of myself as a person because I am a person to them.

Being an authentic teacher meant bringing their whole selves to the classroom, which opened up participants' teaching.

Unlike the *gay poster child* phase of gay teacher development, participants in the *authentic teacher* phase wove in gay and lesbian topics naturally instead of treating them as add-ons. Carolyn used the phrase "dating relationships" instead of separating out same-sex relationships as she did in the past. Lauren made it clear that "there's a lot of stuff in the class that I do that is not, 'Here's the gay unit.' It's simply teaching it as part of the overall curriculum. When I started, I think I actually did do more of that.... It's getting smaller every year as I make the thing more inclusive."

For Duncan, a student asking "how do you spell homosexual?" epitomized this integration. For Carolyn, this occurred when students discussed her partner in the context of a class discussion when she used a personal anecdote as an example of addiction:

> "It wasn't just me drinking my coffee. My partner was drinking the coffee, too." Then this other kid goes, "Was your partner addicted?" All of a sudden they were having this whole conversation about my partner and it was just totally normal. It was just so wonderful. And it wasn't like people were worried about saying partner or asking me about my partner. It was just like asking Mr. Bridle about his wife. And you have these kinds of experiences and you realize . . . there are probably a vast majority that are ok with it, especially at this juncture.

For openly gay participants, coming out reduced the stigma attached to homosexuality.

Presenting gayness as one aspect of humanity and integrating gay and lesbian topics into the curriculum helped naturalize gayness for students and colleagues. Taking a stand led to feelings of "empowerment," as Duncan described: "I've been fully empowered as an individual person because I have allowed myself to recognize or reveal the full depth of my character." Opening the closet door meant opening schools to new understandings of gayness and teaching.

CONCLUSION

For participants, telling their stories involved both identifying with categories of sexual orientation and using cause and effect to make sense of their own experiences. In this chapter, I explore how participants presented their gay teacher identity development. As participants described the constant interaction between gay identity development and teacher identity development, it became clear that it would be impossible to address one without addressing the other, as Tony explained: "I don't know how much of it is evolution as a teacher versus evolution as a gay person. I don't know where the boundaries are between those two."

NOTES

1. All participant names are pseudonyms.

REFERENCES

Epstein, D., and Johnson, R. (1994). On the straight and the narrow: The heterosexual presumption, homophobias and schools. In D. Epstein (Ed.), *Challenging lesbian and gay inequalities in education* (pp. 197–230). Buckingham: Open University Press.

Evans, K. (1999). When *queer* and *teacher* meet. In W. Letts and J. T. Sears (Eds.), *Queering elementary education* (pp. 237–46). Lanham, MD: Rowland and Littlefield.

Jennings, K. (1994). *One teacher in ten*. Boston: Alyson.

Lipkin, A. (1999). *Understanding homosexuality, changing schools*. Boulder: Westview.

Ponse, B. (1978). *Identities in the lesbian world: The social construction of self* (Vol. 28). Westport, CT: Greenwood.

Rensenbrink, C. W. (1996). What difference does it make? The story of a lesbian teacher. *Harvard Educational Review, 66*(2), 257–70.

Rich, A. (1993). Compulsory heterosexuality and lesbian existence. In H. Abelove, M. A. Barale, and D. M. Halperin (Eds.), *The lesbian and gay studies reader* (pp. 227–54). New York: Routledge.

Sears, J. T. (1993). Responding to sexual diversity of faculty and students: Sexual praxis and the critically reflective administration. In C. A. Capper (Ed.), *Educational administration in a pluralistic society* (pp. 110–72). Albany: State University of New York Press.

Woods, S., and Harbeck, K. (1992). Living in two worlds: The identity management strategies used by lesbian physical educators. In K. Harbeck (Ed.), *Coming out of the classroom closet* (pp. 141–66). New York: Harrington Park.

Woog, D. (1995). *School's out*. Boston: Alyson.

Chapter Six

Teachers as Sexual Strangers[1]

Steve Fifield

After a particularly bad day as a student teacher in biology at Middletown High School, Lee had a dream.

> I showed up at school and there were signs on all the doors that asked students to boycott the school because I was gay. There were not many students in school, but my class was there. They asked me if it was true. I could not respond before one student claimed I had molested him. The students all started accusing me and left the room. The teachers would not speak to me and before I knew it, school administrators came with the police to arrest me. They took DNA evidence. No one believed me. I had no one to turn to. That was how the dream ended.

For student teachers, dreams are part of the psychic struggle to re-present themselves and what they teach as coherent subjects (Britzman, 2003; Brown 2006; Evans, 2002).

Lee's dream illustrates how dominant cultural storylines and the values, beliefs, and images they contain shape the sense we make of ourselves and how we desire others to see us. Lee conjured the familiar cultural image of gay teachers as sexual predators lurking among their prey—the pernicious equation, homosexual + children = danger (Evans, 1999). In his dream, heterosexist cultural debris obscured Lee's view of other possibilities for what it might mean to be gay and a teacher. He saw himself labeled a child molester and abandoned by his colleagues, his identity out of his control, determined instead by others' perceptions. The police collected DNA, so often fetishized as the foundation of personality and sexuality, to tie Lee to the alleged crime.

Dreaming and awake, Lee was an active sense maker. But he was not the autonomous individual of western psychological tradition, actualizing an innate and enduring, if repressed, identify. His ability to present his self to himself, and to others, was enabled and constrained by social ties manifested in meanings and ways of knowing that circulate in schools and broader culture. I am interested in this relationship of identity and knowledge, of being and knowing, of becoming and learning. This chapter examines the complementary nature of identity and knowing (ourselves, others, and the world) and how this relationship can both impoverish and enrich ways of thinking and being in classrooms and beyond.

In this chapter, I draw on Lee's experiences as a student teacher to explore how ways of being and ways of knowing enable and constrain each other. We see how Lee's real or perceived status as an outsider to heterosexuality—as a sexual stranger (Phelan, 2001)—ran up against cultural norms of heterosexuality that acted to limit who it was possible to be and what it was possible to know in his classroom. Heteronormativity conditioned Lee's and his students' knowledge of bodies, and their bodies of knowledge. But we will also see that Lee's ongoing effort to create identities as a gay man and a teacher profoundly transformed the sense he made of biology, the school subject he taught.

I use Lee's story to examine the relationship between knowledge and identity from two interpretive stances that seem to me to offer different prospects for knowing and being. The first orientation calls for gay teachers to come out of the closet—to defy shame, ignorance, and intolerance and to live out their true identities as fully normal human beings. The second reading applies Shane Phelan's (2001) notion of the sexual stranger to challenge the determinism, essentialism, and desire for normality that infuse standard coming out stories, and to wonder instead about the epistemological prospects of strangeness.

My hope is that reading Lee's story in two ways will help us see further possibilities for how the differences that teachers and students bring to classrooms can be valued as ever-evolving standpoints for knowing and being.

STORIES FROM STUDENT TEACHING

Lee was a student in my science education methods course. The following semester he was a student teacher in biology at Middletown High School under the supervision of another faculty member. Lee first came out as gay to his parents and a few friends during the semester he was in my methods course. At the time I did not know Lee was in the process of coming out, and he did not know I was gay. He was selective and cautious in coming out and he had plenty of issues to work through.

A few weeks before he came out to his parents, he ended a serious relationship with his girlfriend. He also struggled to reconcile his deeply held religious beliefs with his sexuality. I was not in contact with Lee when he was student teaching, until one evening when he walked into a campus support group for LGBTQ students that I sometimes attended. Shortly after that unexpected meeting Lee and I began to talk and write together about our experiences as teachers (Fifield and Swain, 2002).

My analysis of Lee's experiences coming to understand himself as a gay teacher examines how cultural norms of heterosexuality shape the possibilities for identity and knowledge (Nixon and Givens, 2004; Nobles and Letts, 2000). These are heteronormative cultural practices that reflect an underlying "view that institutionalized heterosexuality constitutes the standard for legitimate and prescriptive sociosexual arrangements" (Ingraham 1994, p. 204). In other words, in a heteronormative culture, heterosexuality is typically taken-for-granted as normal, natural, and proper.

This ambient heterosexuality is typically experienced as nothing special, unremarkable, normal (Murray, 1995). But cultural practices that establish, maintain, and defend heteronormativity come sharply into view in the lives of those who refuse the norms, or are perceived by others as somehow not fitting in. By looking at episodes of transgression, when the rules of heterosexuality are bent or broken, we can see the disciplining effects of heteronormativity, *and* how individuals who refuse the norms can create new identities and ways of knowing.

The Personal in Professional Life

Although school cultures are already (and profusely) heterosexualized, practices that make the broader diversity of sexual and gender identities visible are criticized for sexualizing supposedly asexual educational spaces and relationships. As Lee looked ahead to student teaching, he wanted nothing more than to follow the heteronormative rules so he could keep his emerging, and very private, gay life out of his classroom. He understood himself to be a biology teacher, not a *gay* biology teacher.

Looking back on his early feelings he wrote, "Before student teaching I did not think that [being gay] would really matter; that somehow my personal life could easily be kept separate from my professional life." But his mother worried about what he would face as a gay teacher. "Kids can be so mean," he recalled her saying. He shrugged off her concern. He did not plan on telling anyone at school that he was gay, so he figured it would not be an issue.

Lee soon discovered that it was an issue. Heteronormativity in the classroom collapsed the distance he tried to maintain between his personal and professional lives. For instance, his students' everyday language resisted his efforts to create a classroom space, and a teacher identity in that space, that were cleanly separated from ways of knowing and being outside the classroom. "Oh, that's so gay!" and "fag" were ordinary exclamations in his students' conversations.

One of the ways that heteronormative sexual and gender boundaries are maintained is by using terms for stigmatized sexual practices and identities as *general* markers of disapproval and disdain (Nayak and Kehily, 1997; Steinberg, Epstein, and Johnson, 1997). Lee saw that relationships in his classroom were shaped by language beyond the vocabulary of the official curriculum. Coming out (even if just a little, and outside of school) made him more sensitive to homophobic language, and this awareness sharpened his concern about the risks of challenging this language:

> I never confronted this [homophobic language] because . . . I was paranoid that they would pick up on my defensiveness or [my] personal investment in the issue. It was always easy to confront racist or sexist comments or cursing. These types of statements are different. It's obvious that they are offensive to certain groups . . . that are represented in the room. It is also the norm to confront these comments. But confronting heterosexism or homophobia was different. I felt as if I could not do so without implicating myself or revealing a piece of me I was not ready to reveal.

He later regretted letting heterosexist language go unchallenged. He knew that treating heterosexism as acceptable had sent the wrong message to everyone in his class, and he was particularly concerned that his inaction had left some students "more alone and more fearful then they were previously."

Girlfriends and Poop-Chute Raiders

Lisa Weems (1999) observes, "heteronormativity operates to police the boundaries between normal and pathological forms of desire" (p. 34). Heteronormativity does more than passively mark a border beyond which the straight should not wander.

To a teacher in the closet, otherwise innocuous and even endearing encounters with students and colleagues can threaten to expose them. Like most student teachers, Lee quickly learned that his students were interested in his personal life. They wanted to know where he was from, what kind of car he drove, and what he did for fun. Two girls asked him to the school prom—he gently declined. Students grilled him on his dating history, and were concerned that he did not have a girlfriend. They reminded him that he was getting older and needed to find a wife if he wanted to have kids. In the tradition of closeted teachers, Lee did his best to bob and weave around these questions.

Lee was not sure what tipped them off, but some of his students decided he was inadequately heterosexual. Some of them reacted by creating a more complete heterosexual biography for Lee. They saw him at a local shopping mall with a female friend and playfully decided that she must be his secret girlfriend. Students wrote notes to him from his girlfriend, complete with pictures of her clipped from magazines, and left them around the room for him to discover. Lee failed to produce a suitably heterosexual life story, so his students invented one for him. He thought all this was a sign of affection for him, which it may well have been. But it was also a clear application of the cultural norms that would set Lee straight.

A small group of tenth-grade boys took a different approach by drawing on heterosexist cultural images of gay men to mark and distance Lee as a repulsive and threatening Other (Redman, 1997). Here is how Lee described one incident:

> I was teaching one day and one student . . . stopped me and said "Mr. Swain, what's that on the board?" I hadn't noticed anything previously, but I looked and it said "poop chute raider." I had actually seen this comment scrawled on a desk a few days before, but had just cleaned it up and not thought much about it. I told the class that someone in second period probably wrote it and proceeded to erase it off. He asked me what it said and at this point [my] paranoia is kicking in again . . . well not even paranoia, because at this point, I am sure they know. I read it and the class giggled. And I smiled. It pissed me off that I was smiling, but once again I didn't want to show my disdain for the comment because of how it might affect me. He asked what it meant and I responded with "I don't pretend to know what the student who wrote this was thinking." A few of the guys in the class continued to giggle here and there.
> Later in the class, one of the antagonists asked me a question. As I walked up behind him to help, he cringed and smirked at his friends, as if I were going to engage in anal sex with him. This made me very angry. I helped him with his question, but I am sure the whole class could sense the change in my mood. I wanted nothing more than to get out of there at that point.
> Throughout the rest of the semester, occasionally students would yell out "poop-chute raider" or make other comments. It was always the same few and I found myself becoming biased against these students. I didn't screw with their grades or anything, but I found that my tolerance became smaller and smaller for these students. It probably affected the quality of education the whole class received, because I dreaded starting the third-period class every day, and had little motivation to plan anything new for them. I found that I preferred to have them work quietly on worksheets or simply stick to lecture rather than . . . discussion[s] or interactive activities. I felt no obligation to the small group of students who tormented me, but my reaction to these students adversely affected the whole class.

In reaction to harassment from a few students, Lee adopted pedagogies that promised more control over students' interactions and conversations. But pedagogical strategies that constrain classroom social relationships also constrain the understandings of subject matter that students and teachers create together. We see in this episode of students behaving badly how cultural

Sex, God, and the Natural Way of Things

norms that discipline teachers' sexual identities can affect classroom social relationships in ways that shape pedagogies, subject matters, and students' opportunities to learn.

Sex, God, and the Natural Way of Things

Heterosexual norms denied the separation Lee wanted to maintain between his personal and professional lives, troubled his relationships with students, and shaped his classroom teaching practices. Still, when it comes to the actual content of what he taught, can't we expect a science subject like biology to be free of this cultural baggage? By sticking to the facts of life (science), perhaps Lee could keep the spotlight on what he taught, and off of who he was. But the sciences are fully human activities. Scientific practices and understandings shape and are shaped by the cultural imagination. The links between popular and scientific understandings are particularly intimate in schools, institutions that reproduce the sciences and broader cultures (Letts, 2001; Millar, 1989; Rudolph, 2002; Weaver, Morris, and Applebaum, 2001).

Like scientists, Lee's students used the cultural resources they had at hand to construct their understandings of nature. During a unit on genetics he asked students to pair off as hypothetical parents, and to flip coins to determine the genes they would pass along to their offspring. There were more girls than boys in the class, so some girls paired up as parents. According to Lee, some students "had a fit, and said that two women can't have a kid." His students' resistance to transgressing heterosexuality heightened a growing tension in his understanding of biology, his identity in science, and his sexuality.

> Throughout the genetics unit I stated that males paired with females, as if that's what nature dictates. That did not feel natural to me, and it was where the scientist in me conflicted with my personal feelings. The natural "laws" I had learned and was teaching about conflicted with what I felt about myself. I had learned that homosexuality is not natural, yet it is one of the most natural feelings to me. Teaching about the 'natural' way of things forced me to consider whether I was somehow flawed or a genetic reject. I wondered if my homosexuality was a choice, rather than something I have no control over.

Later in the genetics unit, Lee asked his students to read an article from *Life* magazine about genetic and environmental influences on characteristics like thrill-seeking, obesity, and homosexuality (Colt, 1998). Most of his students seemed to accept that genes affect personal characteristics, but they were not eager to talk about the causes of homosexuality. The few who spoke up favored some sort of environmental explanation for homosexuality, rather than a genetic foundation. Some students added that the Bible says homosexuality is wrong. God, they said, would not give humans an immoral genetic trait.

The students' selective and strategic application of nature (i.e., genetics) versus nurture (i.e., environment) pressed Lee to confront his own uncertainties about what science and religion had to say about him as a gay man. Neither biology nor religion, as he understood them, regarded homosexuality as natural. But homosexuality *felt* natural to him. Genetic explanations appealed to him because, he said, "then I have to deal with it, rather than try to change it." To embrace the notion that his genes made him gay seemed to Lee to make his feelings more natural and to justify his recent decision to "deal with" his sexuality, instead of resisting it.

Like his students, Lee also tried to reconcile the power of genetics with the word of God. "I have read and reread those scriptures," he said, "yet it is still an area of uncertainty that bothers me. It was hard for me to concentrate on teaching the lesson because my thoughts were on other matters."

In class discussions, there were no clear boundaries between science and religion, nature and culture, knowing and being. Lee was faced with a quandary familiar to those who are strangers in their own cultures: How do we understand ourselves when the cultural norms we internalize (and the science textbooks we use [Snyder and Broadway, 2004]) do not reflect our lived experiences? The students, too, drew from a cultural imagination that shaped the sense they made of human reproduction and genetics. Some of them read heterosexuality as a moral code that God built into our genetic code. Heteronormativity disciplined students' understandings of science, nature, and God, which speaks to its powerful influence on beliefs about what is normal, natural, and right.

While some of his students naturalized (and deified) heterosexuality, Lee also tried to reconcile his understanding of himself with his understanding of nature. Was he a genetic reject because being gay felt natural, or was that natural feeling a normal consequence of his genetics? As a biologist, he knew that reducing the complexity of who he was to a question of nature versus nurture was simplistic and misleading.

Nevertheless, by appealing to genetics he affirmed himself as a gay man. In this he joined many who identify as LGBTQ, not to mention most straight folks, who look to genetics, or simply nature, to normalize their sexualities and to justify claims to civil rights and privileges (Allen, 1997; Rosario, 1997). Genetics also provided Lee with some cover from Biblical assaults on his worth as a human being. He was bothered that he could not find clear affirmation of his sexuality in the Bible, but he understood his genetic self, his gay self, all of who he was, as part of God's creation.

TWO READINGS

What does Lee's story illustrate about the epistemological possibilities of being a gay teacher? How might we imagine relationships between knowing and being that create new possibilities for gay (and straight) teachers and their students? The analytical perspectives we bring to bear will shape our answers to these questions. I offer two readings from distinct interpretive stances.

The first is an account of the hardships of closeted gay and lesbian teachers, and how, by coming out, teachers can live more authentic and fulfilling lives as normal members of society. The second reading imagines gay teachers as *sexual strangers* (Phelan, 2001), ambiguous figures who transgress normal ways of being and knowing. The strangeness of gay teachers is the central concern in both accounts, but they treat the value of and prospects for strangeness very differently.

Coming Out

The first reading of Lee's story follows the familiar narrative of being gay as being subject to social stigma and internalized shame, seeking shelter in the closet, and when denial and deception finally become too much to stand, personally accepting and publicly proclaiming one's real identity in an act of self-affirmation and disclosure called *coming out*. Teachers' stories told through the metaphors of the closet and coming out are in books like *Coming Out of the Classroom Closet: Gay and Lesbian Students, Teachers and Curriculum* (Harbeck, 1992), *One Teacher in 10: Gay and Lesbian Educators Tell Their Stories* (Jennings, 1994), *The Last Closet: The Real Lives of Lesbian and Gay Teachers* (Kissen, 1996), and *Poisoned Ivy: Lesbian and Gay Academics Confronting Homophobia* (McNaron, 1997).

Reading Lee's experiences as a coming-out story, we can see how ambient heterosexism pressed Lee back into the closet, just as he was inclined to cautiously open the door. Life in the classroom closet takes a tremendous physical and psychological toll on teachers' lives. Lies, cover stories, and evasions mediate relationships with colleagues and students. Being in the closet makes it more difficult for teachers to develop trusting relationships with students and to address their vulnerabilities and needs as learners. Teachable moments are squandered when the real lives of gay and lesbian teachers are hidden and institutionalized heterosexism goes unchecked.

These accounts then turn to the transformative potential of coming out of the closet. By coming out, gay and lesbian teachers can reclaim their voices, embrace their true identities, counter stereotypes, serve as role models, and enjoy more fulfilling lives in and outside of the classroom. Advocates of coming out acknowledge its personal risks, but see each individual act of courage as a step toward creating the social and institutional conditions in which the potential benefits of coming out far outweigh its risks. In *One Teacher in 10*, Kevin Jennings (1994) describes what is at stake:

> A school with an openly lesbian or gay teacher is a better school. It is a school where truth prevails over lies; it is a school where isolated students at last have a place to turn to for support; it is a school where our nation's rhetoric about equality moves one step closer to becoming a reality. As gay and lesbian teachers win our freedom, we help to free our students, our colleagues, and our communities of the burden of bigotry that has, for so long, taught some members of families to hate their own sisters, brothers, mothers, and fathers. We are the true upholders of "family values." (p. 14)

In coming-out narratives, the closet hides the truth about gay and lesbian teachers. Teachers in the closet remain strangers to others, and in some ways to themselves. When gay teachers come out of the classroom closet, stereotypes dissolve in the face of the reality that gay and lesbian teachers are pretty much like everybody else. Coming out transforms gay and lesbian teachers from strangers into normal people. Paradoxically, although coming out brings teachers' sexual identities to the foreground, it also promises to clear the air and let teachers get on with the business of teaching. By dealing more honestly with sexuality as a part of who we are, we move beyond it.

Rather than a strange aberration, homosexuality becomes a natural, and so less remarkable, companion with heterosexuality. Coming out helps gay and lesbian teachers to fit in. In a more tolerant institutional climate, Lee would perhaps have felt safe enough to come out of the classroom closet. And by coming out he would have given his students the opportunity to notice, question, and move beyond cultural stereotypes by getting to know a real gay man.

Sexual Strangers

For an alternative to the coming-out narrative, let's turn to queer theory, an eclectic collection of approaches that examine how sexualities and genders are constructed and regulated, and how they shape and are shaped by intersecting identities, social relationships, and cultural institutions (Jagose, 1996; Sullivan, 2003; Turner, 2000). I use *queer* as a verb, not as a catchall noun for LGBTQ people and identities (Broadway, 2011).

Queer theory queers by casting a skeptical eye on putatively natural, fixed, and transcendental categories like male and female, gay and straight, and self and other. It is a tool for excavating historical and cultural processes by which ways of knowing and being come to be seen as natural or unnatural, normal or abnormal, moral or immoral, just or unjust. My aim is to offer a different, and I believe more fruitful, account of Lee's story by challenging what coming-out narratives take for granted about knowing oneself, being known, and strangeness.

The first step in rereading Lee's story is to imagine strangers as those who might share critical insights from life experiences and standpoints that are unfamiliar to us. Shane Phelan (2001) notes the paradoxical nature of strangers as "neither us nor clearly them, not friend and not enemy, but a figure of ambivalence who troubles the border between us and them" (pp. 4–5).

The sociologist Zygmunt Bauman developed the stranger as an analytical concept in his study of the historical position of Jews in social and political systems in Europe. Jews who were native borne, lifelong residents, and next-door neighbors, were not regarded as full members of society and they were not afforded the full rights and privileges of citizenship. Phelan (2001) adapts Bauman's work to argue that in the United States, gays and lesbians and other sexual minorities are *sexual* strangers, because they are not citizens in the "full political sense" (p. 5).

To the extent that their differences from the straight norm remain intact, sexual strangers are denied equal membership in the political community. Sexual strangers live and work among the majority, but do not fully belong to the majority. They are troubling because they are close at hand and often hard to distinguish from nonstrangers. Phelan (2001) writes that they "disrupt seemingly natural boundaries and borders" (p. 29), and "undermine and crack open from inside all polar categories of social order" (pp. 29–30).

But Phelan (2001) argues that "the position of the stranger is not only difficult, it is rewarding" (p. 8). Sexual strangers can act from positions of difference to challenge current social, political, and sexual relations, and to "offer one another and others new ways of questioning the current tight fabric of citizenship and national identity" (p. 8).

Let's think about sexual strangers through a conception of the self as manifesting in stories we (and others) tell ourselves (and others) about ourselves. The self in this sense is not fundamental, not the "starting point of experience," but an ongoing accomplishment, "the end product of an elaborate process of assimilating data, constructing meaning and building a world of local experience" (Olendzki, 2006, p. 256).

Identities circulate as groups and individuals imagine, desire, try on, impose, refashion, and resist being certain kinds of people. Our self-understandings are strands of this cultural identity work, as we variously take up, attach to, reproduce, transform, refuse—and live in ignorance of—the many identities imposed on us. In this way the labor of identification (Pinar, 1998) can be a practice of contemplative inquiry into self that fosters curiosity, compassion, and humility.

Unfortunately, our stories of self easily narrow into habitual patterns that limit how we think and act. We mistake particular storylines for something inherent and enduring about who we really are. Our selves become trapped in their own rigid constructions—what we like, what we dislike, what we need to be happy—that leave us with a gnawing sense of dissatisfaction in a world that so often fails to meet our expectations (Olendzki, 2003).

This strange stance challenges the tale of coming out as accepting and affirming an inherent and enduring identity that is waiting to be acknowledged and actualized. Teachers who come out are said to counter distorted images of gays and lesbians by revealing their authentic selves to students. It is as if one's closeted self preexists, bound up within, homunculus-like, pressing against the constraints of personal shame and social stigma until, finally, they fall away and one's true self expands to life size. But as anyone who has come out knows, you never do it just once, and you are never certain what you and others will make of these moments of self-revelation.

When coming out, we exchange one set of stories that have failed to serve us well for others that seem more authentic and hopeful. The trick is to not mistake the new stories of self for transcendental, unchanging truths about who we really are, which sets us up to be confined by the very insights that could liberate us. As Phelan (1994) says, coming out "is a project rather than an event" (p. 52). Coming out as a singular, seminal moment of revelation here breaks down in favor of a historically and culturally-situated, open-ended inquiry into "(be)coming out" (Phelan, 1994, p. 51),"lifelong learning of how to become and of inventing the meaning of being a lesbian or gay man in this historical moment" (Blasius, 1992, p. 655).

Across this lifelong process, we are neither pawns of a preordained or genetically determined identity, nor fully autonomous to be and become whatever we wish. Being gay, being straight, just being, is a collectively improvised performance that draws on (and transforms) ways of being that are culturally, politically, and psychologically available (Tierney, 1997). We are always to some extent strangers to ourselves and others because we are all unfinished and endlessly revised stories in progress. To relax into never knowing ourselves completely can be a gateway to boundless inquiry rather than a confining closet that limits who we can be.

Lee, like the rest of us, participated in the sociocultural construction of his identities; he could not autonomously create or claim identities as a teacher and a gay man. In classrooms, as elsewhere, identities are collectively constructed as teachers project qualities that students read, reinterpret, and project back on their teachers, who continue the cycle of interpretation with their own readings of students' readings (Talburt, 2000).

As much as (be)coming out is an act of self-determination, it also entails opening one's self to reconstruction by others. The understandings that others develop of gay and lesbian teachers might not resemble the authentic selves that teachers intend to reveal (Talburt, 2000). As such, coming out has a more complex and ambiguous relationship to individual empowerment and cultural change than most advocates of coming out acknowledge.

But let's leave this criticism aside for the moment and grant coming out its due. Coming out is celebrated in LGBTQ communities because it often does allow us to publicly present our selves in ways that feel more genuine. The act of self-disclosure can clarify and so dissipate the vague strangeness that so often surrounds those in the closet.

Gay teachers who come out (or wish they could) commonly say that they want their students (and colleagues) to see them, and by extension other gay people, as normal, not as figures clouded by deception or by cultural stereotypes and prejudice (Kissen, 1996). By doing so they want to counter misguided motivations for intolerance that their students may hold toward gays, lesbians, and other minorities. This is part of their calling as educators.

This is a compelling vision, which it why the potential pedagogical and epistemological costs of exchanging strangeness for normalcy are so rarely explored. If the price of admitting gay teachers into the cultural norm is to occupy identities that make no consequential demands on the heterosexual cultural imagination, then the pedagogical and liberatory virtues of coming out are being oversold.

If the result of coming out is to fix gays and lesbians as natural complements to heterosexuals, then it serves more to silence difference than to voice it. If we seek equality by dissolving difference, we end up with neither. If coming out in the classroom dissolves strangeness into a novelty that is easily accommodated by a liberal recasting of hetero and homo, then the epistemological prospects of strangeness have been forfeited with little to show for the loss.

Let me take one more analytical step and shift perspectives from coming out and being a sexual stranger as ways of being, to ways of knowing about oneself, others, and the world (including school subjects). As an orientation to understanding, coming out reflects a commitment to resolve the unfamiliar within familiar interpretive and epistemological frameworks.

It is a move to reveal that which exists but is hidden, to normalize that which does not fit, to discipline diversity through transcendental unity, to assimilate the strange into a stable and unquestioned ontology. This fundamentally conservative orientation allows us to settle comfortably into an illusion of knowing and being known.

In contrast, knowing as a sexual stranger invites us to bring undomesticated differences to the surface where unexpected and unfamiliar perspectives are available. When we inquire from intentional standpoints as sexual strangers, we discover ways to deny heteronormativity its claims to common sense, which suggests that other unmarked assumptions in our thoughts and practices can be thrown into relief when we take up different interpretive perspectives, ask new kinds of questions, and evaluate answers using new criteria (Broadway, 2011).

Thinking of Lee as a sexual stranger, we can see how teachers who teach from positions of difference might see in themselves, and offer to their students, fruitful new ways of knowing and being. Lee was most insightful (and inciting) when he was most like a sexual stranger, unable or unwilling to fully hide or clarify his difference. He was surprised to find himself thinking about his self and the school subject matter of biology in and through the other, "disrupt[ing] seemingly natural boundaries and borders" (Phelan, 2001, p. 29).

Lee tried to keep his private life separate from his public identity, only to find that his students' heteronormative discourse denied his attempts to partition his life. He thought his sexuality would have nothing to do with being a teacher, but by trying to keep his sexuality out of the classroom he only attracted curiosity and suspicion. All he wanted was a neutral position so he could focus on explaining biology instead of himself. But some of his students were troubled by this ambiguity, this strangeness. They desired a fuller and more familiar account of who Lee was, and of who they were in relation to him.

To resolve the ambiguity that resisted their habitual ways of knowing others and themselves, ambiguity they rightly sensed might conceal new ways of knowing that would threaten their current self-satisfied selves (Luhmann, 1998), they needed Lee to be either a straight us, or a gay other.

By the time Lee taught the genetics unit, it was clear to him that his students' beliefs about sexuality, sometimes including their perceptions of *his* sexuality, were elements of the larger belief systems that they used to make sense of themselves, others, and school subjects. Similarly, as Lee's understanding of his sexuality changed, so did the interpretive perspectives he brought to bear on himself, others, and the topics he taught. He became more aware of the ways in which biology, as he had learned it, failed to account for what he knew and felt as a gay man.

Textbook knowledge he once accepted as factual accounts of the "natural way of things" no longer seemed complete or even truthful to him. Along an increasingly fuzzy boundary between knowledge and identity, Lee said, "was where the scientist in me conflicted with my personal feelings." This was a transformational conflict that undermined some understandings and identities, and spawned new ones that enriched Lee's life and ways of thinking, as a gay man and as a teacher.

Two years after student teaching, Lee reflected back on the changes in his understandings of science and his self-in-science:

> I was initially attracted to science because it was based on facts, logical processes, and predictable outcomes. I found the mysteries of science intriguing and the search for an ultimate, unwavering truth was exciting. I thought I could be secure in the truth and value of the facts, content, and skills I learned, and

would someday teach. But after student teaching, I began to see science as a social construct that is not isolated from the outside world. The scientific "facts" I taught about were not as reliable as I once thought. I felt like a hypocrite when the subjects I taught questioned, devalued, and denied the credibility of my sexual orientation. I did not feel connected to the field, I did not see myself reflected in it.

Despite his own best efforts to maintain a polite separation between his personal and classroom lives, Lee came to better understand his self through its very absence from the biology he taught. He came to understand the social construction of science in the process of uncovering and participating in the social construction of his self. He learned that truth is mediated by values, facts are malleable in the face of social interests, and biological knowledge is simultaneously shaped by, and used to legitimate, heterosexual ideologies (Fausto-Sterling, 2000).

Lee came to understand himself as a stranger in relation to the biology he thought he knew, unrepresented in the Nature it constructed, and devalued by this silence. He created new understandings of biology that secured a place for his self in the natural way of things. His insights about himself and biology illustrate how the sciences and the cultures in which they arise shape each other, which in turn is a resource for thinking about how school science can be made more accessible and meaningful to more people.

CONCLUSION

Lee's experiences as a sexual stranger also invite us to wonder, what if schools valued strangeness? Can we create a curriculum in which students and teachers are invited to acknowledge strangeness and to inquire into what they might learn through it about themselves (Britzman, 1995; Luhmann, 1998)? Can we imagine schools as places where teachers who, like sexual strangers, queer cultural norms, are valued for the diversity and differences they offer to their students (Leck, 1999)? Can we create classrooms in which students are strangely educated—raised in the dominant culture *and* empowered by difference to ask unsettling questions toward understandings and selves that exceed the dominant cultural imagination?

Recalling his last day of student teaching, Lee wrote:

> [I] was cleaning my room. On the front of a book of overhead transparencies someone had written "Mr. Swain is gay." At first I tried to wipe it off, but [I] realized that wasn't working. I decided to just leave it on there.

NOTES

1. Earlier versions of this chapter were presented at the University of Delaware, Newark, Delaware, in April 2004, and Charles Sturt University, Bathurst, New South Wales, Australia, in October 2004.

REFERENCES

Allen, G. (1997). The double-edged sword of genetic determinism: Social and political agendas in genetic studies of homosexuality, 1940–1994. In V. A. Rosario (Ed.), *Science and homosexualities* (pp. 242–70). New York: Routledge.
Blasius, M. (1992). An ethos of lesbian and gay existence. *Political Theory, 20*(4), 642–71.
Britzman, D. P. (1995). Is there a queer pedagogy? Or, stop reading straight. *Educational Theory, 45*(3),151–65.
Britzman, D. P. (2003). *Practice makes practice: A critical study of learning to teach.* Albany: State University of New York Press.
Broadway, F. S. (2011). Queer (v.) queer (v.): Biology as curriculum, pedagogy, and being albeit queer (v.). *Cultural Studies of Science Education, 6*(2), 293–304.
Brown, T. (2006). Negotiating psychological disturbance in pre-service teacher education. *Teaching and Teacher Education, 22,* 675–89.
Colt, A. (1998, April). Were you born that way? *Life, 21*(4): 38–42, 44, 46, 48–49.
Evans, K. (1999). When queer and teacher meet, In W. J. Letts and J. Sears (Eds.), *Queering elementary education: Advancing the dialogue about sexualities and schooling* (pp. 237–46). Lanham, MD: Rowman and Littlefield.
Evans, K. (2002). *Negotiating the self: Identity, sexuality, and emotion in learning to teach.* New York: RoutledgeFalmer.
Fifield, S., & Swain, H. L. (2002). Heteronormativity and common sense in science (teacher) education. In R. M. Kissen (Ed.),*Getting ready for Benjamin: Preparing teachers for sexual diversity in the classroom* (pp. 177–89). Lanham, MD: Rowman and Littlefield.
Fausto-Sterling, A. (2000). *Sexing the body: Gender politics and the construction of sexuality.* New York: Basic.
Harbeck, K. M. (1992). *Coming out of the classroom closet: Gay and lesbian students, teachers and curricula.* New York: Harrington Park.
Ingraham, C. (1994). The heterosexual imagery: Feminist sociology and theories of gender. *Sociological Theory, 12*(2): 203–19.
Jagose, A. (1996). *Queer theory: An introduction.* New York: New York University Press.
Jennings, K. (1994). *One teacher in 10: Gay and lesbian educators tells their stories.* Los Angeles, CA: Alyson.
Kissen, R. M. (1996). *The last closet: The real lives of lesbian and gay teachers.* Portsmouth, NH: Heinemann.
Leck, G. M. (1999). Afterword. In W. J. Letts and J. Sears (Eds.), *Queering elementary education: Advancing the dialogue about sexualities and schooling* (pp. 257–62). Lanham, MD: Rowman and Littlefield.
Letts, W. J. (1999). How to make "boys" and "girls" in the classroom: The heteronormative nature of elementary-school science. In W. J. Letts and J. Sears (Eds.), *Queering elementary education: Advancing the dialogue about sexualities and schooling* (pp. 97–110). Lanham, MD: Rowman and Littlefield.
Letts, W. J. (2001). When science is strangely alluring: Interrogating the masculinist and heteronormative nature of primary science. *Gender and Education, 13*(3): 261–74.
Luhmann, S. (1998). Queering/querying pedagogy? Or, pedagogy is a pretty queer thing. In W. Pinar (Ed.), *Queer theory in education* (pp. 141–55). Mahwah, NJ: Lawrence Erlbaum.
McNaron, T. A. H. (1997). *Poisoned ivy: Lesbian and gay academics confronting homophobia.* Philadelphia: Temple University Press.

Millar, R. (Ed.). (1989). *Doing science: Images of science in science education.* London: Falmer.

Murray, A. (1995). Femme on the streets, butch in the sheets (a play on whores). In D. Bell and G. Valentine (Eds.), *Mapping desire: Geographies of sexualities* (pp. 66–74). London: Routledge.

Nayak, A., & Kehily, M. J. (1997). Masculinities and schooling: Why are young men so homophobic? In D. L. Steinberg, D. Epstein, and R. Johnson (Eds.), *Border patrols: Policing the boundaries of heterosexuality* (pp. 138–61). London: Cassell.

Nixon, D., & Givens, N. (2004). "Miss, you're so gay." Queer stories from trainee teachers. *Sex Education, 4*(3), 217–37.

Nobles, C., & Letts, W. (2000, April). *"Queering science education? You don't say."* Paper presented at the annual meeting of the National Association for Research in Science Teaching, New Orleans.

Olendzki, A. (2003). Buddhist psychology. In S. R. Segall (Ed.), *Encountering Buddhism: Western psychology and Buddhist teachings* (pp. 9–30). Albany: State University of New York Press.

Olendzki, A. (2006). The transformative impact of non-self. In D. K. Nuriyal, S. Drummand, and Y. B. Lal (Eds.), *Buddhist thought and applied psychological research: Transcending the boundaries* (pp. 250–61). London: Routledge.

Phelan, S. (1994). *Getting specific: Postmodern lesbian politics.* Minneapolis: University of Minnesota Press.

Phelan, S. (2001). *Sexual strangers: Gays, lesbians, and dilemmas of citizenship.* Philadelphia: Temple University Press.

Pinar, W. F. (Ed.). (1998). *Queer theory in education.* Mahwah, NJ: Lawrence Erlbaum.

Redman, P. (1997). Invasion of the monstrous others: Heterosexual masculinities, the "AIDS carrier" and the horror genre. In D. L. Steinberg, D. Epstein, and R. Johnson (Eds.), *Border patrols: Policing the boundaries of heterosexuality* (pp. 98–116). London: Cassell.

Rosario, V. A. (1997). Homosexual bio-histories: Genetic nostalgia and the quest for paternity. In V. A. Rosario (Ed.), *Science and homosexualities* (pp. 1–25). New York: Routledge.

Rudolph, J. L. (2002). *Scientists in the classroom: The cold war reconstruction of American science education.* New York: Palgrave.

Snyder, V. L., & Broadway, F. S. (2004). Queering high school biology textbooks. *Journal of Research in Science Teaching, 41*(6), 617–36.

Steinberg, D. L., Epstein, D., & Johnson, R. (Eds.). (1997). *Border patrols: Policing the boundaries of heterosexuality.* London: Cassell.

Sullivan, N. (2003). *A critical introduction to queer theory.* New York: New York University Press.

Talburt, S. (2000). *Subject to identity: Knowledge, sexuality and academic practices in higher education.* Albany: State University of New York Press.

Tierney, W. G. (1997). *Academic outlaws: Queer theory and cultural studies in the academy.* Thousand Oaks, CA: Sage.

Turner, W. B. (2000). *A genealogy of queer theory.* Philadelphia: Temple University Press.

Weaver, J. A., Morris, M., and Appelbaum, P. (2001). *(Post) modern science (education): Propositions and alternative paths.* New York: Lang.

Weems, L. (1999). Pestalozzi, perversity, and the pedagogy of love, In W. J. Letts and J. Sears (Eds.), *Queering elementary education: Advancing the dialogue about sexualities and schooling* (pp. 27–36). Lanham, MD: Rowman and Littlefield.

Chapter Seven

The Personal Is Professional

Understanding Schools as Cultural Institutions through the Identities of Mother/Educator/Lesbian

Laura A. Bower

A teacher's identity is central to her pedagogical decisions and interactions with students and colleagues (Korthagen, 2001; Loughran, 2006; Palmer, 1998). Yet individual identity is complex, fluid, and subject to governance by societies, cultures, and institutions (Bullough, 2008; Foucault, 1978). As identities are continually reconstructed within and across various contexts, teacher identity may reveal as much about societal and institutional discourses as about individual teachers (Zembylas, 2005).

In this chapter, the author explores the policing of teachers' identities. The chapter provides insight into the narratives of teaching that are privileged and those that are marginalized, which has significance for the status of teaching as a profession as well as the professional (and personal) lives of teachers.

The chapter presents an exploration of the identities and public identity performances of five women who are mothers, educators, and lesbians.[1] This allows for consideration of two highly contested icons within teaching: that of homosexual as teacher and that of teacher as mother. Investigating how the (re)enactment of these icons are both rewarded and punished demonstrates the ways educational systems and societies police teachers' identities.

Although "coming out" as lesbian is an important element in this study, the focus is not on whether lesbian mothers and teachers should disclose their sexual orientation. Rather, the choices mothers/educators/lesbians (MELs) make around disclosure provide important insight into the role schools, as social institutions, play in shaping identity.

The following questions guided the inquiry: How do certain women define and perform their identities as educators, as mothers, and as lesbians? What informs these definitions and performances? What are the perceived punishments and rewards associated with these identities?

PERSPECTIVES ON IDENTITY

This chapter draws on poststructural conceptions of identity, meaning "culturally intelligible" performances of personhood (Butler, 1990, p. 23) that institutions govern by rewarding some performances and punishing others (Foucault, 1978). Identities are complex and fluid, "an identity tenuously constituted in time, instituted in an exterior space through a *stylized repetition of acts*" (Butler, 1990, p. 179). These identities are not natural, innate states, but rather are constructed (and reconstructed) across various contexts (Foucault, 1978; Morris, 1998; Taubman, 1993). Bullough (2008) argues, "Identity formation necessarily leads to both self and institutional criticism and perhaps toward change and renewal" (p. 53).

At the same time, juridical discourses, such as medicine, education, and the law, govern identity formation and performance as some identities are rewarded and others are labeled as deviant and subsequently punished (Foucault, 1978). Therefore, the power to shape identity and institutions is shared between individuals, collective groups, and institutions (Zembylas, 2005). Schools, as cultural institutions, have both shaped and been shaped by lesbian teachers' and lesbian mothers' identities.

The mutual shaping of schools and lesbian teachers can largely be seen through the lesbians' choices around disclosure of sexual orientation. Lesbian teachers "manage their sexuality at work" (Ferfolja, 2009, p. 384), meaning that they consciously make choices about which aspects of their identities they put forth as public knowledge and which they conceal.

When teachers choose to disclose their sexual orientation, they do so to shape schools, contextualizing their choices as a means to promote lesbian, gay, bisexual, and transgender visibility within schools (Jennings, 2005). Further, some teachers feel that their minority sexual orientation leads them to prioritize safety, social justice, and rapport with students, which influences schools as institutions (Jackson, 2007).

Conversely, many lesbian teachers choose not to disclose their sexual orientation for fear that making their sexual orientation known will cause them to be categorized as a danger to students (Evans, 2002). Teachers' fears are buttressed by historical efforts to fire gay and lesbian teachers (Blount, 2000) and the lack of national antidiscrimination legislation that includes sexual orientation (Human Rights Campaign, 2009).

Educators' disclosure of sexuality may also negatively affect students' perceptions of teacher credibility (Russ, Simonds, and Hunt, 2002). In this context, schools shape lesbian teachers as beings who do not talk about their personal lives. In addition, teachers are shaped through being made to feel that gay and lesbian teachers must attempt to become perfect teachers to compensate for their sexual orientations (Litton, 1999).

Like lesbian teachers, lesbian mothers have been described as managing their sexuality while at school (Gabb, 2005). The intentional (non)disclosure of sexual orientation within schools also applies to lesbian mothers and their children (Lindsay, Perlesz, Brown, McNair, deVaus, and Pitts, 2006).

A great deal of parental stress reported by lesbian mothers pertains to if, when, and how to disclose sexual orientation to school personnel (Mercier and Harold, 2003). Lesbian mothers fear the effects disclosure of sexual orientation will have on teachers' interactions with the lesbian mothers' children (Casper and Shultz, 1999). Some lesbian mothers wait until the teacher has come to know the child as an individual before introducing their entire family, thus disclosing sexual orientation (Bower and Klecka, 2009).

While schools significantly shape lesbian mothers' identities, particularly the disclosure of these identities, lesbian mothers also shape schools. Lesbian mothers have discussed intentionally selecting the best school for their children, with the following criteria for "best" schools: multicultural student populations, gay and lesbian staff, and incorporation of gay and lesbian families into the curriculum as their (Gartrell, Deck, Rodas, Peyser, and Banks, 2005).

This intentional selection of schools is particularly important in contexts in which schools compete for funding on the basis of student enrollment. Lesbian mothers also shape schools through advocating for their children, particularly in their promoting curricular materials that are inclusive of gay and lesbian families and making teachers aware of bullying and teasing of children with gay and lesbian parents (Mercier and Harold, 2003; Ray and Gregory, 2001).

IDENTITIES OF MOTHER/EDUCATOR/LESBIAN

Given the choices that lesbian mothers and lesbian teachers make in managing identities and the ways these choices shape and are shaped by schools as cultural institutions, an examination of the identities of MELs can probe the ways that multiple aspects of identities are shaped and managed within school contexts. In this chapter, the identities of five women are examined through the lens of MEL identities.[2] With concern for anonymity and confidentiality, pseudonyms are used to protect the women. Each self-identified as lesbian, actively parented at least one school-aged child, and served either as a teacher or an administrator at the K–12 level.

Penny, a white elementary special education teacher, had a partner of nine years. Together, they parented their two year old son and Penny's seven year old nephew. Kelli, a white woman, taught within an elementary gifted program. She and her partner of nine years were raising Kelli's fourteen year old son. Michele and Abigail, both white high school teachers, were partners. Abigail's six year old daughter lived with them, and they coparented the six year old son of Abigail's ex-partner. Nyla was a Middle Eastern administrator at an elementary school. She and her partner of two years were raising Nyla's five year old daughter and three year old son.

The five women worked in a large, urban school district. It is important to note that sexual orientation was included in the school district nondiscrimination policy and that the school district provided domestic partner benefits for all employees. In terms of the community climate for sexual minorities, the state in which the school district is situated does not recognize same-sex marriage, a condition of a state amendment. The ability of LGBTQ parents to adopt their partners' children is not explicitly prohibited; second-parent adoption within LGBTQ families varies from case to case, depending on individual judge's rulings. However, sexual orientation is listed within anti-discrimination laws at the state level (Human Rights Campaign, 2009).

UNPACKING MOTHER/EDUCATOR/LESBIAN IDENTITIES

This section, based on an analysis[3] of a series of interviews[4] with each woman, describes how the five MEL articulated their identities within a particular role, what informed their performance of these identities, and the perceived rewards and punishments of these performances.

PERFORMING MOTHERHOOD

Each MEL articulated a coherent sense of how to perform the role of "good mother," particularly making children a top priority. This required sacrificing the mother's own desires, needs, and professional obligations for the sake of her children. Abigail explained, "You put your kids first. You sacrifice. Sometimes you've got to put your stuff down and play with them and then come back to your other work." Kelli discussed the way she and her partner make their son a priority.

> We have been very active parents. [Our son] is and has always been a large part of how we plan our lives, so whether it's homework [or something else], we also have that priority. We don't mind giving up a weekend of going out of

town when we know that he has a large project or something that he needs to do. Because that's what we do. We spend a lot of time doing educational things. For instance we just came back from Spring Break. We could have done other things, but we chose to take him and do things that would interest him as well as us.

Kelli, like the other participants, also focused on providing a multitude of educational experiences for children. This will be further examined in the "teachers as mothers" section. Each MEL also mentioned the importance of doing homework and working on school projects with their children. Abigail, for example, expressed, "Education is important to me; it's a priority. We spend a lot of time reading. Part of that is I'm always trying to read so that I model that for [my daughter]. And we do math and we try to do educational games."

MELs' performances of good mother were largely shaped by emulating or resisting the practices of their own parents. As Abigail explained, "I think we obviously model both the things we like about our mothers and change the things we disliked about our mothers. I think it's a combination of both." And Michele said, "I think a lot of it is the environment in which you were raised. Because some people grow up in a crappy home, and then they're like, 'I'm not going to do this to my child.' Of course they're going not to do what their mothers did to them. And sometimes you grow up in a wonderful household with a wonderful family, and it just carries on."

Additionally, Penny mentioned learning from other parenting models, "You learn from people around you. From family. I've got family members. From people you work with. It comes from a wide range of people. Because I didn't have a strong mother role growing up." MELs also discussed their roles as teachers being instructive in the way they parented, which is discussed in detail in the "Teachers as Mothers" section later in this chapter.

MELs linked the rewards for being good mothers with outcomes for their children. Specifically, they expected that as good mothers, they would be rewarded with close relationships with their children and with children who were emotionally secure, well educated, and successful. Nyla specifically connected her parenting goals with her relationship with her children:

> I think for me it has a lot to do with developing a relationship that's interdependent. So I want them to become independent human beings, productive members of society, etc., but I also want them to really value relationships with family and to connect with family.

Kelli explained, "You get to know what your child's about and what they're doing. It shows your child that what he does or what she does during the day is important."

In terms of punishments, MELs described the types of parents they did not want to be. They complained about parents who were uninvolved in their children's lives, particularly in their education, and parents who failed to teach their children social skills. Penny described these as parents who "get all in a wad if you ask for anything extra that involves taking away time from their daily life. I don't see parents parenting, putting education high. They don't put it as something to value and something to enjoy. It's something that's a hardship on them, not something that they're teaching the kids that this is the best thing ever and they're game for it."

MELs connected uninvolved parenting with low academic success for children. Michele said, "I wish more parents in our community were involved. I think that would make a world of difference in attendance and grades. If a child is not coming to class or slacking off and you try to call but no one returns your phone calls, it's hard to be successful when there's no one on the other end to help you." Penny suggested that academic learning time was compromised because of these parents:

> We spend so much time as educators teaching manners and social skills that their education suffers. If they come to school with bad social skills, bad behavior skills, no manners, it takes up a lot of the day. Half the day is over and they haven't even gotten to any [academic] skills yet.

The connection between "good" parenting and academically successful children was evident across categories.

TEACHERS AS MOTHERS

MELs described themselves as better mothers as a result of teaching. Their professional knowledge as teachers and interactions with students informed their expectations of and engagement with their children. Abigail explained how her interactions with students informed her parenting, "I believe from all these years of teaching, you don't [begin to] parent at thirteen. You parent at two, three, four, five, six. If I don't set boundaries and structure now, I'm dead when she's a teenager. Because I see; I know what good kids do."

Kelli captured her professional knowledge as, "Understanding child development, early childhood, and gifted education." She explained, "[My son's] friends are all looking to me at different times in their children's growth, 'how do you know this' or 'how do you know that?' Because you're a teacher, you should know that." Penny also discussed the effect her professional knowledge has on her parenting, "You know what they need as a teacher, the tons of reading, the tons of everything. Everything revolves around learning, when we're in the car and when we're at school. And then when we get home, there's not spelling or math problems; it's just problem solving learning, like games. It's all the time. It never seems to end. It's just really hard to turn it off."

Given the priority MELs placed on good mothers creating educational opportunities for their children, they viewed the ability to create appropriate learning environments for their own children as a reward for being a mother who also teaches. Their professional status and educational background were also rewarded by easier navigation of educational systems. Most mentioned hand-selecting their children's teachers. Kelli described her son's teachers as "all hand picked." This reward was a result of interactions with co-workers and access to administrators. MELs did not mention any punishments or negative effects on parenting as a result of being teachers.

MOTHERS AS TEACHERS

MELs named improvements in their teaching after becoming mothers. Nyla explained, "My teaching experience and training made me a much better parent than I think I ever would have been. And now my parenting experiences make me a better educator." Specific improvements in teaching practice included increased compassion and treating students as the MELs would want their own children to be treated. Abigail said,

> Since I had a child, I am probably more compassionate in my classroom. I look at them, no matter how much I want to rip their head off. And I think, you are somebody's child. Somebody loves you. I don't. But somebody cares about you and I need to realize that maybe you're not the piece of you know.

MELs allowed their identities as mothers to inform their teaching practices, for the perceived rewards of being more effective educators. Unlike the emphasis on professional knowledge in the previous category, the connection between motherhood improving teaching practices focused on affective elements.

LESBIANS AS MOTHERS

In talking about motherhood and sexual orientation, each MEL stated the need to be open. Penny explained, "I'm so open. I don't have to hide anything. It's hard for me to imagine that someone wouldn't accept it, even though I know they don't." In terms of school, the mothers suggested approaching personnel prior to the school year to garner a more favorable classroom climate for children. Nyla explained her strategy:

> Be brave, make an appointment before the school year starts with the teacher, go in, and lay it out on the table. Don't let the year start and allow homophobia

to infect your child. Be very open. Start with the teacher and then, if you need to, let the school administration or higher know that this is your family, and your child's not going to be discriminated against and is not going to be excluded.

And Abigail suggested, "I think you need to be honest with their teachers. You can't hide it. You just show up."

MELs perceived better school environments as a reward for disclosing maternal sexual orientation to school personnel. This was evident in MELs' beliefs that they could prevent or minimize discrimination their children experienced in schools, indicating a belief that disclosing sexual orientation would lead to positive change. Nyla explained how she would perform lesbian motherhood if she were not a school administrator.

> I would try to get parent groups together, because you know every school has a number of glbt [gay, lesbian, bisexual, and transgender] parents. And then I would try to work within the district to get parents involved and really make some positive change. And not just for the parents, but then also for the time they get to upper elementary and then middle and high school when kids are coming out to themselves and to their friends. And I would try to work toward making a safer environment for them.

MELs assumed that the negative consequence (or punishment) for failing to talk openly about their sexual orientation would be teaching their children to be ashamed of the children's families. Abigail captured this in talking about the parents' of her daughter's friends. "I am [out to them]. Because, you know what, if they have a problem with it then their kid cannot come to my house. I really don't care, because I'm not going to hide that. Because then I teach [my daughter] that she needs to hide things. And I refuse to do that." For this reason, MELs allowed their identities as lesbians to inform their parenting practice.

LESBIANS AS TEACHERS

Whereas MELs were very open about their sexuality as mothers, they worked to keep their sexual identities apart from their teaching identities. Nyla highlighted the distinction between being openly gay as a principal and as a mother: "It's more appropriate for me to establish myself as an effective leader first, no matter what my sexual orientation. But as a mom, I'm very proactive and very out and will be more and more as the kids get older."

MELs explained their need to conceal being lesbian in terms of concerns for professional and personal safety and effectiveness in schools. They felt that sexual orientation was irrelevant in teaching. Kelli stated, "I do tend to personalize myself to my students, but not in that respect. I think sexuality needs to stay out of the classroom. It's not relevant what your sexual orientation is to be a good teacher." Michele echoed this, "I don't talk about my personal life." Abigail said, "I don't talk about it in my [class]room, and I don't bring it up. It's a non-issue, because it just needs to be."

They feared specific punishments for disclosing sexual orientation, such as negative effects on student learning, lessened respect from students and students' families, or job loss. Abigail explained, "I want to be a teacher that they remember ten years later as someone who pushed them. Not as the gay teacher they had." And Nyla said, "It would be very easy for a group of teachers with a brand new principal who just comes right out [as gay] on the first morning, to accuse me of having an agenda and get me moved. You know, with the right amount of complaints."

MELs' efforts to keep their sexual identity separate from their teaching identity were informed by their perceptions both of administrators' wishes and of students' families' beliefs. Penny mentioned,

> A lot of parents have ethics and morals that would not be able to handle it. They would think that it's going to be a predator on their child or inflict my opinions on them just because their own beliefs are so strong against it. That's not something that I want to spend my time battling, trying to changes someone's mind when there's a very slim chance. And meanwhile their kid suffers. The parent and I are battling and it's going to be awkward for him. He loses his chance of really receiving an education in my class because if the child is hearing his parents' opinion, then all respect is gone. And then there goes his expectation of learning.

Penny's fears connected to the punishment MELs associated with lesbians as teachers.

CONCLUSIONS

From the perspective of the women whose lives are examined in this chapter, it seems that culturally appropriate performances for educators can include being a mother, but not a lesbian. Perceived punishments for being a lesbian educator comprised negatively influencing student learning, garnering less respect from students and students' families, and losing one's job.

Yet the perceived rewards for mothers who are teachers included improved teaching practice, greater educational experiences for one's own children, and higher-quality parenting practices. Importantly, the women's identities as educator and mother were mutually shaped. They talked about being better mothers because of being educators and better educators because of being mothers. Sexual orientation influenced MELs' performances of mother, but they strove to keep their educator and lesbian identities separate.

The identities of the women presented in this chapter indicate a championing of the icon of "teacher as mother/mother as teacher" as well as a persistent fear of the "homosexual as teacher." Both have implications for teacher education and for the lives of teachers. The promotion of teaching as mothering is troubling in light of concerns regarding the feminization of the teaching profession. Within the United States, teaching has been a female-dominated occupation for at least the past 150 years (Spencer, 2001).

A major concern is that, as an occupation with a largely female workforce, teaching receives less respect and lower pay than other professions (Griffin, 1997). The conflation of teaching with mothering allows for the deprofessionalization of education, promoting maternal instinct over professional knowledge. Grumet (1988) writes, "And so, even though we secretly respect this maternal pedagogy of ours, it seems personal to us, not quite defensible in this public place, and we provide this nurturant labor without demanding the recompense it deserves" (p. 87).

This chapter provides insight concerning the persistent discrimination against lesbian educators. The work that MELs did to separate their sexual orientation from their teaching required a great deal of thought and effort not required of heterosexual teachers. MELs were reluctant to reveal their sexual identity in their roles as educators but were quick to disclose their sexuality as mothers. MELs' fears around disclosure are not unfounded, given that only twenty states within the United States prohibit employment discrimination based on sexual orientation (Human Rights Campaign, 2009).

The mother as teacher and lesbian as teacher identities are emblematic of sanctioned and unsanctioned performances of identity within contemporary schools. Given the mutually shaping nature of identity and institutions, teacher education can have a powerful role in both identity formation and schools. The role of schools in socializing teachers' professional identities has long been acknowledged (e.g., Lortie, 1975). MELs had been socialized to allow their mother and teacher identities to shape one another but to hold their lesbian identities separate from their teaching.

Teacher education classrooms can be a place for preservice and inservice teachers to explore their complex identities and the ways these identities can and do shape teaching practices. This will challenge the strict binary of personal and professional identities. Such conversations have been promoted around race for some time now, with fears that white teachers lack the cultural knowledge to connect with students of color (e.g., Howard, 1999).

These racially based conversations champion the personal cultural experiences of teachers of color, relying on these experiences to make school experiences more relevant for students of color (Ladson-Billings, 1995). In understanding the teacher identity as complex and as both personal and professional, discussions of identity must be expanded to include sexual orientation and family structure, among other formative aspects of identity.

Further, in exploring the ways complex identities shape teaching practices, teacher educators must be careful not to privilege certain identities, including mother or heterosexual. Understanding teacher identity as inherently linked to personal identity creates space for diverse perspectives, backgrounds, and beliefs in teaching, which will ultimately benefit learners. Teacher education must recognize the personal as professional in an institutional critique that makes schools safer for individual difference.

NOTES

1. A major part of content for this chapter was taken from a qualitative research study presented in 2010 at the annual meeting of the American Educational Research Association in Denver. The study, which focused on the identities of mother/educator/lesbian, took place in a large, urban school district over the course of three months (see Bower, 2010). The data reported here were gathered as part of a larger study (Bower, 2008) but were reanalyzed to highlight the complex, fluid identities of mother/educator/lesbian.

2. The five women whose identities are examined in this chapter were originally participants in the research study (Bower, 2010) and were selected through purposeful sampling (Creswell, 1998) via social networking within the gay and lesbian communities and through school district contacts. The purpose of seeking participants within both of these networks was to encourage participation from women with diverse professional and personal identities. The small sample size of this study may be reflective of educators' reluctance to disclose their sexual identities, as discussed in the literature review. Several participants asked multiple questions about anonymity and confidentiality before consenting to participate. For this reason, minimal demographic details were provided about each participant and the school district context in which the participants worked.

3. Analysis of transcripts entailed inductive coding (Patton, 1990) coupled with the constant comparison method (Lincoln and Guba, 1985). Initial codes included nine categories: description of self as mother, description of self as educator, description of self as lesbian, description of self as "other," parenting beliefs, educational beliefs, beliefs surrounding sexuality, practices as educator, practices as mother. Owing to the complex nature of identity, many statements fit more than one category and were coded with two or more categories simultaneously. Categories were later collapsed to form five categories: performing motherhood, mother as teacher, teacher as mother, lesbian as mother, and lesbian as teacher. Each of these five categories was then examined to determine what informed the identity performance and the perceived rewards and punishments for each.

4. Each woman engaged in an initial semistructured interview, ranging in length from thirty to sixty minutes. Questions focused on professional practice, views of parenting, and experiences within schools and communities. Transcripts were used to generate questions for follow-up interviews, which lasted thirty to forty-five minutes and provided an opportunity for member checking (Lincoln and Guba, 1985) and probing issues from initial interviews.

REFERENCES

Blount, J. M. (2000). Spinsters, bachelors, and other gender transgressors in school employment, 1850–1990, *Review of Educational Research, 70*(1), 83–101.
Bower, L. A. (2010). The personal is professional: Unpacking cultural sanctions through the identities of mother/educator/lesbians. Paper presented at the Annual Meeting of the Association of Teacher Educators, Denver, CO.
Bower, L. A. (2008). *Finding the other in mother: Queering social scripts for mothers and teachers in K–12 schools.* (Doctoral dissertation, University of Nevada, Las Vegas).

Bower, L. A., & Klecka, C. L. (2009). Lesbian mothers' bids for normalcy in their children's schools. *The Educational Forum, 73*(3), 230–39.

Bullough, R. V. (2008). *Counternarratives: Studies of teacher education and becoming a teacher.* Albany: State University of New York Press.

Butler, J. (1990). *Gender trouble: Feminism and the subversion of identity.* New York: Routledge.

Casper, V., & Schultz, S. (1999). *Gay parents/straight schools: Building communication and trust.* New York: Teachers College Press.

Creswell, J. W. (1998). *Qualitative inquiry and research design: Choosing among five traditions.* Thousand Oaks, CA: Sage.

Erickson, F. (1986). Qualitative methods in research on teaching. In M. Wittrock (Ed.), *Handbook of research on teaching* (third edition, pp. 119–61). New York: Macmillan.

Evans, K. (2002). *Negotiating the self: Identity, sexuality, and emotion in learning to teach.* New York: RoutledgeFalmer.

Ferfolja, T. (2009). Stories so far: An overview of the research on lesbian teachers. *Sexualities, 12*(3), 378–96.

Foucault, M. (1978). *The history of sexuality* (R. Hurley, Trans. Vol. I). New York: Random House.

Gabb, J. (2005). Locating lesbian parent families: Everyday negotiations of lesbian motherhood in Britain. *Gender, Place and Culture: A Journal of Feminist Geography, 12*(4), 419–32.

Gartrell, N., Deck, A., Rodas, C., Peyser, H., & Banks, A. (2005). The national lesbian family study: 4 interviews with the 10-year-old children. *American Journal of Orthopsychiatry, 75*(4), 518–24.

Griffin, G. (1997). Teaching as a gendered experience. *Journal of Teacher Education, 48*(1), 7–18.

Grumet, M. (1988). *Bitter milk: Women and teaching.* Amherst: University of Massachusetts Press.

Howard, G. R. (1999). *We can't teach what we don't know: White teachers, multiracial schools.* New York: Teachers College Press.

Human Rights Campaign. (2009). *Statewide employment laws and policies.* Retrieved June 17, 2009, from http://www.hrc.org/documents/Employment_Laws_and_Policies.pdf.

Jackson, J. M. (2007). *Unmasking identities: An exploration of the lives of gay and lesbian teachers.* Lanham, MD: Lexington.

Jennings, K. (Ed.). (2005). *One teacher in 10: LGBT educators share their stories* (second edition). Los Angeles: Alyson.

Korthagen, F. A. J. (2001). The realistic approach: Its tenets, philosophical background and future. In F. Korthagen, J. Kessels, B. Koster, B. Langerwarf, and T. Wubbels (Eds.), *Linking practice and theory: The pedagogy of realistic teacher education* (pp. 69–87). Mahwah, NJ: Lawrence Erlbaum Associates.

Ladson-Billings, G. (1995). Toward a culturally relevant pedagogy. *American Educational Research Journal, 32*(3), 465–91.

Lincoln, Y. S., and Guba, E. G. (1985). *Naturalistic inquiry.* Beverly Hills, CA: Sage.

Lindsay, J., Perlesz, A., Brown, R., McNair, R., de Vaus, D., and Pitts, M. (2006). Stigma or respect: Lesbian-parented families negotiating school setting. *Sociology, 40*(6), 1059–77.

Litton, E. F. (1999). Stories of courage and hope: Gay and lesbian Catholic elementary school teachers. Paper presented at the Annual Meeting of the America Educational Research Association, Montreal.

Lortie, D. C. (1975). *Schoolteacher: A sociological study.* Chicago: University of Chicago Press.

Loughran, J. (2006). *Developing a pedagogy of teacher education: Understanding teaching and learning about teaching.* New York: Routledge.

Mercier, L. R., and Harold, R. D. (2003). At the interface: Lesbian-parent families and their children's schools. *Children and Schools, 25*(1), 35–47.

Morris, M. (1998). Unresting the curriculum: Queer projects, queer imaginings. In W. F. Pinar (Ed.), *Queer theory in education* (pp. 275–86). Mahwah, NJ: Lawrence Earlbaum Associates.

National Center for Education Statistics. (2006). Schools and staffing survey, public school teacher data file, 2003–04. Washington, DC: US Department of Education.

Palmer, P. (1998). *The courage to teach: Exploring the inner landscape of a teacher's life.* San Francisco: Jossey-Bass.

Patton, M. Q. (1990). *Qualitative evaluation and research methods* (second edition). Newbury Park, CA: Sage.

Ray, V., & Gregory, R. (2001). School experiences of the children of gay and lesbian parents. *Family Matters (Australian Institute of Family Studies), 59,* 29–34.

Russ, T., Simonds, C., & Hunt, S. (2002). Coming out in the classroom. . . . An occupational hazard? The influence of sexual orientation on teacher credibility and perceived student learning. *Communication Education, 51*(3), 311–342.

Spencer, D. A. (2001). Teachers' work in historical and social context. In V. Richardson (Ed.), *Handbook of research on teaching* (fourth edition, pp. 803–25). Washington, DC: American Educational Research Association.

Taubman, P. (1993). Separate identities, separate lives: Diversity in the curriculum. In L. Castenell and W. Pinar (Eds.), *Understanding curriculum as racial text: Representations of identity and difference in education* (pp. 287–306). Albany: State University of New York Press.

Zembylas, M. (2005). Discursive practices, genealogies, and emotional rules: A poststructuralist view on emotion and identity in teaching. *Teaching and Teacher Education, 21,* 935–48.

Chapter Eight

Dismantling Straight Privilege

Alternate Conceptions of Identity and Education

Tonette S. Rocco, Hilary Landorf, and Suzanne Gallagher

This chapter examines the nature and consequences of straight privilege on education and practice. The nature of straight privilege includes binary thinking, moralizing, and myths. Binary thinking and moralizing support the negative myths surrounding lesbian, gay, bisexual, transgender, and queer/questioning (LGBTQ) identity. These myths include gays as pedophiles, nature versus nurture, the myth of choice, the conversion myth, and counterfeit marriage myth.

The consequences of straight privilege are evident in the construction, the influence, and the pervasiveness of the myths on personal experience and teaching and learning. LGBTQ people choose to remain silent and (straight or gay) teachers choose not to engage on the issues surrounding sexual minorities, which then has an influence on educational options and teaching for social justice.

LGBTQ people are "[s]exual minorities [who] are denied civil rights, the right to work, and other human rights because of their sexuality and sexual orientation" (Rocco, Landorf, and Delgado, 2009, p. 8). Sexual minorities are people who are or are perceived to be not heterosexual. Nonheterosexual groups include but are not limited to lesbian, gay, bisexual, transsexual, and transgender people.

Throughout this paper, *LGBTQ* as initials is used to encompass the subgroups. The individual name such as *lesbian* is used when referring to this specific group. The authors use *sexual minorities*, *sexual orientation*, and *queer* in specific contexts. The term *sexual minorities* represent a denial of civil and legal rights; *sexual orientation* represents a human characteristic; *queer* represents a political attitude. *Queer work* intends to destabilize the boundaries around sex, sexual orientation, and gender (Hill, 2004).

CONSTRUCTING STRAIGHT PRIVILEGE

"Privilege is the systematic conferral of benefit and advantage" (Wildman, 1996, p. 29) and straight privilege is when these benefits and advantages go to straight people. Privilege is composed of a triarchy of interlocked psychosocial, reciprocal, and structural realms that result in discriminatory beliefs, practices, and policies (Rocco and West, 1998). *Psychosocial* "refers to internalized, uncritical acceptance of assumptions gained through socialization" (Rocco and West, 1998, p. 176). The reciprocal realm comprises our interactions with others. The structural realm is reflected in a consistent history of "norms, policies, and language which maintain and sanction" (Rocco and West, 1998, p. 177) the status of the dominant culture.

Our social system is, then, built on a foundation of coercive power that validates the legal system as just based on what is in the best interest of the dominant group that writes and enforces the law. This invisibility of privilege to those who are privileged leads to a belief in being innocent and not complicit in the oppression of others.

> Heterosexism or heterosexual privilege is a system of oppression that reduces the experience of sexual minorities to medical or criminal causes while victimizing through violence or diminished opportunity people that are seen as sexual minorities. Heterosexism sustains a legal system that denies equal protection and property rights (such as marriage) and holds in contempt the personal relationships of sexual minorities. (Rocco and Gallagher, 2006, p. 2)

To maintain heterosexual or straight privilege, the boundaries surrounding sex, gender, and sexuality must be fixed and without ambiguity (Ruffulo, 2005). A *boundary* is something that marks or fixes a limit; in the case of sexuality, it is the limit of what is moral or conforming to standards of right behavior (*Webster's*, 1999). A male is expected to be heterosexual and masculine and a female is conditioned to be heterosexual and feminine. Oppression, domination, and violence are used to maintain these definitions and boundaries, which also exist within a classroom. These definitions reduce the issue to who one's sexual partner is, which then bolsters male dominance (Pharr, 1988) and heterosexism.

Creating and Maintaining Binaries and Boundaries

Binary categorization and reductionism underlie the American economic, legal, and political systems (Delgado and Stefanic, 2001). Each of us has certain characteristics such as gender, race, sexual orientation, and ethnicity, which can be seen as binaries—a person is one thing or the other. This binary system supports the "fixed and clear meanings" (Arriola, 2000, p. 322) of each characteristic. The binary system defines and creates the boundaries for other concepts such as *sex*, *gender*, and *sexuality*, and reactions such as lust, love, attraction, and desire.

Sex is defined as either male or female. Gender is a learned response of what it is to be masculine or feminine, including behavior, appearance, and affective orientation. This is the sociopsychological side of sex in which people learn gender roles and how to enact them (Haeberle, 2001–2005). *Sexuality* is defined as "heterosexual" or "homosexual." The adjective *heterosexual* is defined as "intercourse between individuals of the opposite sex" (Merriam-Webster, 2003), and the adjective *homosexual* means "involving sexual intercourse between persons of the same sex."

Reductionism is the process of using one identity characteristic to represent a person's whole identity. In the process of reducing a person's identity to one characteristic, the person's other characteristics are denied (e.g., the reduction of a person's whole identity to lesbian while denying that the person is also Cuban). Each characteristic of a person has fixed meanings; some characteristics, such as sexual orientation, have no legal basis for federal discrimination claims (Arriola, 2000).

Reductionist assumptions "create false dichotomies and false power relationships and promote limited visions of equality" (Arriola, 2000, p. 322). For instance, an incident in a college class went something like this: A straight student made a report in class about a telemarketing organization, mentioning that most of the people on the phones were women. Someone in the class made an off-the-cuff remark that the remaining workers must be gay. A gay student asked the instructor to pursue this incident as an issue of social justice, equity, and blatant stereotyping. The instructor asked the student how the discussion should proceed. The student felt this remark was dismissive of his concern, thus silencing the student.

Other students viewed the teacher's action as trying to address his concerns. However, had the remark been about race, class, or gender, the instructor would not have needed to ask how to proceed. In education, characteristics are reduced by what we feel comfortable discussing. Scholars discuss certain characteristics in the public realm like gender and race while neglecting others such as disability, ethnicity, and sexual orientation (Hill, 1996). Queerness in any of its forms can be dismissed and the concerns of a gay or lesbian student in a class can also be dismissed as not relevant to course content.

Unfortunately many instructors proclaim that they are concerned with social justice and equity issues while reducing this concern to a few marginalized groups or characteristics. This incident is representative of the dilemma faced by social justice educators who use pedagogical skills on behalf of race and gender but who cannot translate these skills to issues of sexual orientation. Reasons for this inability may be a lack of knowledge or motivation to learn about sexual orientation.

Sexual orientation may be dismissed as not belonging to the same class of concerns as racial or gender minority group issues of power and privilege. The inability to address LGBTQ student concerns can also be due to stereotyping and discrimination. We recognize that it is difficult to see beyond these binary categorizations, to refrain from reductionism, and to quit blaming the victim or minority group member for his or her plight.

Moral/izing and Family Values

Morality is socially constructed and based on *morals* which are generally accepted customs of behavior in a society defined by socially accepted conventional principles or standards of right or wrong conduct (Ianinska and Garcia-Zamor, 2006). Because morals are socially constructed, they are bound by space and time, creating the possibility for multiple and conflicting systems of moral principles to coexist. More than one system of moral principles, even conflicting systems, may exist side by side (Walther cited in Ianinska and Garcia-Zamor, 2006).

Moralizing from a position of heterosexual privilege requires strict boundary maintenance of the binaries that determine who is normal and moral and who is deviant and immoral. Goffman (1963) defines *social deviants* as "the folk who are considered to be engaged in some kind of collective denial of the social order . . . perceived as failing to use available opportunity for advancement in the various approved runways of society; they show open disrespect for their betters; they lack piety; they represent failures in the motivational schemes of society" (p. 144). The social order is prescribed and defined by heterosexuals who maintain the strict binary to support the notion of heteronormativity as synonymous with humanity and morality (Gamson, 2000). The consequences of being a social deviant include discrimination, oppression, domination, myth perpetuation, and "marginalization and silencing at best, violence and death at worst" (Hill, 2004, p. 86).

Often morality and family values have been used to deny civil rights and liberty to individuals deemed deviant in a specific time and context. Values are attitudes and beliefs about issues such as abortion, gay rights, or gender roles in childrearing. The term *family values* originated in 1974 and means values "especially of a traditional or conservative kind which are held to promote the sound functioning of the family and to strengthen the fabric of society" (Merriam-Webster Dictionary, 2003).

In 2004, Tavis Smiley interviewed Jesse Jackson about the upcoming presidential election. The Reverend Jackson observed how deeply held values in this society that demean one group while reinforcing institutional power evolve (Smiley, 2004). For instance, Jackson said there was a time when slavery, disenfranchisement, and white supremacy were deeply held family values.

Another widely held value in the United States is the antimiscegenation stand that many states wrote into law. These statutes made it a crime for consenting adults of different races to cohabitate even if married in another state. The Lovings, who were arrested in 1958 in Virginia after being married in Washington, D.C., sued Virginia and won, ending all antimiscegenation laws (*Loving v. Virginia*, 1967). The Supreme Court decision rendered the laws unconstitutional by stating that marriage was a fundamental civil right (Clarkson-Freeman, 2004).

Warren J. Blumenfeld (2008), in an essay distributed via listservs, has made the point that marriage for straight couples of different races had to be supported by the Supreme Court as a civil right because states "would [not] have voluntarily relinquished the practice of arresting and incarcerating" adults of different races who wished to marry. This practice was based on a widely held family value that nonwhite races were inferior to the white race, and the stance that interracial sexual relationships were immoral. This same argument of immorality is used against same-sex marriage.

The rhetoric of *special rights* further demeans same-sex marriage as a civil right. Special rights are "those invocations of rights that seek to oppose or to qualify other forms of rights mobilization [e.g., the gay rights movement] by reference to the excessive quality of the original rights claims. As a mark of this excess, opponents often say these claimants are seeking 'special rights'" (Goldberg-Hiller and Milner, 2003, p. 1076). We would like to believe that the Reverend Jackson's remark about the evolution of values that demean others will soon extend to the current debate concerning same-sex marriage.

Mythmaking and Consequences

Discrimination based on race, sexual orientation, gender, and other factors is ancient practice based on a myth. As Montagu (1942/1997) wrote, "A myth is a faulty explanation leading to social delusion and error" (p. 41). The problem is that we do not see how we share responsibility across time and place with others in perpetuating myths. Many myths are an attempt to justify the inhumane and discriminatory treatment of one group by another group.

For instance, adoptions by gay and lesbian people are illegal in some states based on two myths: first, that gays are pedophiles and, second, that children raised by LGBTQ people will become gay because nurture will win out over nature.

Challenging the first myth, *The Stop Child Molestation Book* (Abel and Harlow, 2001) states "more than 70 percent of the men who molest boys rate themselves as heterosexual in their adult sexual preferences. . . . The majority of men who molest boys are also married, divorced, widowed, or living with an adult partner" (p. 2). Only 8 percent of those surveyed identified as homosexual.

Science challenges the second myth, nature versus nurture. In reality, *all* LGBTQ people are the product of the union of a man's sperm and a woman's egg. This reality of straight parents procreating queer children (in which nurture did not win out over nature) is frequently ignored in favor of the myth of choice, the myth that one chooses a bohemian life and turns one's back on a moral life. This myth forms the basis of discriminatory practices against LGBTQ people and is contrary to reality. Many LGBTQ people turn to God, prayer, and other forms of spirituality to make peace with the world that tells them they are an abomination and immoral (Sweasey, 1997). LGBTQ people turn to the God they grew up with in organized religions, a God who loves all; yet LGBTQ people are surrounded by church members who display raw disgust with and discriminate against LGBTQ people. The consequences of oppressive religious traditions on LGBTQ people include suicide, a sense of shame, hiding, denial of spirituality, invisibility, and the loss of community (Clark, 1993). The consequences include a denial of religiosity within the LGBTQ community as a reaction to being spurned by organized religion. This makes it doubly hard for LGBTQ people seeking solace in spirituality to affirm and practice their spirituality (Sweasey, 1997).

This notion of choice and immorality affects educational opportunities and career development. We know many LGBTQ people who chose religious lives and careers as a way to come to terms with their personal struggles between the biological and erotic impulses and the standards family and society maintained as moral and acceptable behavior. This struggle then keeps people from seeking other career and educational options until years later, if ever.

The choice for LGBTQ people is between living a true life with acceptance of identity or of living a false life and hiding one's true identity in an effort to live a socially accepted (but false) life. However, we acknowledge that the choice may not be as simple as choosing between living a true or false life because heterosexism creates times when safety dictates that there is no choice but to be in the closet. As Sedgwick (1993, p. 46) reminds us, "few of even the most openly gay people . . . are not deliberately in the closet with someone personally or economically or institutionally important to them."

For every new introduction or encounter, a decision is made about amount, timing, and the consequences of a decision to disclose. The concept of choosing to pass as straight (live a false life) may not be a free choice at all, if the person's economic survival or family relationships are based on keeping one's true identity secret. There is no guarantee that choosing to live a false life by passing as straight can be maintained indefinitely.

The conversion myth suggests that if a LGBTQ person engages in any form of sexual expression, physical contact, or emotional closeness with a straight person, the straight person can be converted (i.e., choose to be gay) (Meijer, 1993). This conversion myth is the most powerful aspect of the logic behind violence against LGBTQ people; if LGBTQ people can convert straight people to be gay, then they must be stopped.

The immorality of violence is neutralized by an action seen as saving the species. The conversion myth is extended to rationalize violence against lesbian women. An example of this myth is that if a straight man rapes a lesbian woman, she will see the light and rejoin the straight majority and procreate responsibly. The truth is that a violent criminal act has been committed that has nothing to do with procreation or species maintenance; instead, it is all about male dominance and sexism (Pharr, 1988). The conversion myth is based on the notions that only the binary is real, that sexual acts are only for procreation, and that eroticism and pleasure are outside the norm.

The rhetoric around procreation extends to the myth of marriage between same-sex people as counterfeit. Cahill (2007) writes, "Marriage traditionalists have increasingly relied on a particular rhetoric of deception—counterfeiting—to convey what in their view is a species of public fraud—same-sex marriage and its close approximations, civil unions and domestic partnerships" (p. 394).

The public fraud is perpetuated by misinformation distributed by organizations like the Family Research Council (FRC). The FRC stand is that same-sex marriage "degrades a time honored institution," creates unstable home environments, "redefines marriage to include virtually any sexual behavior," and "will lead to the persecution of those who object on moral or religious grounds" (Dailey, 2009, n.p.). The persecution that has occurred, however, has been by organizations like the Westboro Baptist Church, who demonstrated at Matthew Shepard's funeral calling him names and proclaiming he would burn in hell.

Myths about LGBTQ people lead to discrimination that denies access to employment, education, political, civic, and social opportunities while reserving access for a privileged few. Oppression consists of:

systematic institutional processes which prevent some people from learning and using satisfying and expansive skills in socially recognized settings, or institutionalized social processes which inhibit people's ability to play and communicate with others or to express their feelings and perspectives on social life where others can listen. (Young, 1990, p. 38)

Young (1990) summarizes this idea by writing, "oppression is the institutional constraints on self-development, and domination is the institutional constraints on self-determination" (p. 37). Going further, Young states that "[d]omination consists in persons having to perform actions whose rules and goals they have not participated in determining, under institutionalized conditions they have not had a part in deciding" (p. 218). For instance, LGBTQ people pay taxes, and these taxes support public adoption and foster care agencies, yet many states use these tax dollars to support processes that deny LGBTQ people the right to adopt or participate in the foster care system.

Domination is organized and reproduced to reinforce the normality of the domination. At the same time, domination compresses difference into a binary of normal (straight) and superior versus abnormal or deviant (queer) and inferior.

DISMANTLING STRAIGHT PRIVILEGE: ALTERNATE CONCEPTIONS OF IDENTITY AND EDUCATION

Audre Lorde (1985) wrote, "Some of the ways in which I identify myself make it difficult for you to hear me" (p. 3). The negative experience that occurs when a person is struggling with emergent identity produces emotional responses. For learning to occur from experience, feelings need to be processed. For some learners, there is no safe space to process feelings of being deviant or immoral.

Miller (2005) cautions that "the considerable struggle often involved in turning unpleasant aspects of experience into learning" (p. 79) should be acknowledged by educators. How do educators facilitate learning from experience? More to the point, how do educators facilitate learning from negative experiences when we cannot even name or recognize the experience of coming out in a society that condemns this as an immoral choice?

As educators, we need to see that, until equity is established for all of our students, none of our students will be truly free to speak and learn in a supportive environment. Few of us endeavor as researchers or instructors to understand what the polyrhythmic realities (Sheared, 1999) of our students really mean. For instance, a student in a marginalized group for whom we are actively seeking inclusion might also be in a group we discount, a privileged group, or a group invisible to us.

Moving the Boundaries of Identity

The fundamental nature of reality is fluid and indeterminate (Heisenberg, 1971). By extension, identities are fluid and based on interactions in relationships with self, others, and society. Fluid identities are consistent with a relational view of self (Tennant, 2000) and the nonunitary self (Clark and Dirkx, 2000). Identity can be viewed as "a dynamic web of interrelated events" (Capra, 1996, p. 39).

Consistent with queer theory, identity is fluid and indeterminate (Grace, Hill, Johnson, and Lewis, 2004). Sex is not a predetermined structure that someone is; rather, it is a range of possibilities that someone is becoming. The social construction of choice influences the "becoming" of all persons, not just queer people. The biological, social, economic, and political forces are currently defined by straight privilege to hide the social construction of heterosexuality. By redirecting these forces by reducing the negative implications of being queer, everyone's sexuality will be seen as an emerging possibility or pattern of becoming (Johnson, 2003).

Even though we believe a genetic predisposition or biology determines sexual orientation, how this predisposition plays out is influenced by historical and social contexts. During different periods of time, same-sex attraction has had a positive value, a negative value, and has been invisible. Certain concepts are used at different points in time to assign differential value to the social construction of sexual identity.

We posit six conditions that influence the social construction of sexual identity through time: (1) the strength of the genetic predisposition to be or not to be straight or queer; (2) the strength of the genetic predisposition to be male, female, or intersexed; (3) how each of us acts on these predispositions; (4) how our actions are perceived and interpreted by ourselves and others; (5) the strength of the response of family and community to these actions; and (6) how these actions are dictated by the social and cultural mores of the time.

The interplay of the conditions and binary characteristics in different contexts creates comfort or discomfort with sexual identity for both student and teacher. Using these six concepts, we can move the boundaries of identity by recognizing that identity is not static; at times, identity is internally or externally reduced to one characteristic and sometimes others.

So, for instance, if we view our students for the most part on a single facet of their identities—we see them first as male or female, black or white—we assume certain things about this single facet of their identities and use our power as teachers to sustain those assumptions. Teachers do not have to deconstruct assumptions because when most of us do social justice work, we assume we are already socially just. We don't see that we believe in different degrees of justice for different students or that we rank certain student's voices as more desirable to be heard.

One reason for only seeing a single facet of identity is because students with certain characteristics are observed as not moral and therefore can be dismissed. We can't know something exactly; rather, the very act of observing influences the perception (Heisenberg, 1971). The position and perspective of observer and observed influence what is seen and what is known.

The teacher and the learner are both observers to the teaching moment. For instance, the student who was offended by a remark about gay men felt silenced by the teacher. By his observation, the concern about stereotyping of LGBTQ people was set aside and was treated as not important enough to discuss. The teacher's observation was that the student would not assist with discussing this issue the teacher was not familiar with.

Mythmaking and Educational Consequences

The effects of straight privilege, moralizing, and myths about gay and lesbian people are felt in learning, educational opportunities, and teaching. Gay and lesbian adult learners are invisible, harassed, silenced, and in some cases physically assaulted. A student was outed by a dissertation committee member during her defense because the faculty member thought the "elephant in the room" or the student's "lesbianism" needed to be addressed in the findings of the dissertation. This created an uncomfortable situation and a forced disclosure of something not related to the task at hand just because the straight male faculty had the power to do so. When do we consider that a person's heterosexual orientation or heterosexism should be addressed in terms of the findings of any study?

Imagine being LGBTQ in formal sessions at work or in higher education and being asked to share experiences. A common assumption of adult education programs, theories, and teaching is that adults learn "throughout their lives, from their work and leisure, from their experience in social and domestic contexts, and from their personal relationships" (Miller, 2005, p. 72). Learning from experience and discussing the actual experiences in open forums may be too dangerous or uncomfortable for LGBTQ people who fear retaliation, misinterpretation, and prejudgment.

For instance, in an adult teaching and learning course I (Tonette) once taught, a woman whom I suspected was a lesbian stayed quiet through most class discussions and always when the discussion involved sharing personal stories. To my surprise, during the last session in a discussion about barriers to learning and pursuing higher education, she disclosed and announced that she had put off having a child. She and her partner would procreate once she graduated, indicating that family planning was a concern for lesbians, too. Obviously, she felt comfortable enough by that time to disclose such information but the fact is that she is a school teacher and teachers can and still do lose their jobs because of the myths surrounding sexual orientation.

Because of the invisibility, silencing, and discrimination, LGBTQ learners do not learn from experience in a safe space. Gay and lesbian learners are struggling with forming a positive self-identity in a discriminatory environment, pulling energy away from achieving lifelong learning goals. Straight learners are diminished through a lack of exposure, understanding, tolerance, and affirmation.

Educational opportunities are reduced through lack of engagement, fear, and oppression. Career opportunities are reduced when LGBTQ role models are not visible. Teachers who affirm LGBTQ experience in their classrooms may risk harassment and discrimination. Teachers may be fired or not even hired because of sexual identity.

Practicing Inclusive Pedagogy

Inclusive pedagogy advocates teaching practices that affirm the whole student in the learning process. This holistic vision includes a sense of the whole person who is connected to his or her surrounding context and environment. Inclusive pedagogy rejects the labeling and segregating of students, and encourages the use of a wide range of teaching and learning strategies to reach diverse populations.

One inclusive approach to learning is the use of various strategies, such as constructivist learning, which is based on the assumption that students construct their own meaning and understandings. This is facilitated through inquiry learning and problem solving. Knowledge is viewed as more fluid and less fixed. Another strategy acknowledges the inner life of the student and views education as a process wherein the student can transform him or herself (Miller, 2007).

In traditional (transmission) education, on the other hand, the teaching and learning exchange is seen as fixed and the teacher and learner have fixed roles. Behaviorism, cognitivism, and social learning theory predict that the teacher will have a specific type of influence on the student such as being able to change behavior, deposit new knowledge, or transform feelings and values. In this mechanistic view of learning, the teacher views the student as an object and a single-faceted entity to be manipulated. What we see as instructors when we look at our students is influenced by our values, morals, and the myths we believe about different characteristics of people.

If our moral code seeks equity for blacks and women, but we believe being gay is a lifestyle choice rather than a genetic trait, how then do we interact with a student who is black or a woman and also gay? Do we think issues around sexual orientation are important for us to learn about, speak about, and include in our concern for equity? Then if we think of the inherent power differential between teachers and learners, that teachers shape what is to be learned, and learners are there to learn it, what happens to the observer's power in creating reality?

Both players in the teaching-learning exchange influence each other by virtue of observing this reality. But is knowledge truly cocreated as we like to think when the teacher's very attitude toward specific characteristics such as sexual orientation creates a hostile environment for learning?

Current educational practices privilege "certain identities and hierarchies of knowledge" (Wells, 2004, p. 197). Heterosexual privilege results in controlling the knowledge of LGBTQ people through invisibility, silence, and oppression. The lives and experiences of LGBTQ students are marginalized in society and by extension in the classroom. By transforming our understanding of identity to a fluid movement rather than a fixed essence, everyone has the opportunity to be valued through observation, discussion, and learning.

Learners are patterns of becoming (Rocco and Gallagher, 2006) with sexual identity seen as a moment of permanence in an ocean of possibilities. With fluid identities, knowledge is not controlled; rather it influences the flow and pattern of experience (Burris, 2004).

Educators concerned with inclusive pedagogy argue that one's position and privilege (or lack of privilege) influences the learning process (Tisdell, 2001). Learning is about screening information in our environment (Taylor, 2001) and one's heterosexual privilege often screens out or makes invisible the experience of LGBTQ people. In higher education classrooms when LGBTQ issues are raised by the teacher, most students assume this is an external discussion and that no one in the class is queer.

The positionality of queer individuals deconstructs heteronormative privilege (Grace et al., 2004) and creates knowledge of queer experience. Hart (2001) writes, "My own location determines the possibilities of and limitations on what I can or should learn, unlearn, or relearn" (p. 180). The observer effect gives us an additional voice to acknowledge the power of one's position in the teaching-learning exchange.

Queer people advocate that there is a deeper pattern of just social relationships that emerge from allowing people to self-determine and self-develop their identities (Grace et al., 2004). Classroom experiences facilitate or inhibit self-determination through the dynamics of teacher-student, student-student, student-content, and class-institution interactions.

Many of our images of classroom dynamics are based on closed-system thinking in which we (teachers) have control over the inputs, processes, and outcomes (Pratt, 1998) when the reality is that we are part of an open, fluid environment that results in complex, often unintended learning. Yet teaching and learning is "a highly complex psychosocial drama" in which personalities of all players are displayed and observed, and in which the context and "prevailing political climate crucially affect the nature and form of learning" (Brookfield, 1986, p. vii).

A fear expressed in heterosexual-privileged discourse is that by acknowledging the variations in sex, sexuality, and gender, social control will be lost (Johnson, 2003). Hierarchical relationships supported by straight privilege include the male dominating the female, the heterosexual limiting the life choices of the homosexual, and the masculine over the feminine.

The network or web image of relationships allows us to see that everyone is connected to everyone else (Capra, 1996). In a network, "A person is defined by the relationship to others. . . . [T]his means then that my personal growth does not hinder yours. On the contrary it enhances it. . . . Anyone else's diminishment diminishes me" (Capra and Steindl-Rast, 1991, pp. 95–96). We do not see the pattern of just social relationships now because we are blinded by binary thinking (Johnson, 2003).

Teachers are challenged to practice inclusive pedagogy that affirms the presence of LGBTQ students and the contributions of LGBTQ people in their subject area (Macgillivray, 2004). One term, I (Tonette) taught a course on adult learning and teaching, raising queer issues whenever I could. This was disconcerting to the straight majority but some ventured forth honestly. Students talked about having co-workers who feared gay men as carriers of disease or lesbian women being dangerous because lesbians want to have sex with straight women.

Once students speak their truth, there exists a teachable moment or at least a moment when these attitudes might be deconstructed. I asked the class how it might feel to be a gay student in this class and hear this conversation. (That anyone might be gay in the class never occurred to anyone.) Because most of my students are Latina/o, I also asked whether they would be able to work comfortably at their jobs if they had to hide their Latin identity because myths about Latinas/os are that they carry disease and are hypersexed? At that point, the class had something to think about because in fact both these myths exist about Latinas/os.

CONCLUSION

There is no way to know if attitudes were changed. All I can say is my dean did not receive any letters of complaint and in several student presentations sexual orientation appeared as a discussion point. I believe it is the responsibility of those in privileged positions and those born with privilege to understand it. We talk about this in education, but how many of us are willing to risk our positions to take a stand? Inclusive pedagogy allows us to deconstruct the privilege that oppresses and marginalizes. Reconceptualizing the binary characteristics around sexuality can aid teachers in creating safe spaces for all learners.

REFERENCES

Abel, G., & Harlow, N. (2001). *The stop child molestation book.* Philadelphia: Xlibris.
Arriola, E. (2000). Gendered inequality. In R. Delgado and J. Stefanic (Eds.), *Critical race theory: The cutting edge* (second edition, pp. 322–24). Philadelphia: Temple University Press.
Blumenfeld, W. J. (2008, June 19). National versus states rights: A reflection. Essay posted to AERA Queer Studies Special Interest Group.
Brookfield, S. D. (1986). *Understanding and facilitating adult learning.* San Francisco: Jossey-Bass.
Burris, E. D. (2004). The "reality" of the classroom: Epistemological errors in teaching. In B. Davis, R. Luce-Kapler, and R. Upitis (Eds.), *Proceedings of the 2004 complexity science and educational research conference* (pp. 33–54). Chaffey's Locks, Ontario, Canada.
Cahill, C. M. (2007). The genuine article: A subversive economic perspective on the Law's procreationist vision of marriage. *Washington and Lee Law Review, 64,* 393–468.
Capra, F. (1996). *The web of life: A new scientific understanding of living systems.* New York: Anchor.
Capra, F., & Steindl-Rast, D., with T. Matus. (1991). *Belonging to the universe.* New York: HarperCollins.
Clark, J. M. (1993). *Beyond our ghettos: Gay theology in ecological perspective.* Cleveland: Pilgrim.
Clark, M. C., & Dirkx, J. M. (2000). Moving beyond a unitary self: A reflective dialogue. In A. L. Wilson and E. R. Hayes (Eds.), *Handbook of adult and continuing education* (pp. 101–16). San Francisco: Jossey-Bass.
Clarkson-Freeman, P. A. (2004). The defense of marriage act (DOMA): Its impact on those seeking same sex marriages. *Journal of Homosexuality, 48*(2), 1–19.
Dailey, T. J., (2009). InFocus: Ten facts about counterfeit marriage. *Family Research Council.* Retrieved on July 14, 2009, fromhttp://www.frc.org/content/ten-facts-about-same-sex-marriage.
Delgado, R., & Stefanic, J. (2001). *Critical race theory: An introduction.* New York: New York University Press.
Gamson, J. (2000). *Sexualities, queer theory, and qualitative research.* In N. K. Denzin and Y. S. Lincoln (Eds.), *The handbook of qualitative research* (second edition, pp. 347–65). Thousand Oaks, CA: Sage.
Goffman, E. (1963). *Stigma: Notes on the management of a spoiled identity.* New York: Simon and Schuster.
Goldberg-Hiller, J., & Milner, N. (2003, Autumn). Rights as excess: Understanding the politics of special rights. *Law and Social Inquiry, 28*(4), 1075–118.
Grace, A. P., Hill, R. J., Johnson, C. W., & Lewis, J. B. (2004). In other words: Queer voices/dissident subjectivities impelling social change. *International Journal of Qualitative Studies in Education, 17*(3), 1–24.
Haeberle, Erwin J. (2001–2005). Archive for sexology, critical dictionary of sexology. Retrieved June 25, 2005, fromhttp://www2.hu-berlin.de/sexology/index.html.
Hart, M. (2001). Transforming boundaries of power in the classroom: Learning from *La Mestiza.* In R. M. Cervero and A. L. Wilson (Eds.), *Power in practice: Adult education and the struggle for knowledge and power in society* (pp. 164–83). San Francisco: Jossey-Bass.
Heisenberg, W. (1971). *Physics and beyond.* New York: Harper and Row.
Hill, R. J. (1996). Learning to transgress: A sociohistorical conspectus of the American gay lifeworld as a site of struggle and resistance. *Studies in the Education of Adults, 28,* 253–79.

Hill, R. J. (2004). Activism as practice: Some queer considerations. In R. St. Clair and J. E. Sandlin (Eds.), The welfare-to-work challenge for adult literacy educators (pp. 85–94). *New Directions for Adult and Continuing Education* (p. 102), San Francisco: Jossey-Bass.

Ianinska, S., & Garcia-Zamor, J. C. (2006). Morals, ethics, and integrity: How codes of conduct contribute to ethical adult education practice. *Public Organization Review: A Global Journal, 6*(1), 3–20.

Johnson, T. (2003). *Gay perspective: Things our homosexuality tells us about the nature of God and the universe.* Los Angeles: Alyson.

Loving v. Virginia, 388 U.S. 1, 3 (1967).

Lorde, A. (1985). *I am your sister: Black women organizing across sexualities.* New York: Kitchen Table.

Macgillivray, I. K. (2004). *Sexual orientation and school policy.* Lanham, MD: Rowman and Littlefield.

Meijer, H. (1993). Can seduction make straight men gay? In J. P. DeCecco and J. P. Elia (Eds.), *If you seduce a straight person, can you make them gay? Issues in biological essentialism versus constructionism in gay and lesbian identities* (pp. 125–36). Binghamton, NY: Harrington Park.

Merriam-Webster's Collegiate Dictionary (2003, eleventh edition). CD-Rom Version 3. Springfield, MA: Merriam-Webster.

Miller, J. (2007). Holistic education: Learning for an interconnected world. In R. V. Farrell (Ed.), *Encyclopedia of life support systems (EOLSS).* Oxford, UK: EOLSS.

Miller, N. (2005). Learning from experience in adult education. In A. L. Wilson and E. R. Hayes (Eds.), *Handbook of adult and continuing education* (pp. 71–86). San Francisco: Jossey-Bass.

Montagu, A. (1942/1997). *Man's most dangerous myth: The fallacy of race* (sixth edition). Walnut Creek, CA: AltaMira.

Pharr, S. (1988). *Homophobia: A weapon of sexism.* Iverness, CA: Chardon.

Pratt, D. D. (1998). *Five perspectives on teaching in adult and higher education.* Melbourne, FL: Krieger.

Rocco, T. S., & Gallagher, S. J. (2006). Deconstructing heterosexual privilege with new science metaphors. In M. Hagen and E. Goff (Eds.) *Proceedings of the 47th adult education research conference* (pp. 312–17). Minneapolis–St. Paul: University of Minnesota.

Rocco, T. S., Landorf, H., & Delgado, A. (2009). Framing the issue/framing the question: Inquiry, inclusion, advocacy, or hostility? In T. S. Rocco, J. Gedro, and M. Kormanik (Eds.), Sexual minority issues in HRD: Raising awareness. *Advances in Developing Human Resources, 11*(1) 7–23.

Rocco, T. S., & West, G. W. (1998). Deconstructing privilege: An examination of privilege in adult education. *Adult Education Quarterly, 48*(3), 171–84.

Ruffulo, D. V. (2005, June). *Queering educational research in the academy: Disturbing binary sexualities for queer subjectivities.* Paper presented at Lesbian, Gay, Bisexual, Transgender, Queer, and Allies Preconference at the annual Adult Education Research Conference, University of Georgia, Athens, GA.

Sedgwick, E. K. (1993). Epistemology of the closet. In H. Abelove, M. A. Barale, and D. M. Halperin (Eds.), *The lesbian and gay studies reader* (pp. 45–61). New York: Routledge.

Sheared, V. (1999). Giving voice: Inclusion of African American students' polyrhythmic realities in adult basic education (pp. 33–48). *New Directions for Adult and Continuing Education, 82,* San Francisco: Jossey-Bass.

Smiley, T. (Broadcaster). (2004, November 4). The Tavis Smiley Show [Radio Broadcast]. Washington DC: National Public Radio and the African American Consortium.

Sweasey, P. (1997). *From queer to eternity: Spirituality in the lives of lesbian, gay, and bisexual people.* London: Cassell.

Taylor, M. C. (2001). *The moment of complexity: Emerging network culture.* Chicago: The University of Chicago Press.

Tennant, M. (2000). Adult learning for self-development and change. In A. L. Wilson and E. R. Hayes (Eds.), *Handbook of adult and continuing education* (pp. 187–100). San Francisco: Jossey-Bass.

Tisdell, E. J. (2001). The politics of positionality: Teaching for social change in higher education. In R. M. Cervero and A. L. Wilson (Eds.), *Power in practice: Adult education and the struggle for knowledge and power in society* (pp. 145–63). San Francisco: Jossey-Bass.

Webster's New Explorer Dictionary and Thesaurus. (1999). Springfield, MA: Federal Street.

Wells, K. (2004). Post perspectives: The critical roots of complexity-informed discourses in education. In B. Davis, R. Luce-Kapler, and R. Upitis (Eds.), *Proceedings of the 2004 Complexity Science and Educational Research Conference* (pp. 193–205). Chaffey's Locks, Ontario, Canada.

Wildman, S. M. (1996). The missing element. In S. M. Wildman, *Privilege revealed: How invisible preference undermines America* (pp. 25–42). New York: New York University Press.

Young, I. M. (1990). *Justice and the politics of difference*. Princeton, NJ: Princeton University Press.

Chapter Nine

Teaching the Taboo

*Including Sexual Orientation
in Teacher Preparation Courses*

Stephanie L. Daza

Taboo means "excluding something from use, approach, or mention because of its sacred and inviolable nature" (*American Heritage Dictionary*, 2001). Using this definition, I refer to this research project as "teaching the taboo" because the courses under study—my own courses—attempt to interrupt what often is considered natural and sacred, such as normative discourses about US society and the assumption of education as library. At the same time, they include subjects, such as privilege and sexual orientation, rarely mentioned in noncritical, multicultural education diversity courses.

Most participants—often preservice teachers who plan to work with PK–12 students or practicing teachers who already work with PK–12 students—take these courses to fulfill a so-called diversity requirement of some sort. Most participants do not expect to be asked to dig deep into their own backgrounds and schooling experiences or to imagine schooling and teaching as part of the problem of inequity instead of the solution. (To avoid confusing students in these courses with PK–12 students and because neither "preservice teachers" nor "teachers" accurately reflects all the participants in the courses, I use the term *participants* to refer to the students who take these courses.)

The following anonymous comments help to illustrate participant expectations:

> In the course, I hope to gain knowledge on getting the students to understand and to learn about every student's culture and how to create a mathematics curriculum that can reach to all students from all backgrounds.

> The main things I would like to learn about in this course are how to create a diverse community in the classroom where everyone can learn and learn to embrace differences in others. I want to learn what are the proper ways to incorporate different aspect of cultures and background into the classroom without making others feel uncomfortable.
>
> When I first started this course, I had to sit down and think about myself in terms of how my upbringing has affected my current views on education. As I looked at that autobiography, I began to fear that I would be misunderstood and stereotyped into the typical suburban white girl. [I asked] is this also racial profiling? However, once I attended class I realized that this was one of the points this course was trying to make; how to avoid stereotyping.

As these comments show, participants often begin these courses expecting to study about cultural diversity in ways that are comfortable, apolitical or neutral, and not about them. When they find out the courses asks them to go deeper, they sometimes express trepidation.

Some participants also come to the course with more critical expectations or develop them after being introduced to the course, as captured in the following kinds of comments:

> Before Thursday I had no idea what I wanted from this course, but after going to the first class I found what I wanted to take away. If nothing else I would like to take away the ability to look at things in a more critical manner. I would like to learn not to take things at face value and learn how to ask the hard questions as to why something is the way it is. Asking these questions I can make a difference in life.
>
> I want to learn how to respect student differences while asking students to question some of their deepest values. . . . I want to interrogate my own assumptions about education as both a tool for liberation and oppression. I want to learn about teacher self-disclosure of identity(ies) in the classroom and its positive and negative effects on student learning.

Although many participants reveal more critical expectations, overall participants come to the course expecting to focus on "all" students and "others" (e.g., students of color), but for the most part not on themselves or whites and white privilege (Solomona, Portelli, Daniel, and Campbell, 2005), let alone LGBTQI (lesbian, gay, bisexual, transgender, queer/questioning, and intersex) populations and heteronormativity.

Heteronormativity refers to discourses, practices, and policies of power that produce heterosexuality as normal (Pillow, 2004). It is underpinned by other normalizing discourses about sex, gender, and sexual orientation and in turn helps to construct and maintain such discourses. Of course, norms are social constructs. As Varney (2001) explains, "for normal to exist, one must have deviants" (p. 88); so heteronormativity works in conjunction with sex and gender "norms" to produce and maintain binary norms of sexual orientation (gay-straight and heterosexual-homosexual) that rely on, as well as reinforce, binary norms of sex (male-female biology) and gender (men and boys–woman and girls).

"While sex concerns one's anatomy and physiology," Blount (2005) explains, "gender is a set of stories that people tell themselves and each other about what it means to be men and women. The stories are as varied as the individuals and the cultures in which they live. Sex-related anatomy and physiology can vary substantially: therefore a person's sex is not always as clearly drawn as the polarized female/male model might indicate" (p. 14). Blount continues, "Sexual orientation . . . concerns sexual desire, [but] gendered behaviors, characteristics, or identities assist individuals in navigating sexual choices within their cultures" (p. 14). Like gender, sexual orientation is partly socially constructed, not completely fixed, and can vary depending on cultural and historical context (Foucault, 1985/1990, 1986/1988, 1978/1990).

The research and analysis represented here has implications for "teaching the taboo" both in higher education and PK–12. It specifically argues for the inclusion of sexual orientation in teacher education and against teacher education that fails to provide teachers with the theoretical tools required to perceive and interrupt deficit frameworks that maintain inequalities in school and society.

This chapter reflects some preliminary analysis of data that I have been collecting from mostly teacher preparation courses, especially diversity courses, over the last decade at both the graduate and undergraduate level in three institutions. To help contextualize the study and me as a queer of color teacher-researcher, I review relevant literature and terms, as well as provide two short vignettes of my own experiences. Then I discuss the ongoing collection and analysis of data from these courses and some of the emerging implications for teaching the taboo in teacher education.

MULTICULTURE NOT MULTICULTURAL

Ellsworth (1999) demonstrates, and not purely in the grammatical sense, that "multicultural" as the descriptor in "multicultural education," subordinates multicultural education to education, positioning education as regular, normal, valued, and mainstream. The same could be argued about "multicultural society."

Whatever or whoever are not the main subjects are the "others"—and what is different than the main subject (the norm) often is considered less than or deficient (Bartolomé, 2008). Instead, Ellsworth (1999) uses the term *multiculture* and I employ that term herein. Neither an ideology nor a choice, multiculture, although not static, just is (Ellsworth, 1999; Oakes and Lipton, 2007).

Who is "othered" and questions of whether or not to school so called "others" and how to do it are neither new, nor unique to the United States, although they play out differently for different groups and contexts given that they are (re)produced through distinct local and global contexts and forces, power-knowledge dynamics, histories, and logics (Cochran-Smith, 2004; Ladson-Billings and Brown, 2008). In the United States, trends in educating "others" (particularly as part of, or separate from, all multiculture) ebb and flow; focus on race and ethnicity, ability, and language; and may vary for different groups (Anderson, 1988; Coloma, 2006; Lomawaima and McCarty, 2006; MacDonald, 2004; Sadker and Sadker, 1994; Spring, 2005; Yoshino, 2006).

DIVERSITY COURSES, IDENTITY MARKERS, AND (DE)POLITICIZATION: SOME RELEVANT LITERATURE

Although the content of diversity courses is difficult to determine, some research points to the limited inclusion of sexual orientation. In Jennings's (2007) research, race and ethnicity are the most covered diversity topics and sexual orientation is ignored or the least covered diversity topic in the teacher education programs he surveyed. Gender, a separate concept but thoroughly intertwined with sexual orientation, is the next least covered topic.

In addition to lack of time relative to other necessary topics in the program, student disinterest, and university opposition, Jennings's (2007) study found that lack of interest, knowledge, and comfort of teacher education faculty, regardless of their own identity markers, affected inclusion of diversity topics in their programs. Although *Getting Reading for Benjamin: Preparing Teachers for Sexual Diversity in the Classroom* (Kissen, 2002) and other materials (Gay, Lesbian, and Straight Education Network [GLSEN], 2003a; Lipkin, 2004) are available, there is little to indicate that they are being adequately used by teacher educators or teachers (Kosciw, Diaz, and Greytak, 2008).

Blackburn and Donelson (2004) explain that, although:

> progress has been made in the past decade by those who seek to encourage a more tolerant and pluralistic society by recognizing sexual orientation as a legitimate identity marker ... [and] there has been wider acceptance in the popular culture of individuals whose sexual identities deviate from those of the dominant culture ... conversations that merge discussions of what it means to be outside the mainstream in terms of sexual identities with schooling [may still be considered taboo]. (p. 99)

Likewise, Blount's (2005) history, *Fit to Teach: Same-Sex Desire, Gender, and School Work in the Twentieth Century*, documents that, despite a variety of promising events for sexual minorities in the early twenty-first century, ultimately "school workers learn that to remain above reproach, they must modify any personal behavior, fashion, relationships, or other facet of their lives that might cast doubt on their sexual orientation or gender identity" (p. 1). According to Blount, "just as they were 100 years ago, school workers today are hired in part to model and preserve normative sexuality and gender" (p. 182).

Diversity courses often focus on education for and about others from a "depoliticized anthropological perspective that focuses on group descriptions and the implications of such descriptions for teaching" (Jennings, 2007, p. 1265) and not on critiquing privilege or examining underlying policies and practices that stratify society and schooling (Kumashiro, 2002). They also essentialize heterogeneous population groups (e.g., gays, Asian-Americans, women, whites) as homogeneous, teach tolerance but not equity, and often reinforce rather than interrupt deficit thinking about difference and others (Gorski, 2005). For example, "others" are positioned as problems and subordinated to "regular" (mainstream) students and groups, while education and teachers often are positioned as the liberators (saviors) of oppressed, disadvantaged, and nonprivileged population groups (Ladson-Billings, 1998).

A politicized, complicated, and nuanced view of education and public schooling as both tools of liberation *and* subordination may not be presented (Ayers, Quinn, and Stovall, 2009; Spring, 2005). Often privileged groups and privilege within populations groups are not really included, let alone the structures, policies, practices, and discursive norms (e.g., heteronormativity, patriarchy, white privilege, etc.) that underpin inequalities (Sleeter, 1996).

Diversity may be narrowly defined as race and even more specifically in the United States within a black-white binary (Subedi and Daza, 2008). Also, differences (e.g., ability, race, enthnolinguistic affiliation, sexual orientation, gender, etc.) may be simplified and compartmentalized rather than complex and intersectional (Crenshaw, 1991, 1995; Lugg, 2003). Members of such courses may be asked neither to examine their own identity markers and center or periphery positions in groups nor to interrogate and interrupt their own complicity, and the complicity of education, in deficit thinking and maintaining inequity.

Diversity courses may become significant when it is time to show how diversity requirements of certification and accreditation are being met, but may be positioned as less important than content and method courses and sometimes as an add-on or extra burden, rather than vital (Cochran-Smith, 2004). "Yet," as Oakes and Lipton (2007) clearly evince, "persistent patterns of unequal conditions, resources, and opportunities in and outside of school that are related to students' race and social class underlie the disparities in students' achievement" (p. 5) and teachers often do not have the "professional groundwork of social theory and educational research" required to teach multiculture in such an "unequal landscape" (p. xx). Therefore, as Bartolomé (2008) argues, educators need to be prepared to recognize and counter negative, deficit views of "others" that influence teacher education and also may be normalized and internalized by them.

THE LIMITED VALUE OF VALUE-NEUTRAL

Unfortunately, US education today generally (re)enforces a depoliticized (noncritical, apparently value-free) approach to teaching "diversity" to teachers (or eliminates it all together in some cases) and backpedals toward reductionist ways of thinking about and teaching multiculture (hooks, 1994; Sleeter, 2008). This is adequately described by Taubman (2009) as "teaching by numbers" in his book of the same title. According to Sleeter (2008),

> In this context, teacher education programmes are being compelled to jettison not only explicit equity-oriented teacher preparation, but also learner centered teaching, in order to prepare technicians.... Some of this pressure has taken the form of revisions to standards for teacher preparation, reducing or eliminating reference to social justice, multicultural education, or bilingual education. (p. 1952)

This reductionist, depoliticized approach is ineffective and rejected by those who recognize difference as (re)produced through power relationships and its influence on multiculture (Kumashiro, 2004, 2008; Nieto, Bode, Kang, and Raible, 2008). Value-neutral languages, curricula, policies, and practices only appear colorless, genderless, and so forth; they are anything but.

Whereas sexual orientation has begun only recently to be considered an identity marker and topic in teacher diversity courses, race as an identity marker and topic is well established. Thus, although different from sexual orientation, a look at how this work on race is playing out is informative. Pollock's (2004) research makes clear that so-called value-neutral approaches to race (e.g., colormuted approaches) actually have everything to do with skin color and race; indeed, she states, there is "talk of education for 'all'.... [but] race is deeply buried in the word—and as a policy word that is colormute and race-loaded simultaneously, 'all' can be both a useful and dangerous word for equality efforts" (p. 74).

Moreover, Ladson-Billings and Brown (2008), writing about curriculum and cultural diversity specifically, note that the articulation of this work in schools "never goes beyond what Banks calls the contributions and additive approaches" (p. 154). Rather, they explain that "the mainstream United States curriculum functions as a default against which all efforts to challenge it either fail or are incorporated in ways that fail to result in real change" (p. 154). In other words, depoliticized (value-neutral) language is not value-neutral at all but rather mainstream views of identity are embedded within it; it also can be both mute and loaded at the same time.

While education for "all" might be mobilized for equality efforts, it also may serve to maintain the status quo, where *mainstream* is actually white-stream, malestream, and straightstream. As I described at the beginning of this chapter, this is similar to how multicultural education remains subordinate to education (Ellsworth, 1999).

Thus, efforts like this edited volume and my research herein do provide some hope for the inclusion of sexual orientation in diversity studies for educators and for politicized, or not depoliticized, diversity studies that may lead to more socially just schooling for multiculture in the twenty-first century. However, this hope is tempered by the magnitude of both the quantity and quality of work needed if we want US education and schooling institutions to be more equitable and less sexist, racist, homophobic places to work and study. Many have begun to argue, albeit in diverse ways, that this work must be done not only in the name of equity but if we want these places to exist as public spaces at all (Darling-Hammond, 2010; Giroux, 2009; Newfield, 2008; Quinn and Meiners, 2009).

Yet many members of the multiculture navigated PK–16 schooling and have gone on to live, work, and write against the grain as scholars, activists, parents, and so on. Some opened up concrete and intellectual spaces for the rest of us. In spite of being schooled in such places, exemplars such as Gloria Anzuldúa, Audre Lorde, and bell hooks became writers, researchers, and educators and found ways to hope, to survive, to thrive, to tell their counter-tales (Anzaldúa, 1987/1999; Lorde, 1984), and to teach to transgress (hooks, 1994). Following their lead, in the following section I tell and partially analyze two personal narratives with the intent of contextualizing my study of teaching the taboo and myself as a researcher.

VIGNETTE 1: "POWER IS THE ABILITY NOT TO HAVE TO LEARN"

After teaching multiculture student populations for about five years in California public schools, I served as a US Peace Corps volunteer (PCV) in Bolivia between 1998 and 2000. I was among a handful of PCVs who started a friends, lesbians, and gays (FLAG) group for volunteers. At our conference for all Peace Corps employees, we had one of our first meetings. As we introduced ourselves, most people took this opportunity to identify as "friend," "lesbian," "gay," or "bisexual." Some who identified as "friends" also shared that they had family members, co-workers, and others who were gays and lesbians.

Many commented that it felt good to be "out" among PCVs. This event remains particularly salient for me for several reasons. First, when it was my turn to introduce myself, I struggled to find a fitting term and rambled something about being more than a friend, not a lesbian, not straight, and kind of bi. The term *queer* was not yet part of my vocabulary, let alone a descriptor. Second, one of our Peace Corps program coordinators stated that he was glad PCVs were coming out and that he, as a coordinator, "should have been one of the first . . . leading the way."

This coordinator's disclosure has helped give me the courage to be queer in the academy. As an academic, this particularly translates into writings like this chapter and an ongoing commitment to LGBTQI peoples and queer issues.

In retrospection, this experience also made me ask why a certified, practicing teacher in the 1990s lacked fluency in the basic vocabulary of sexual orientation? The simple answer is Bateson's (1989): "power is the ability not to have to learn." I grew up, was schooled, and taught in a heteronormative world that constructed me as heterosexual. As a female who publicly dated a male, I didn't have to recognize heteronormativity or learn much about LGBTQI communities, even though I did not self-identify as straight.

With few exceptions, my teacher preparation and subsequent professional development provided a technocratic view of education (Labaree, 1997; Shumar, 1997; Taubman, 2009), a deficit view of diversity (Cochran-Smith, 2003), and no view at all of sexual orientation. I was not asked to interrogate my white privilege as a light-skinned, brown woman, nor was I pushed to complicate my complicity in meritocracy as a graduate of a high-priced, private liberal arts college or my shame at being the poor kid on that campus. Perhaps this is just as well, because I had limited theoretical lenses required for such tasks and my analysis likely would have been skewed by and incorporated into mainstream (default) sense-making (see Ladson-Billings and Brown, 2008).

In my view, one of the major limitations of teacher education programs is the emphasis on content to the detriment of educational foundations, theory, and pedagogy. In my particular case, however, my content background in English provided me with some limited theoretical lenses and analytical skills. As an English major, I acquired at least some background in feminist literary theory (e.g., Dillard, 1982), limited exposure to (mostly white) lesbian perspectives (e.g., Rich, 1980), and some theoretical literacy needed to analyze texts and experiences. By "theoretical literacy," I mean social practices and conceptions of reading, writing, and interpreting the word and the world (Freire and Macedo, 1987; Street, 1984).

Developing, appropriating, and modifying theoretical literacies to analyze texts and experiences from multiple perspectives is an ongoing living-process; my limited exposure as an undergraduate was helpful but not sufficient to prepare me for understanding my own identity markers or for teaching diverse populations. As I further developed theoretical literacies through graduate school and also lived experiences with diverse (especially indigenous) populations, I was able to make different kinds of sense out of my experiences—sense-making that did not rely on interpreting experience from a mainstream perspective to fit mainstream views of what and who is normal, valued and devalued, or deviant.

Perhaps the PCV FLAG meeting was the first time I tried to say out loud that I was queer. Even though I had not yet reclaimed the once pejorative word *queer* that I use to describe myself today, I was grasping for a way of naming my own sexual orientation. Certainly at that time, I was uncomfortable talking about sexuality or sexualities that were not reducible to a gay-straight binary (Kumashiro, 2002).

Because I could "fit in" to the heteronormative mainstream and because I was not pushed in my education to learn otherwise, I also failed to learn what I needed to teach for a more socially just world. Now, as a postsecondary educator, I am arguing for education programs and courses that will help build theoretical literacy and teach the taboo.

VIGNETTE 2: SEXUALITIES, EDUCATION, AND THE BIG THREE

Before I was given the economic privilege of a university fellowship, I was a busy high school teacher by day and a graduate student by night. Assigned to hall duty at my large public high school in a city district, I first saw two students who were half-carrying another student. Then I saw blood. The student, who was out as a lesbian, had been beaten and tossed in a trash dumpster on school property. The friends had already called the student's mom. It's important to note that administration and some teachers had labeled this student "a problem kid." It probably had a lot to do with her public and performed self-identity as a lesbian, such as holding hands with her partner and her multiple face piercings, buzzed hair, and so called "boy" clothes. When we entered the main office, which was where both the principal and the nurse were located, the principal's first question was not "Are you okay?" or "What happened?" but "Have you been drinking?" In my view, his interrogation of the victim continued to get worse. The student's mom, who had arrived, and the rest of us, knew her daughter was beaten for her gender expression and her sexual orientation.

Theory is often discredited and politicized, as if value-neutral practice exists, but in this situation I saw the value of theoretical literacies that allowed for a more complicated and nuanced interpretation of this experience. I saw that different people in different positions interpreted the same situation differently. It seemed to me then, and still seems now, that some interpretations were more socially just than others. Clearly, interpretations may be at odds and contested. Because institutional and policy norms, not to mention curricula, are grounded in mainstream ideology, they often mitigate educational experiences (e.g., administrator actions) to fit mainstream conceptions.

This experience greatly reinforced my commitment to develop coursework to build theoretical literacy around the needs of LGBTQI communities. At the same time, a group assignment in one of my graduate seminars was to analyze an existing diversity education course or to develop a new one. My group chose to develop a new course on sexualities and education. We would conduct the research not just on the course topic, but on estimated enrollment, policy, and law; write the new course and its proposal; develop a syllabus; successfully navigate its inclusion on various programs of study and for meeting certain general education requirements; and eventually shepherd the course through the various committees until it was offered.

As the only member of the group still around after this process was complete, I was the first to teach the course. As a teacher, I have always assessed my courses but this experience ushered in a more systematic effort. Since that time, I have been analyzing my own teaching and courses and this article stems from that work.

As a graduate student at a flagship institution, I think it is rare to be able to develop a new course and see it institutionalized (and especially to be approved to meet some general education requirements). And it is probably rarer when the topic is sexual orientation and education. But through this experience, I learned that institutional norms can be navigated towards *teaching the taboo*. For that year only, three professors—to me "the big three"—were self-identifying lesbians and feminists and one was in a strategic administrator role.

More than having an identity marker in common, however, I believe these professors were committed to the idea of teaching the taboo and working within and against mainstream institutional norms. From my perspective, this triad helped make possible the fertile ground from within which the institutionalizing of a new course on sexual orientation and education could emerge. They had the skills and power (and graduate students) to navigate institutional dynamics.

I wonder if this course would have made it onto the books in other years. It existed well before the recent attention to LGBTQI research called for by the Queer Study Special Interest Group of the American Educational Research Association or LGBTQI needs in the wake of 2010s teen suicides, which only serve to solidify the need for more curricula, courses, and research.

RESEARCH METHODS FOR TEACHING THE TABOO

As Ayers, Quinn, Stovall, and Scheiern (2008) clearly delineate, narrative approaches, although perhaps "difficult for some researchers," are necessary to teacher education research that wants to avoid putting "teacher experience into brief, general, neatly outlined packages," but rather wants to analyze "the messy, complicated picture of teacher work with multiple contexts, interpretations, and impositions of curriculum" (p. 309). Thus, "autobiography that makes a difference in the way children are educated is grounded in social action" (p. 309) and "historically, [these approaches] have been a foundation for qualitative research because they focus on social fractures and contradiction as well as personal ones" (Ayers, Quinn, Stovall, and Scheiern, 2008, p. 307), particularly in efforts to produce different knowledge differently (St. Pierre, 1997).

Qualitative research together with critical theoretical perspectives of difference interrupts empirical inquiry as value-neutral; deconstructs mainstream ideologies that subordinate "others"; and (re)generates methodologies like counter storytelling for academic inquiry. Qualitative inquiry is heterogeneous on purpose. Data, participants, and researchers are analyzed as (re)produced through relations of power and not left to "speak for themselves." For a discussion of the role of critical race theory, see Ladson-Billings and Brown (2008, p. 154). For queer, postcolonial, and "post" perspectives in qualitative research, see Daza (2008, 2009), Rhee and Subreenduth (2006), and Lather (2009).

At the end of the day, "assessing the complexity and messiness of practice-in-context is the strength of qualitative research" (Lather, 2009, p. 10). In this sense of qualitative research, a limitation of the analysis presented in this article is the space to better complicate the data analysis, especially the quoted material and vignettes. A more nuanced analysis might better emphasize the researcher as instrument and would not let the data simply "speak for itself;" in this sense, I am providing somewhat of a "realist-tale" (Van Mannen, 1988) that might be critically reinterpreted in subsequent work and by readers.

Data for this chapter come from an ongoing study of education courses (primarily "diversity" courses) that have been taken by more than seven hundred preservice and practicing teachers at both the graduate and undergraduate level in three institutions in two different geographical regions. Nine different teacher preparation courses, offered in various formats—face-to-face; hybrid format (traditional classroom meetings and online components); and fully online through various course platforms such as WebCT, Blackboard, and ECollege—are included in the study. Several of the courses specifically focus on multiculture and schools for a diverse and democratic society.

Three of the nine courses were undergraduate courses mostly taken by participants preparing to teach in PK–12 school settings. The graduate courses included both preservice teachers seeking certification and practicing teachers seeking a master's degree. Administrators, social workers, corporate trainers, and others also have taken the graduate courses, often in order to fulfill a so-called diversity requirement.

Similar to the national norm for the teaching workforce, members of my courses often self-identify as white, English-speaking, heterosexual, middle-class females. Additionally, my courses include males, LGBTQIs, and participants who identify themselves nationally (e.g., Ukrainian) or racially, ethnically, regionally (e.g. African Americans, Latino/as, Asians, Asian Pacific Islanders, and South Asians), and as biracial or multiracial.

Although much is made of the fact that the US teaching workforce, especially in public schools, is dominated by white women who are less racially and ethnically diverse then the populations they teach (Oakes and Lipton, 2007, pp. 473–74), this group should not be considered homogeneous. Lumping white women teachers together ignores the various backgrounds, experiences, values, and beliefs of this group that were made obvious in the data over and over again. As I have written elsewhere (Daza, 2008), similar language, skin color, and other identity markers do *not necessarily* indicate group affiliations or similar views.

The collection of, and reflection on, participant feedback on the courses I teach is part and parcel of pedagogy for teacher-researchers interested in improving teaching and learning (Fink, 2003). Participant perceptions of the content (readings, videos, websites, etc.), the instruction (format and teaching methods), and the instructors (me and any teaching assistants) are considered. Data include solicited and nonsolicited feedback. Some of this data has been collected in the form of anonymous surveys of teaching given by the institutions.

As part of my regular instructional practice, participants may respond to an anonymous, volunteer survey, as well. Participant feedback found in assignment reflections, course discussions, and email communications also is included. In adherence to my ethical commitments and the parameters of using existing data per my institutional review board, data are shared obscurely to keep participants, specific course offerings, and locations anonymous, as well as to deter to the extent possible connections among participants, courses, and institutions.

For the purpose of this chapter, survey data come from sections of one graduate-level, diversity course in which a reflective survey was available for two consecutive years, and four semesters. In total, 53.8 percent possible course members responded (n = 49). Specifically, one of fifty survey variables directly addresses gay issues. Using a five-point Likert scale ("strongly disagree" to "strongly agree"), course members could respond to the statement "Gay issues and information about people who identify as Gay, Lesbian, Bisexual, Transgender, or Queer should be included in diversity courses for educators."

Although not to be considered value-neutral (Cohen, Manion, and Morrison, 2007; Lather, 2007), a more thorough measurement of survey data will be conducted and reported in subsequent publications of the study. Likert scales, although limited in various ways, are useful because "they build in a degree of sensitivity and differentiation of response while still generating numbers" (Cohen et al., 2007, p. 325).

To address some of these limitations, the data also include open-ended questions (Cohen et al., 2007), material artifacts (syllabi, participant-produced work such as websites, instructor feedback,) and participant observation. As well, analysis considers McCall's (2001) cautions in the use of interval-scaled scores and suggestions for using percentages and collapsed categories.

In this research, theories of critical qualitative research prevail over quantification and data are coded and compared to develop themes and patterns (Denzin and Lincoln, 2005). NVivo qualitative software and SNAP online survey software are used. Although preliminary analysis appears to show differences in perceptions based on course type, program of study, identity and background, and institution, data are not disaggregated here and data collection and analysis is ongoing.

TEACHING THE TABOO EMERGING THEMES

The themes and implications offered here are emerging from my preliminary analysis of the data archive; data will continue to be scrutinized as part of the analysis process. Two findings are discussed.

First, data show course members' perceptions of teaching the taboo. They value and find useful a politicized approach to diversity courses for educators and agree with including gay issues and information about people who identify as gay, lesbian, bisexual, transgender, or queer in diversity courses for educators. Secondly, however, the data also show that some participants express their desire for and use of depoliticized language (neutral, genderless, colormuted, etc.) instead of politicized language (white privilege, etc.).

POLITICIZED DIVERSITY AND GAY ISSUES: OKAY FOR TEACHER EDUCATION

Not only does data suggest that most participants value the course and its perspective that politicizes, rather than depoliticizes, diversity and multicultural education, data also indicate that course participants are on board with including gay issues in diversity courses for educators. Most course participants indicated that multiculture education is needed in rural and suburban schools, not just urban ones; that teachers should teach for social justice; and that privilege, such as a critique of white privilege, should be included.

Only one person identified as LGBTQI on the volunteer survey, but 84 percent of responders agreed gay issues and information about people who identify as LGBTQI should be included in diversity courses for educators. Only six course participants disagreed that this information about LGBTQIs should be included in diversity courses for educators. A more nuanced analysis is needed, but it is interesting to compare this percentage with the percentage agreeing that diversity and multicultural education courses for teachers should include the study of privilege (71 percent), white supremacy (67 percent), issues of ability (98 percent), and critiques of patriarchy (55 percent).

The following anonymous comments are reflective of the perceptions of participants overall:

> Diversity courses should not censor these topics. . . . [I]f they are ignored [in teacher education courses] then teachers will ignore them in the classroom and that can be extremely detrimental for students . . . [including] those raised in white privileged homes or patriarch[al] families.
> I like the way this [course] worked—some of the content made people really mad and I believe that is what gets people thinking.
> Diversity courses should address the underlying issues that are left unspoken. They should address the issues that people do not normally think about. Everybody knows what lies on the surface; we all know the distinct differences amongst each other. The important thing is for us to realize that we may hold underlying [prejudice] that was never realized before.
> Content was appropriate because all views, from one extreme to another, were presented.

In general, course members support a politicized view of difference in their teacher preparation courses and felt that different perspectives on difference were respected.

Participants also used the information in the course to critically analyze policies, curricula, and lived experience in schools and classrooms. Their conversations show the need for the inclusion of sexual orientation in teacher education courses and how it might be useful not only in deconstructing heteronormativity but in supporting students directly. Their comments also show that they already began using the information presented in the course. The following comment refers to an observation of a high school English class done by a course member and the film s/he watched titled *It's Elementary*.

> There was downtime before the bell rang and the students were lounging around, talking and being teenagers. One of the boys was telling a story that ended with someone calling someone else "faggot." He said it loud, laughing. The teacher asked if that was nice language to use, almost half joking herself. [The student] admitted it wasn't, but defended himself by saying he was just telling a story, he wasn't really saying it. Then things went back to normal, no more was said. I thought about the film. And the impact it would have on a young gay or confused student if a teacher pushed back hard against the use of such slurs.

This comment shows how a course member is using content materials in the course, such as films and articles, to critically analyze field experiences.

Data also indicate that course members, especially during and after the course, were not naïve about the implications of teaching the taboo—of the possibilities and dangers of "pushing back hard" against heteronormativity—in PK–12 institutions. The next comment shows that a politicized and nuanced view of diversity in teacher education courses can be very useful, if not crucial, to classroom teachers and their students.

> I want to start educating my second graders to have respect for other cultures and study other cultures in greater depth. For example, just last week one student called another student gay and the student became very upset. When I questioned both students about the meaning of "gay," they had no idea what it meant, but they knew it was something bad. However, I do feel like I have to be very careful because of the politics of my school and the community.

Not only was this teacher able to interrupt the pejorative use of the word "gay" in a second grade glass, s/he was aware of the politics in doing so.

THE MINORITY REPORT

There were also conflicting perspectives about the course. Some participants perceived the course as too focused on one group or another, as illustrated by the following comments:

> It seemed that this entire course was set up to bash white people . . . how about showing the other side of that coin . . . not always having students read about how wrong white people are.
> I think the Gay/Lesbian issue was brought up way more than it had to be.
> In service teachers should be made aware of customs, religious beliefs, mores and norms of a wide variety of cultures, not just Hispanic, in order to value and affirm all our students.
> Because of the magnitude of reading, I think several of the other readings could have been reduced or eliminated especially the ones that just kept going back and harping on white privilege or gay/lesbian issues.

> I strongly urge you not to choose readings that constantly insult, berate, and call us racist. I think it would be much, much more advantageous to offer some positive accolades to the sacrifice and effort we make for our students day in and day out—students of color, white students, diverse learners, homeless students, rich students, abused students, suicidal students, gay, straight, gifted, handicapped, ED, LD, ESL, ELL . . . whatever you want to call them. We, the white, female, middle class get up early every day to inspire, encourage, and teach them—all of them. This class insulted me and my heritage in almost every assignment.

These data demonstrate that some participants perceived the course as focusing too much on one group or topic or another. At this preliminary stage in the analysis, the most polemic feedback tends to be about race, whiteness, and white privilege. Although there are many conversations and comments about the inclusion of gay issues and heteronormativity in schools, only the two comments cited here were coded as explicitly negative.

NEUTRALITY AND COMFORT: EMPOWERING OR DISEMPOWERING?

Some of the comments in this chapter's introduction and in the "Minority Report" section illustrate a desire for, and use of, depoliticized language (e.g., "all our students," "all backgrounds," "where everyone can learn," and "without making others feel uncomfortable"). Some of these comments also seem to illustrate that politicized languages, especially about racial inequity and white privilege, makes some course members uncomfortable (e.g., "harping on white privilege," "readings . . . constantly insult, berate, and call us racist," and "This class insulted me and my heritage in almost every assignment.").

Not only do some participants prefer to be comfortable, some, as one comment suggests, also prefer to be centered and praised as the saviors of "others" (e.g. "offer some positive accolades to the sacrifice and effort we make")—a common positioning for white teachers of "others" (Ladson-Billings, 1998). There is a need to further analyze and perhaps disrupt comfort, safety, and the teacher as savior, given the dominance of (1) the teacher as savoir discourse, (2) (mis)constructions of student-centered pedagogy that treat students as clients and customers (Paris, 2001), and (3) appropriation of safety by the security industry among others (Robbins, 2008).

However, the interruption of comfort—safe spaces—in classrooms is too complex to flesh out here except to mention that it might produce competing meanings, such as inclusivity for "others" (GLSEN, 2003b) and respect for multiple, conflicting, minority views or teaching that avoids challenge and resistance (Dahlgren and Masyada, 2009). It is important to note that safety is at least in part being coopted to (re)produce a depoliticized understanding of diversity and processes that can result in shutting down real learning and change (Loutzenheiser, 2001), and promote the militarization of schools and youth (Robbins, 2008).

Finally, it also should be noted that talking about sexual orientation and other identity markers in politicized ways related to equity and inequity can be dangerous and uncomfortable for instructors and students in both center and the periphery positions for varying reasons.

IMPLICATIONS OF TEACHING THE TABOO IN EDUCATION

Discussions about diversity in society have particular implications to the field of education in the United States because they help us further understand how the schooling process (including interpretations of curriculum) is shaped by dominant viewpoints of knowledge (Subedi, 2010). Some research has shown that students simply reinterpret curriculum based on their own background and experiences in mainstream discourses; thus, often from a position of white or heteronormative privilege, privilege is denied and deficit perspectives reinforced (Solomona et al., 2005).

There is limited research on how participants in teacher education programs interpret curricula on sexual orientation, particularly in online courses. With a specific focus on sexual orientation, this chapter sheds light on the purpose of diversity courses in teacher preparation, the importance of including sexual orientation, how politicized diversity and the inclusion of sexual orientation are both valued and devalued by course participants, and the idea that teacher preparation risks becoming too technocratic and too palatable to address inequity in schools and society.

According to hooks (1994), teaching to transgress goes against the grain of the banking system (Freire, 1970/2002); challenges the status quo; does not separate the mind from the body or the affective; invokes passion; takes more time than traditional teaching; makes participants uncomfortable; values free thinking and disagreement; and requires small class sizes, meeting with each student one on one, doing activities with students beyond the class, creating a space where students are mutually responsible for developing learning experiences and constructing knowledge, and long-term engagement with students as they live their lives.

Given the climate and constraints under which teacher education specifically (Labaree, 1997; Taubman, 2009) and higher education generally (Giroux, 2007; Shumar, 1997) are operating today, it is not surprising that teacher preparation in general and "diversity" courses in particular have been watered down and in some cases eliminated. Ladson-Billings (2004) provides an overview of the meanings, limits, and possibilities of multicultural education specifically.

CONCLUSION

In spite of numerous limitations to teaching the taboo in teacher education and higher education, many course participants in my teacher preparation courses bring or develop critical, theoretical literacies of analysis and politicized views of difference and equity and inequity in school and society. They often seem to take away something useful and something hopeful.

Some indicate how they have brought what they are learning in my courses to their own schools or, as the following comment from an unsolicited email shows, write that they intend to do so. After specifically recognizing and valuing the politicized way diversity is presented in the course textbook, *Teaching to Change the World* (Oakes and Lipton, 2007), the participant wrote:

> I teach at a school that has very little diversity, but I have personally learned so much from this class and have been sharing my experiences with my principal. He has asked me to speak at our inservice at the beginning of school about diversity within the classroom.

In spite of the pressure to depoliticize diversity in teacher education preparation, many educators, including classroom teachers, are trying to teach against the grain and for social justice (Ayers, Quinn, and Stovall, 2009; Oakes and Lipton, 2007). Fortunately, transgression *is* everywhere.

REFERENCES

American heritage dictionary (fourth edition). (2001). New York: Dell.
Anderson, J. (1988). *The education of blacks in the south, 1860–1935*. Chapel Hill: University of North Carolina Press.
Anzaldúa, G. (1987/1999). *Borderlands, La frontera: The new mestiza* (second edition). San Francisco: Aunt Lute Books.
Ayers, W., Quinn, T., & Stovall, D. (Eds.). (2009). *Handbook of social justice in education*. New York: Routledge.
Ayers, W., Quinn, T., Stovall, D., & Scheiern, L. (2008). Teachers' experience of curriculum: Policy, pedagogy, and situation. In F. M. Connelly, M. F. He, and J. Phillion (Eds.), *The Sage handbook of curriculum and instruction* (pp. 306–26). Thousand Oakes, CA: Sage.
Bartolomé, L. (2008). *Ideologies in education: Unmasking the trap of teacher neutrality*. New York: Peter Lang.
Bateson, M. C. (1989). *Composing a life*. New York: Atlantic Monthly.
Blackburn, M., & Donelson, R. (2004). Sexual identities and schooling. *Theory into Practice, 43*(2), 99–101.
Blount, J. M. (2005). *Fit to teach: Same-sex desire, gender, and school work in the twentieth century*. Albany: State University of New York Press.

Cochran-Smith, M. (2003). The multiple meanings of multicultural teacher education: A conceptual framework. *Teacher Education Quarterly, 30*(2), 7–26.
Cochran-Smith, M. (2004). *Walking the road: Race, diversity, and social justice in teacher education.* New York: Teachers College Press.
Cohen, L., Manion, L., & Morrison, K. (2007). *Research methods in education.* New York: Routledge.
Coloma, R. S. (2006). Disorienting race and education: Changing paradigms on the schooling of Asian Americans and Pacific Islanders. *Race, Ethnicity and Education: Special Issue: Asian Americans and Pacific Islanders: The State of Research, 9*(1), 1–15.
Crenshaw, K. (1991). Mapping the margins: Intersectionality, identity politics, and violence against women of color. *Stanford Law Review, 43*(6), 1241–99.
Crenshaw, K. (Ed.). (1995). *Critical race theory: The key writings that formed the movement.* New York: The New Press.
Dahlgren, R., & Masyada, S. (2009). Ideological dissonance: A comparison of the views of eight conservative students with the recruitment document from a southeastern college of education. *Social Studies Research and Practice, 4*(1), 1–12.
Darling-Hammond, L. (2010). *The flat world and education: How America's commitment to equity will determine our future.* New York: Teachers College Press.
Daza, S. (2008). Decolonizing researcher authenticity. *Race, Ethnicity and Education, 11*(1), 71–85.
Daza, S. (2009). The noninnocence of recognition: Subjects and agency in education. In R. S. Coloma (Ed.), *Postcolonial challenges in education* (pp. 326–43). New York: Peter Lang.
Denzin, N. K., & Lincoln, Y. S. (2005). *The Sage handbook of qualitative research* (third edition). Thousand Oaks, CA: Sage.
Dillard, A. (1982). *Living by fiction.* New York: Harper and Row.
Ellsworth, E. (1999). Multiculture in the making. In C. Grant (Ed.), *Multicultural research: A reflective engagement with race, class, gender and, sexual orientation* (pp. 24–36): New York: Routledge.
Fink, L. (2003). *Creating significant learning experiences: An integrated approach to designing college courses.* San Francisco: Jossey-Bass.
Foucault, M. (1985/1990). *The use of pleasure: The history of sexuality.* New York: Vintage.
Foucault, M. (1986/1988). *The care of the self: The history of sexuality.* New York: Vintage.
Foucault, M. (1978/1990). *The history of sexuality: An introduction.* New York: Vintage.
Freire. (1970/2002). *Pedagogy of the oppressed* (thirtieth anniversary edition). New York: Continuum.
Freire, P., & Macedo, D. (1987). *Literacy: Reading the word and the world.* New York: Routledge.
Giroux, H. (2007). *The university in chains: Confronting the military-industrial-academic complex.* Boulder: Paradigm.
Giroux, H. A. (2009). *Education and the crisis of youth: Schooling and the promise of democracy.* New York: Routledge.
Gay, Lesbian, and Straight Education Network (GLSEN). (2003a), The gay, lesbian and straight education network's tools and tips: Educators. Retrieved September 4, 2010, from http://www.glsen.org/cgi-bin/iowa/all/educator/index.html.
Gay, Lesbian, and Straight Education Network (GLSEN). (2003b). New safe space kit. Retrieved September 12, 2010, from http://www.glsen.org/cgi-bin/iowa/all/library/record/1641.html.
Gorski, P. (2005). Savage unrealities: Uncovering classism in Ruby Payne's framework. Retrieved April 30, 2006, from http://www.edchange.org/publications/Savage_Unrealities.pdf.
hooks, b. (1994). *Teaching to transgress: Education as the practice of freedom.* New York: Routledge.
Jennings, T. (2007). Addressing diversity in US teacher preparation programs: A survey of elementary and secondary programs' priorities and challenges from across the United States of America. *Teaching and Teacher Education, 23*(8), 1258–71.
Kissen, R. M. (Ed.). (2002). *Getting ready for Benjamin: Preparing teachers for sexual diversity in the classroom.* Lanham, MD: Rowman and Littlefield.

Kosciw, J. G., Diaz, E. M., & Greytak, E. A. (2008). *2007 national school climate survey: The experiences of lesbian, gay, bisexual and transgender youth in our nation's schools*. Retrieved from http://www.glsen.org/binary-data/GLSEN_ATTACHMENTS/file/000/001/1290-1.pdf.

Kumashiro, K. (2002). *Troubling education: Queer activism and antioppressive pedagogy*. New York: RoutledgeFalmer.

Kumashiro, K. (2004). *Against common sense: Teaching and learning toward social justice*. New York: Routledge.

Kumashiro, K. (2008). *The seduction of common sense: How the right has framed the debate on America's schools*. New York: Teachers College Press.

Labaree, D. F. (1997). *How to succeed in school without really learning: The credentials race in American education*. New Haven, CT: Yale University Press.

Ladson-Billings, G. (1998). Teaching in dangerous times: Culturally relevant approaches to teacher assessment. *Journal of Negro Education, 67*(3), 255–67.

Ladson-Billings, G., & Brown, K. (2008). Curriculum and cultural diversity. In F. M. Connelly, M. F. He, and J. Phillion (Eds.), *The Sage handbook of curriculum and instruction* (pp. 153–176). Thousand Oakes, CA: Sage.

Lather, P. (2007). *Getting lost: Feminist efforts toward a double(d) science*. New York: State University of New York.

Lather, P. (2009). *Engaging science policy: From the side of the messy*. New York: Peter Lang.

Lipkin, A. (2004). *Beyond diversity day: A Q and A on gay and lesbian issues in schools*. Lanham, MD: Rowman and Littlefield.

Lomawaima, K. T., & McCarty, T. L. (2006). *"To remain an Indian": Lessons in democracy from a century of Native American education*. New York: Teachers College Press.

Lorde, A. (1984). *Sister outsider: Essays and speeches*. Freedom, CA: Crossing Press.

Loutzenheiser, L. (2001). "If I teach about these issues they will burn down my house?": The possibilities and tensions of queer, antiracist pedagogy. In K. Kumashiro (Ed.), *Troubling intersections of race and sexuality: Queer students of color and anti-oppressive education* (pp. 195–214). Oxford: Rowman and Littlefield.

Lugg, C. A. (2003). Sissies, faggots, lezzies, and dykes: Gender, sexual orientation, and a new politics of education? *Educational Administration Quarterly, 39*(1), 95–134.

MacDonald, V. M. (2004). *Latino education in the United States: A narrated history from 1513–2000*. New York: Palgrave Macmillan.

McCall, C. (2001). *An empirical examination of the Likert scale: Some assumptions, development and cautions*. Paper presented at the 80th Annual California Educational Research Association (CERA) Conference, South Lake Tahoe, CA.

Newfield, C. (2008). *Unmaking the public university: The forty-year assault on the middle class*. Cambridge, MA: Harvard University Press.

Nieto, S., Bode, P., Kang, E., & Raible, J. (2008). Identity, community, and diversity: Retheorizing multicultural curriculum for the postmodern era. In F. M. Connelly, M. F. He, and J. Phillion (Eds.), *The Sage handbook of curriculum and instruction* (pp. 176–97). Thousand Oakes, CA: Sage.

Oakes, J., & Lipton, M. (2007). *Teaching to change the world* (third edition). New York: McGraw-Hill.

Paris, D. (2001). Is there a professor in this class? In R. Cole (Ed.), *Issues in web-based pedagogy: A critical primer* (pp. 95–110). Westport, CT: Greenwood.

Pillow, W. S. (2004). *Unfit subjects: Educational policy and the teen mother*. New York: RoutledgeFalmer.

Pollock, M. (2004). *Colormute: Race talk dilemmas in an American school*. Princeton, NJ: Princeton University Press.

Quinn, T., & Meiners, E. (2009). *Flaunt it! Queers organizing for public education and justice*. New York: Peter Lang.

Rhee, J.-E., & Subreenduth, S. (Eds.). (2006). De/colonizing education: Examining transnational localities. *International Journal of Qualitative Studies in Education, 19*(5), 545–48.

Rich, A. (1980). Compulsory heterosexuality and lesbian existence. *Signs, 5*(4), 631–60.

Robbins, C. (2008). *Expelling hope: The assault on youth and the militarization of schooling.* Albany: State University of New York Press.

Sadker, M., & Sadker, D. (1994). *Failing at fairness: How America's schools cheat girls.* New York: Charles Scribner's Sons.

Shumar, W. (1997). *College for sale: A critique of the commodification of higher education.* London; Washington, DC: Falmer.

Sleeter, C. E. (1996). *Multicultural education as social activism.* New York: State University of New York Press.

Sleeter, C. E. (2008). Equity, democracy, and neoliberal assaults on teacher education. *Teaching and Teacher Education, 24*(8), 1947–57.

Solomona, P., Portelli, J., Daniel, B., and Campbell, A. (2005). The discourse of denial: How white teacher candidates construct race, racism and "white privilege." *Race Ethnicity and Education, 8*(2), 147–69.

Spring, J. H. (2005). *The American school, 1642–2004* (sixth edition). Boston, MA: McGraw-Hill.

St. Pierre, E. A. (1997). Methodology in the fold and the irruption of transgressive data. *International Journal of Qualitative Studies in Education, 10*(2), 175–89.

Street, B. (1984). *Literacy in theory and practice.* Cambridge, UK: Cambridge University Press.

Subedi, B. (Ed.). (2010). *Critical global perspectives: Rethinking knowledge about global societies.* Scottsdale, AZ: Information Age.

Subedi, B., & Daza, S. (2008). The possibilities of postcolonial praxis in education. *Race, Ethnicity and Education, 11*(1), 1–10.

Taubman, P. M. (2009). *Deconstructing the discourse of standards and accountability in education.* New York: Routledge.

Van Mannen, J. (1988). *Tales of the field: On writing ethnography.* Chicago: University of Chicago Press.

Varney, J. A. (2001). Undressing the normal: Community efforts for queer Asian and Asian American youth. In K. Kumashiro (Ed.), *Troubling intersections of race and sexuality: Queer students of color and anti-oppressive education* (pp. 87–104). New York: Rowman and Littlefield Publishers.

Yoshino, K. (2006). *Covering: The hidden assault on our civil rights* (first edition). New York: Random House.

Chapter Ten

Epilogue: Sexual Orientation, Identity Politics and Teaching

LGBTQ Teacher Identities (Re)considered

Patrick M. Jenlink

We live in a society defined by its differences. This we can all agree on, some individuals more so than others. We live in a society defined by its ideological stances on race, gender, and sexual orientation. This we too can all agree on, perhaps some more so than others. We live in a society defined by a myriad of identities, determined in part by society's differences and ideological stances, identities determined by individuals and identities determined by "others" for individuals and groups, not always in the best interest of the individual. This we can all agree on, for the most part.

The caution we face today is grounded historically; what defines us as a country can also divide us in ways that foster hate and violence. We know this all too well. The unfortunate reality of our long history as a country, when considering a teacher's sexual orientation, is that for most, "the teacher's life was[/is] scrutinized inside the classroom as an employee and watched over outside the classroom as a role model for his or her students" (DeMitchell, Eckes, and Fossey, 2009, p. 69).

INTERSECTIONALITY

Whether our society, our communities, and our schools are able to benefit from a democratic way of life, the very essence of who we are and what we stand for as a democracy, depends on how we address tensions that exist around sexual orientation, identity, and teaching. The intersectionality[1] of sexual orientation, identity, and the profession of teaching brings clarity and critical awareness to us as teacher educators with respect to the work that is required if we are to move beyond what has been and is currently a largely heteronormative society.[2] This we also know as a profound and fundamental truth of preparing teachers, both lesbian, gay, bisexual, transgender, or queer/questioning (LGBTQ) and straight, alike.

Jackie Blount, in *Fit to Teach: Same-Sex Desire, Gender, and School Work in the Twentieth Century* (2005), reveals the legacy of many American educators whose lives transcended the hegemony of heteronormativity,[3] transgressing traditional boundaries of gender and sexuality. Importantly, she exposed the role gender and sexual orientation have played historically in redefining the concept of "schoolteacher" in America. Blount explained, "[A]lthough schools attempted to regulate gender and sexual orientation of their workers—and by extension students—they also provided fascinating opportunities for supporting unconventional sexualities and gender behaviors, characteristics, and identities" (p. 16). In this sense, Blount makes visible the perduring presence and turbulent relationship between education, sexual orientation, and teacher identity that exist in schools today (Reilly, 2007).

Students entering teacher preparation programs, matriculating to the status of preservice teachers, completing their preparation programs, and entering school classrooms across the nation today do so in an increasingly diverse and yet decidedly heteronormative society—diverse in the sense of gender, race and ethnicity, and sexual orientation, and heteronormative in the sense of judging LGBTQ teachers by a different set of standards than straight teachers. Teacher educators and policy makers (both state and federal) face the challenges of fostering educational environments in university and public school classrooms alike that are inclusive and welcoming to all students and teachers.

IDENTITY POLITICS

Importantly, many states[4] are addressing the issue heteronormative practices and identity politics by passing legislation and enacting laws to counter discrimination based largely on sexual orientation.[5] Although this is fact, it is also fact that prejudice against LGBTQ teachers is still an accepted practice in the twenty-first century. DeMitchell and colleagues (2009) are instructive on understanding the safety of school culture and climate, particularly for LGBTQ individuals, teachers and students alike. The authors explain:

> If schools are not safe for the most vulnerable, are they safe for anyone? Educators build what they value; they are responsible for the culture of their

school. We must establish a professional culture in which all teachers can be judged for their professional service and not their personal sexual orientation. (p. 105)

The reality of LGBTQ teachers in classrooms is not new; they have "always been in our classrooms; their presence, however, in many cases has been invisible" (p. 105). Specifically, heteronormativity has shaped the organization of public space in university and public school classrooms in ways that are naturalized to the point of invisibility (Woolley, 2013).

This invisibility of sexual orientation is a predominate fact across the history of classroom teaching. However, as DeMitchell and colleagues (2009) argue, invisibility "should not mask the answer to the question whether it makes a difference that a teacher is gay, lesbian bisexual, transgendered, or queer/questioning; "[T]he answer is no. Laws, professional ethics, and community standards should and must make sexual orientation irrelevant in deciding who will teach our children. Quality teachers are the core of a quality educational system" (p. 105). An individual's sexual orientation has no place in defining quality or determining if a teacher is hired or not. At the end of the day, "quality is asexual in practice, and asexual in orientation" (p. 105).

Today, school administrators and teachers must consider whether the educational context facilitates learning for all individuals, including those who are LGBTQ. In a pluralistic society, administrators must consider whether teachers, aides, or other LGBTQ staff members are hindered in the workplace because of discriminatory policies, practices, or comments. LGBTQ issues in education are relevant from PK–12 to higher education as well as in multiple educational contexts from classrooms to college campuses.

(RE)CONSIDERING IDENTITY

Considering and reconsidering one's sexual orientation in terms of being LGBTQ and a teacher requires the teacher educator and the student of teaching to examine and reexamine the surroundings (cultural, ideological, political, spatial) as he/she/they learns to teach, both in the college classroom and the field-based classroom of practice. For the teacher educator, it is important to draw the intersectionality of LGBTQ and teacher identity into an active role and level of understanding. One cannot exist without the other; the intersectionality itself is the space wherein one's identity takes form. Sumara (1998) explains:

> [I]dentity is something that co-emerges with one's ever-shifting geographical, interpersonal, and intertextual experiences, and that identity is always the product of the interpretative work done around the continual fusing of past,

present, and projected senses of self. I try to create literary experiences that facilitate and support this important work. (p. 206)

It is critically important that, as teacher educators, we foster, through pedagogical, situational spaces, the commonplaces for understanding and developing teacher identity for the LGBTQ and straight individuals seeking to become teachers, developing the teachers' spatial identity as self in the classroom and in relation with the self of each student. Such pedagogical, situational space as commonplace occurs within the cumulative and collective intertextual relations among teacher educators, students of teaching, learning activities, biographical narratives, cultural and political texts, and contexts of discourse and practice.

The relationship between identity and pedagogy is complex. Jennings (2010) noted that a teacher educator's teaching and pedagogy emerges from lived experience and the teacher educator's positionality as someone who identifies as LGBTQ or straight will naturally inform his/her/their practice and his/her/their identity. There is need for a pedagogy of identity that understands the necessity of providing a space within which one can become the author of one's own interpretations of one's identity as teacher, whether LGBTQ or straight. These interpretations, however, cannot be extricated from one another. The interpretation of the teacher educator and that of the student overlap and intertwine within an ever-evolving and unstable web of contextualized relations.

FORCES OF HETERONORMATIVITY

We urgently need to target the objective forces of heteronormativity that are at work in society and its educational settings. These forces cause whole lifetimes of guilt and suffering, fear and invisibility. To this point, George Eliot (1866) observed long ago:

> [T]here is much pain that is quite noiseless; and vibrations that make human agonies are often a mere whisper in the roar of hurrying existence. There are glances of hatred that stab and raise no cry of murder; robberies that leave man or woman forever beggared of peace and joy, yet kept secret by the sufferer— committed to no sound except that of low moans in the night, seen in no handwriting except that made on the face by the slow months of suppressed anguish and early morning tears. (p. 84)

Too many individuals, teachers and students alike, live as the "sufferer" in fear because they are lesbian, gay, bisexual, transgendered, or queer/questioning (Watney, 1994). A major responsibility we as teacher educators have in our classrooms is to enable our LBGTQ students of teaching to learn from lived experiences and write their identities in the "safe space" we provide through our pedagogical practices.

These practices must work to mediate the heteronormative forces students have lived with prior to entering teacher preparation. LGBTQ and straight students alike must also learn how to teach in schools and classrooms as a responsibility, a responsibility concerned with always working to free others from the heteronormative forces the pervade our society and our communities and schools.

CONCLUSION

Our greatest concern as teacher educators, in (re)considering LGBTQ teacher identity is that the space wherein our students of teaching form their identity can be claimed, owned by ideological and heteronormative forces, and that the identity of teacher can likewise be owned by the same forces. These forces work to accomplish their political or ideological agendas at the expense of our democratic society, our children, our future, and, most importantly, at the expense of our identity as teachers, LGBTQ and straight alike.

NOTES

1. For the purposes of this chapter, *intersectionality*:

   references the critical insight that race, class, gender, sexuality, ethnicity, nation, ability, and age operate not as unitary, mutually exclusive entities, but as reciprocally constructing phenomena that in turn shape complex social inequalities. (Hill Collins, 2015, 3.2)

2. The effect of heteronormativity's central position in institutions like public schools is significant and deleterious to equity when considering LGBTQ and straight individuals and how they are judged (Woolley, 2013). Macintosh (2007) asks a critical question, embedded in a profound concern about teacher educators:

   [H]ow can we begin to help early-career teachers see the deleterious impact of heternormativism in the everyday lives of their student if they cannot yet begin to see its more immediate presence in their curricula and classrooms? (p. 34)

3. DeMitchell et al. (2009) noted that "Lambda Legal, a civil rights organization focusing on GLBT issues, argues that state laws can have the best impact on bigotry against GLBT individuals in schools" (p. 101).
4. DeMitchell et al. (2009) explained:

   [T]wenty states and Washington, D.C., ban discrimination against employees based on sexual orientation. The states are: California, Colorado, Connecticut, Hawaii, Illinois, Iowa, Maine, Maryland, Massachusetts, Minnesota, Nevada, New Hampshire, New Jersey, New Mexico, New York, Oregon, Rhode Island, Vermont, Washington, and Wisconsin. . . . In most states—Minnesota, Nevada, Hawaii, New

Hampshire, and Illinois, for example—prohibition of discrimination based on sexual orientation is included in prohibitions on other factors like race, religion, or disability. (p. 101)

5. Jennings (2010) noted that, for the teacher educator, this may mean challenging the heterocentric content of literature, textbooks, research, and other course materials. If a teacher educator's past experiences include marginalization based on sexual orientation and identity, that teacher educator's instructional and pedagogical practices might well reflect critical perspectives toward teaching that challenge dominant models of pedagogy, pedagogical practices that may hinder any emancipatory potentials of education and classroom discourse.

REFERENCES

Blount, J. (2005). *Fit to teach: Same-sex desire, gender, and school work in the twentieth century*. Albany: State University of New York Press.

DeMitchell, T. A., Eckes, S., & Fossey, R. (2009). Sexual orientation and the public school teacher. *Public Interest Law Journal, 19*, 65–105.

Eliot, G. (1866/1987). *Felix Holt*. Harmondsworth, UK: Penguin Classics.

Hill Collins, P. (2015). Intersectionality's definitional dilemmas. *Annual Review of Sociology, 41*, 1–20. Retrieved from https://www.annualreviews.org/doi/pdf/10.1146/annurev-soc-073014-112142.

Jennings, T. (2010). "Out" gay and lesbian faculty and the inclusion of sexual orientation topics in teacher preparation programmes in the USA. *International Journal of Inclusive Education, 14*(3), 269–287. DOI: 10.1080/13603110802504531.

Lambda Legal, Working on State Laws to Protect GLBT Students from Discrimination in Schools. Retrieved from http://www.lambdalegal.org/our-work/in-court/other/working-on-state-lawsto.html.

MacIntosh, L. (2007). Does anyone have a Band-Aid? Anti-homophobia discourses and pedagogical impossibilities. *Educational Studies, 41*(1), 33–43.

Reilly, C. (2007). Making the invisible visible: Negotiating (in)visibility and transparency for LGBT Issues in education. *Journal of Gay and Lesbian Issues in Education, 4*(3), 121–30.

Seidman, S. (2002). From identity to queer politics: Shifts in the social logic of normative heterosexuality in contemporary America. *Social Thought and Research, 24*(1 and 2), 1–12.

Watney, S. (1994). Queer epistemology: Activism, "outing," and the politics of sexual identities. *Critical Quarterly, 36*(1), 13–27.

Woolley, S. W. (2013). Identity and difference: Negotiating gender and sexuality in high school contexts. (Doctoral dissertation, University of California–Berkeley). ProQuest ID: Woolley_berkeley_0028E_13179. Merritt ID: ark:/13030/m5cg4c2k. Retrieved from https://escholarship.org/uc/item/2wp2x3q4.

Editor and Contributors

EDITOR

Patrick M. Jenlink is regents professor, E. J. Campbell Endowed Chair in Educational Leadership, and professor of doctoral studies in the Department of Secondary Education and Educational Leadership, Stephen F. Austin State University. Dr. Jenlink's teaching emphasis in doctoral studies includes courses in ethics and philosophy of leadership, research methods and design, and leadership theory and practice. Dr. Jenlink's research interests include politics of identity, democratic education and leadership, social justice and equity, and critical theory. Books published include *Dialogue as a Means of Collective Communication*, *Equity Issues for Today's Educational Leaders: Meeting the Challenge of Creating Equitable Schools for All*, *Dewey's Democracy and Education Revisited: Contemporary Discourses for Democratic Education and Leadership*, and *Teacher Identity and the Struggle for Recognition: Meeting the Challenges of a Diverse Society*. Dr. Jenlink's current book projects include *Ethics and the Educational Leader: A Casebook of Ethical Dilemmas*, *Dewey Studies Handbook*, and *Teacher Preparation at the Intersection of Race and Poverty in Today's Schools*.

AUTHORS

Laura Bower-Phipps is associate professor of education at Southern Connecticut State University, where she also coordinates the undergraduate elementary education program. Laura worked as an educator at the secondary level for seven years before earning her PhD at the University of Nevada, Las Vegas. Her research centers on diversity in teacher education. This work has included lesbian mothers' experiences with their children's teachers; the identities of mother/educator/lesbians; ethnic, gender, and sexual minorities' experiences in their teacher preparation programs; and teacher candidates' capacity to queer their expectations for students. Dr. Bower's current research engages those who identify as "other" in teacher preparation programs in collaborative inquiry groups, and she has won competitive research grants to sponsor participating teacher candidates' travel to present at national conferences. Laura and her wife, Kathleen, live in New Haven, Connecticut. They are both lesbians and educators, and they hope to become mothers in the future.

Stephanie L. Daza is research fellow with the Education and Social Research Institute, Manchester Metropolitan University. She earned her PhD in Social and Cultural Foundations at the Ohio State University. Her lines of inquiry include educational foundations, research methodology, globalizing trends in educational policy, and theorizing difference. Dr. Daza's research has been published in the *International Journal of Qualitative Studies in Education*, *Race Ethnicity and Education*, and *Qualitative Inquiry*. She is an editorial board member of *Educational Studies*, the *Journal of the American Educational Studies Association*, and *Horizons: Postcolonial Directions in Education*. She is the past co-chair of the Postcolonial Studies in Education Special Interest Group (SIG) of the American Educational Research Association (2007–2010). Prior to entering the academy, Stephanie served as a Peace Corps Volunteer (Bolivia, 1998–2000) and taught public school for grades 7–12 and adult education in Ohio and California.

Steve Fifield, PhD, is adjunct assistant professor in the School of Education at the University of Delaware. He is interested in sociocultural, queer, and Buddhist and contemplative perspectives on the intersections of science and technology, education, and self.

Sue Gallagher is the director of research, analysis, and planning at the Children's Services Council of Broward County and is an adjunct professor in the Adult Education and Human Resource Development Department at Florida International University in Miami. Dr. Gallagher won the L. R. Gay Award for best student paper on holistic learning theory and the incorporation of spirituality and learning at work. She has published several articles and book chapters on learning, spirituality, and sexual identity. Dr. Gallagher's work at the Council focuses on integrating government performance measures with community indicator data. She and her colleague, Gloria Putiak, received second place in the Alfred E. Sloan Foundation's international competition on community indicators projects. Her work is grounded in more than twenty years of experience working with people with developmental disabilities and, most recently, for a local government entity that provides leadership, advocacy, and resources to children and families. Her interests include theology and evolution, community planning processes, and social justice.

Adam J. Greteman is adjunct professor of art education at the School of the Art Institute–Chicago, the department of Foundations, Social Policy and Research at Concordia University–Chicago, and a part-time fashion consultant. An emerging scholar who is part educational philosopher, part cultural critic, and is titillated by popular culture, his scholarship centers on issues of sexuality and gender working primarily with queer and feminist theories. A good old Iowa boy, he works primarily with humanities-oriented approaches to research while dabbling in qualitative research. He is currently working on a book-length project on queer intimacies and temporalities in education.

Heather Hickman is an adjunct instructor of education at Lewis University in Romeoville, Illinois, and a full-time high school English teacher in a Chicago suburb. For the university, Heather teaches courses on reading instruction, curriculum, the history of American education, and introductory research. In her more than ten years of teaching high school, she has taught all levels of English language arts and literature. Dr. Hickman's teaching focus, whether at the university or high school level, takes a critical stance examining the status quo and addressing marginalization. This teaching lens was developed through her doctoral program at Lewis University in Educational Leadership for Teaching and Learning. Heather earned her EdD from Lewis in May of 2009. In addition to teaching, Heather has presented and published papers on the topics of heteronormativity and critical theory in education.

Janna Jackson Kellinger is associate professor at the University of Massachusetts Boston. She began her teaching career as a high school English teacher for Fulton County schools in Georgia. After receiving her PhD in curriculum and instruction at Boston College, she published her book, *Unmasking Identities: An Exploration of the Lives of Gay and Lesbian Teachers*. Since then, she has published numerous articles about queer educators and queer theory in education, including "Dangerous Presumptions" in *Gender and Education*, which applies a queer theory lens to dismantle arguments for single-sex education. Her current research projects continue to pursue questions of identity and teaching.

Megan S. Kennedy is chair and associate professor of education at Westfield State University in Massachusetts. As a classroom teacher and then as a gifted and talented facilitator and differentiation coach, Dr. Kennedy was inspired to mentor and guide new teachers into the profession. Dr. Kennedy teaches courses that focus on the interconnection between curriculum, instruction, assessment, and the elementary curriculum. In addition, she teaches graduate courses in advanced pedagogy and is the counselor for the Iota

Iota chapter of Kappa Delta Pi, the International Education Honor Society at WSU. She has written and presented on the topic of queer theory in teacher preparation and on the use of LGBTQ-themed literature in the classroom at both regional and national conferences Additionally, she is a coauthor, along with Annemarie Vaccaro and Gerri August, on a book titled *Safe Spaces: Making Schools and Communities Welcoming to LGBT Youth*. *Safe Spaces* shares powerful narratives of resilient LGBTQ youth and dedicated allies who work to transform schools and communities into safe spaces. Her current research and writing interests include teacher identity in the classroom, creating inclusive spaces in schools and communities for LGBT youth, and literature as a tool for creating socially just classrooms.

Hilary Landorf is associate professor in the College of Education at Florida International University in Miami. She is the executive director of the Office of Global Learning Initiatives. In this position, she leads *Global Learning for Global Citizenship*, a ten-year, university-wide initiative with the purpose to provide every FIU undergraduate with curricular and cocurricular opportunities to gain the knowledge, skills, and attitude of global citizenship through global learning. Dr. Landorf holds a PhD in International Education from New York University, a master of arts from the University of Virginia, and a bachelor of arts in English Literature from Stanford University. Dr. Landorf's current research interests include integrative global learning in higher education and the connection between global learning and human capability development. She has published widely in national and international journals and books, and is regularly consulted for her expertise in globalizing K–20 curricula across the curriculum. Her recent publications include "Global Learning for Global Citizenship," in *Universities and Human Development: A Sustainable Imaginary for the XXI Century* (forthcoming), "Toward a Philosophy of Global Education," in *Visions in Global Education*, and "Education for Sustainable Human Development" in *Theory and Research in Education*.

Tonette S. Rocco, PhD (the Ohio State University) is professor in the Adult Education and Human Resource Development Program and director of the Office of Academic Writing and Publication Support, College of Education, Florida International University. She is a Houle Scholar and a 2008 Kauffman Entrepreneurship Professor. Rocco has published seven books and monographs, winning the 2009 University Continuing Education Association Frandson Book Award for *Challenging the Parameters of Adult Education: John Ohliger and the Quest for Social Democracy* (with Andre Grace, 2009). Her most recent book is *The Handbook of Scholarly Writing and Publishing* (with Tim Hatcher, 2011). She has more than two hundred publications in journals, books, and proceedings. She is the winner of the Elwood F. Holton III Research Excellence Award 2008 for the article "Towards the Employ-ability-link Model: Current Employment Transition to Future Employment Perspectives," published in *Human Resource Development Review* with Jo Thijssen and Beatrice Van der Heijden. She is coeditor of *New Horizons in Adult Education and Human Resource Development*, assistant editor of *Human Resource Development Quarterly*, and qualitative methods editor for *Human Resource Development International*. Editorial board memberships include the *Journal of Mixed Methods Research* (founding board member), *Adult Education Quarterly, Journal of European and Industrial Training*, and *International Journal of Mixed Methods in Applied Business and Policy Research, Journal of Chinese Human Resource Management, PAACE Journal of Lifelong Learning*, and *International Journal of Mentoring and Coaching in Education*. She served on the American Society for Training and Development Certification Institute Board of Directors.

Ira David Soco is educational consultant and advocate, and a researcher and instructor in the College of Education at Michigan State University. He studies the intersections of education, history, concepts of ability, technology, and performance, and uses that research to inform the reimagining of schools. His academic backgrounding in art, architecture, criminal justice, special education, and critical theories of education have mixed with a wide variety of life experiences to support a radically holistic view of what education is, and what education can be. The creator of the "Toolbelt Theory" (a student-centered, task-based technology choice protocol) and "The Iridescent Classroom" (a redefinition of space and time in schools), he spreads his theories primarily through blogging, social media, and direct work with schools, teachers, and students.